DUSU

Path of the Ancient

*"Within every heart sleeps the animal.
The One awakened will be Lord of all."
~ Galemren Proverb*

D U S U
Path of the Ancient

STRANGER
C O M I C S

WRITERS
Sebastian A. Jones
Christopher Garner

ARTIST
James C. Webster

LAYOUT ARTIST
Darrell May

LETTERER AND DESIGNER
A Larger World Studios

EDITOR
Joshua Cozine

DUSU LOGO DESIGNER
Christopher Garner

ASSOCIATES
Ken Locsmandi
Mark Hammond
Terrance Bouldin-Johnson

CHIEF CREATIVE OFFICER
Darrell May

EDITOR-IN-CHIEF
Joshua Cozine

PUBLISHER
Sebastian A. Jones

BASED IN THE WORLD OF ASUNDA CREATED BY SEBASTIAN A. JONES

COND PRINTING. PRINTED IN SOUTH KOREA. ISBN 978-1-939834-28-7

Chapter 1

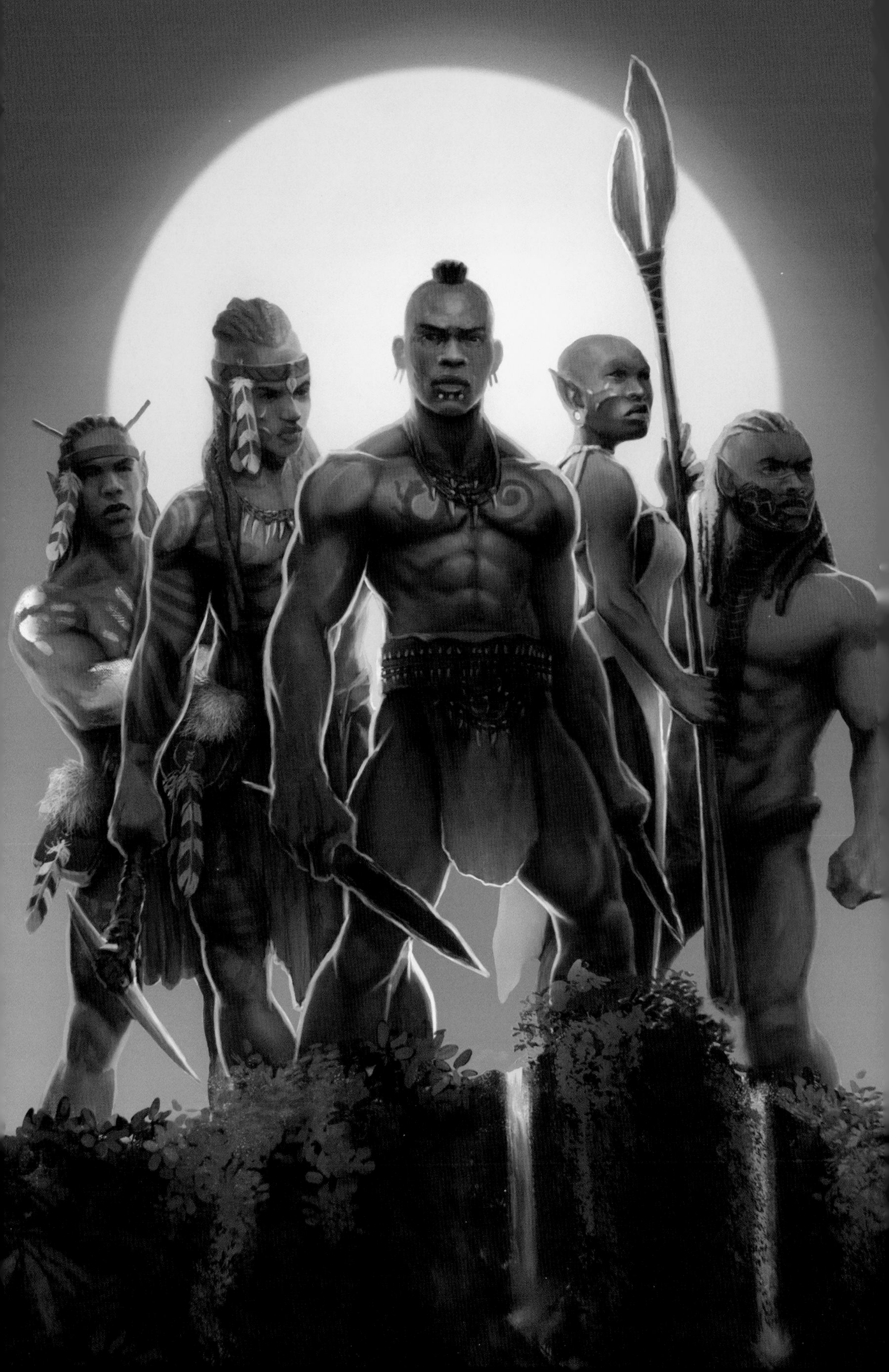

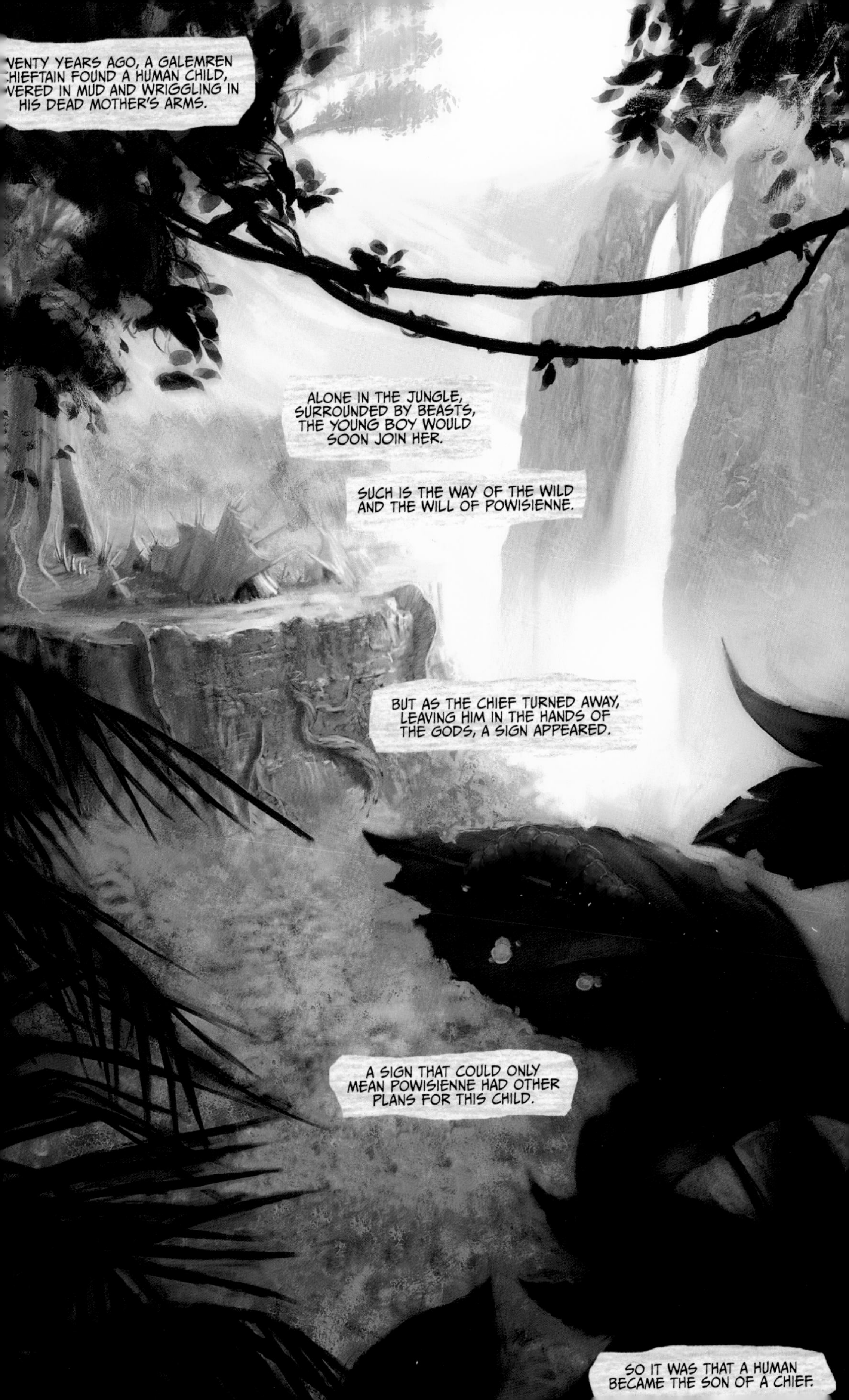
VENTY YEARS AGO, A GALEMREN
CHIEFTAIN FOUND A HUMAN CHILD,
VERED IN MUD AND WRIGGLING IN
HIS DEAD MOTHER'S ARMS.
ALONE IN THE JUNGLE, SURROUNDED BY BEASTS, THE YOUNG BOY WOULD SOON JOIN HER.
SUCH IS THE WAY OF THE WILD AND THE WILL OF POWISIENNE.
BUT AS THE CHIEF TURNED AWAY, LEAVING HIM IN THE HANDS OF THE GODS, A SIGN APPEARED.
A SIGN THAT COULD ONLY MEAN POWISIENNE HAD OTHER PLANS FOR THIS CHILD.
SO IT WAS THAT A HUMAN BECAME THE SON OF A CHIEF.

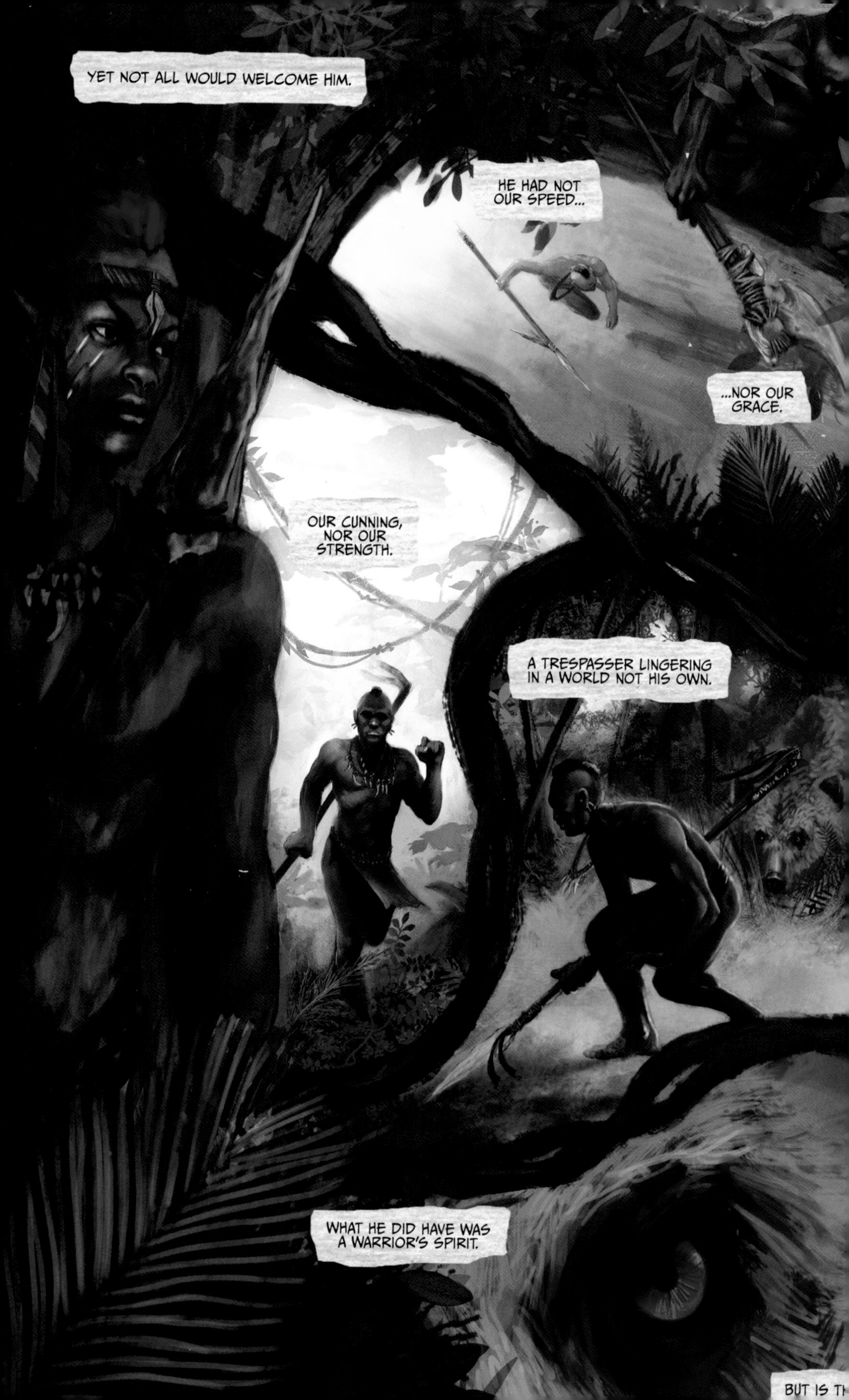
YET NOT ALL WOULD WELCOME HIM.
HE HAD NOT OUR SPEED...
...NOR OUR GRACE.
OUR CUNNING, NOR OUR STRENGTH.
A TRESPASSER LINGERING IN A WORLD NOT HIS OWN.
WHAT HE DID HAVE WAS A WARRIOR'S SPIRIT.

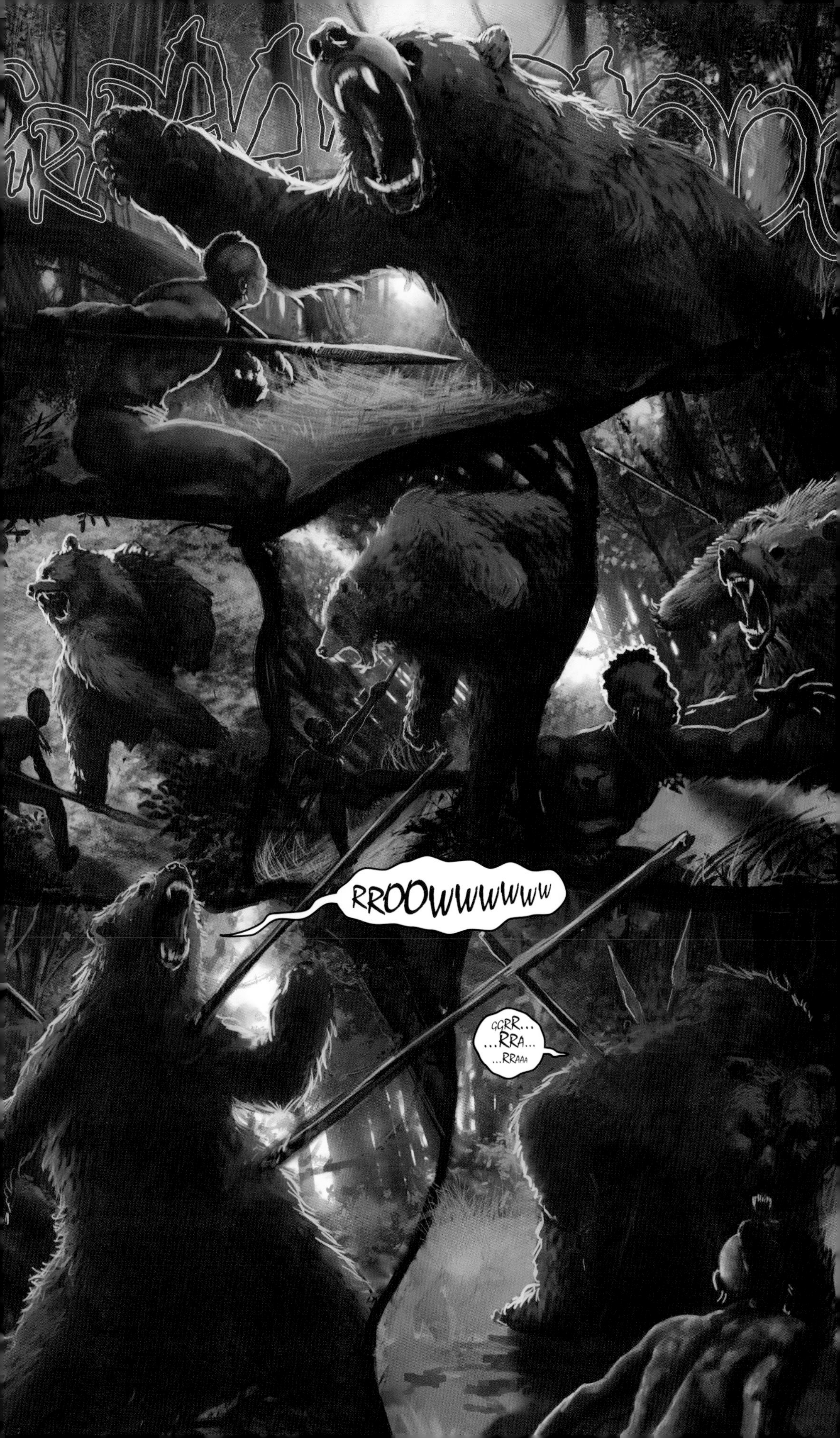
RROOWWWWWW
GGRR... ...RRA... ...RRAAA

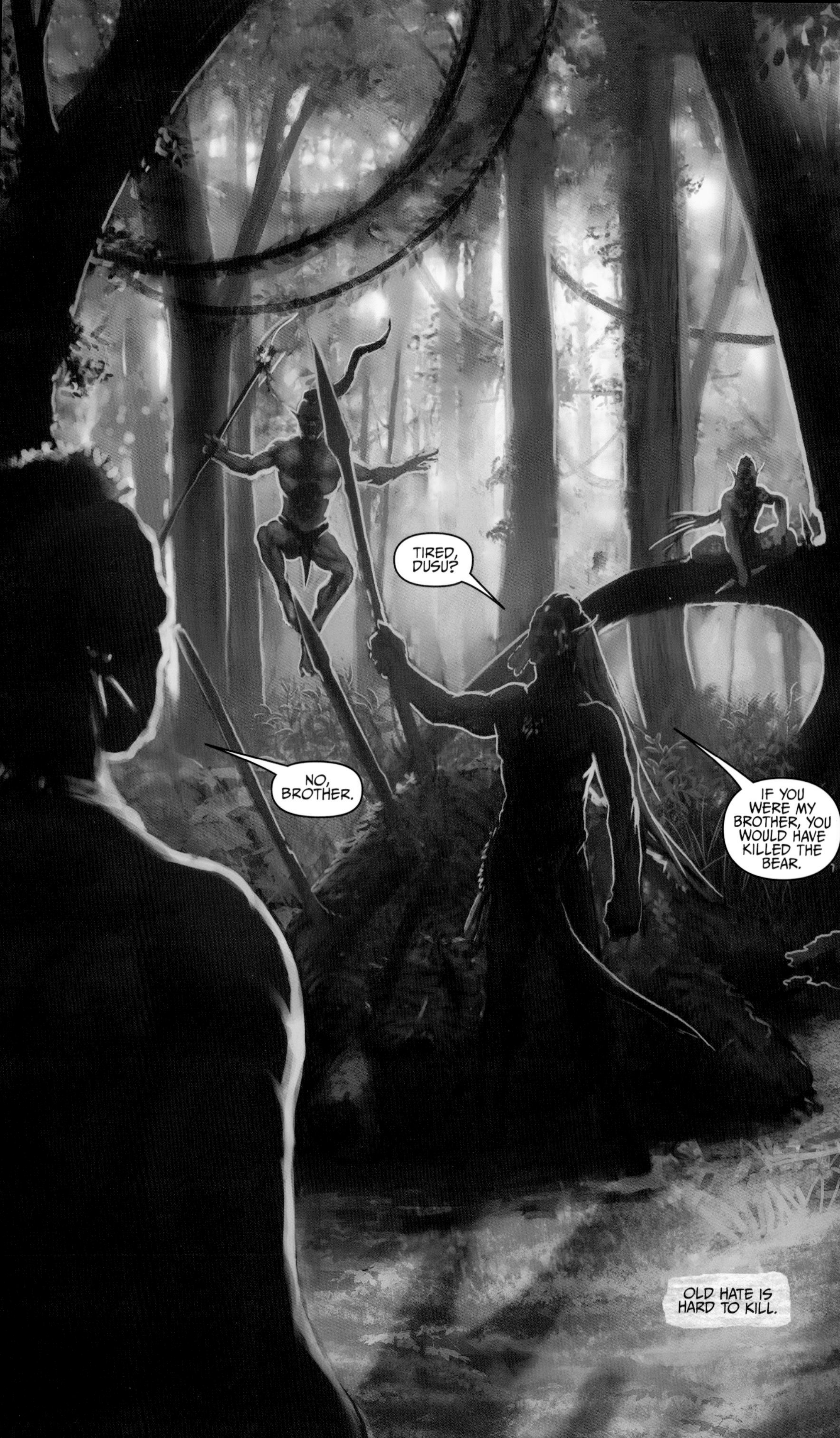
TIRED, DUSU?
NO, BROTHER.
IF YOU WERE MY BROTHER, YOU WOULD HAVE KILLED THE BEAR.
OLD HATE IS HARD TO KILL.

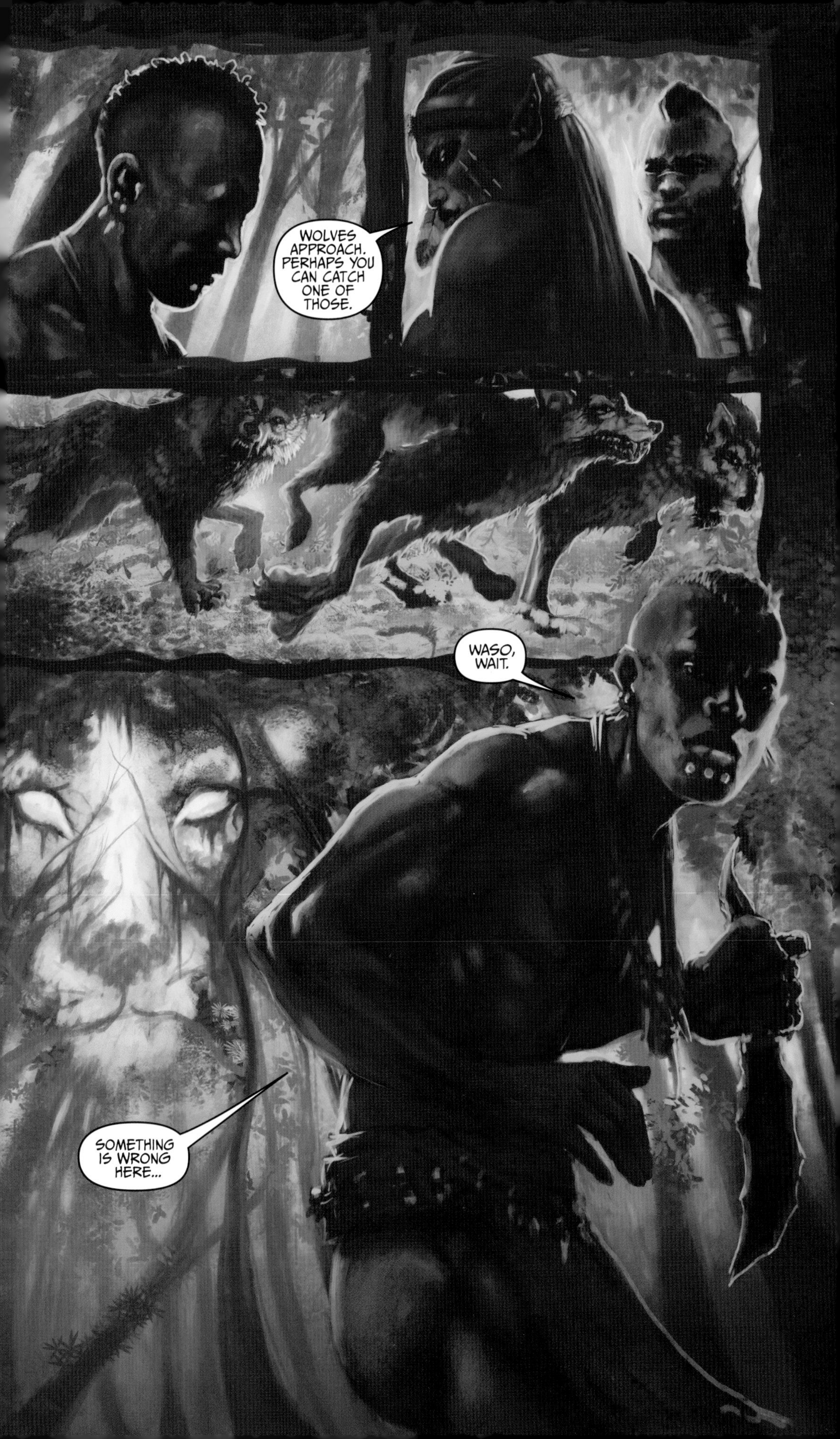
WOLVES APPROACH. PERHAPS YOU CAN CATCH ONE OF THOSE.
WASO, WAIT.
SOMETHING IS WRONG HERE...

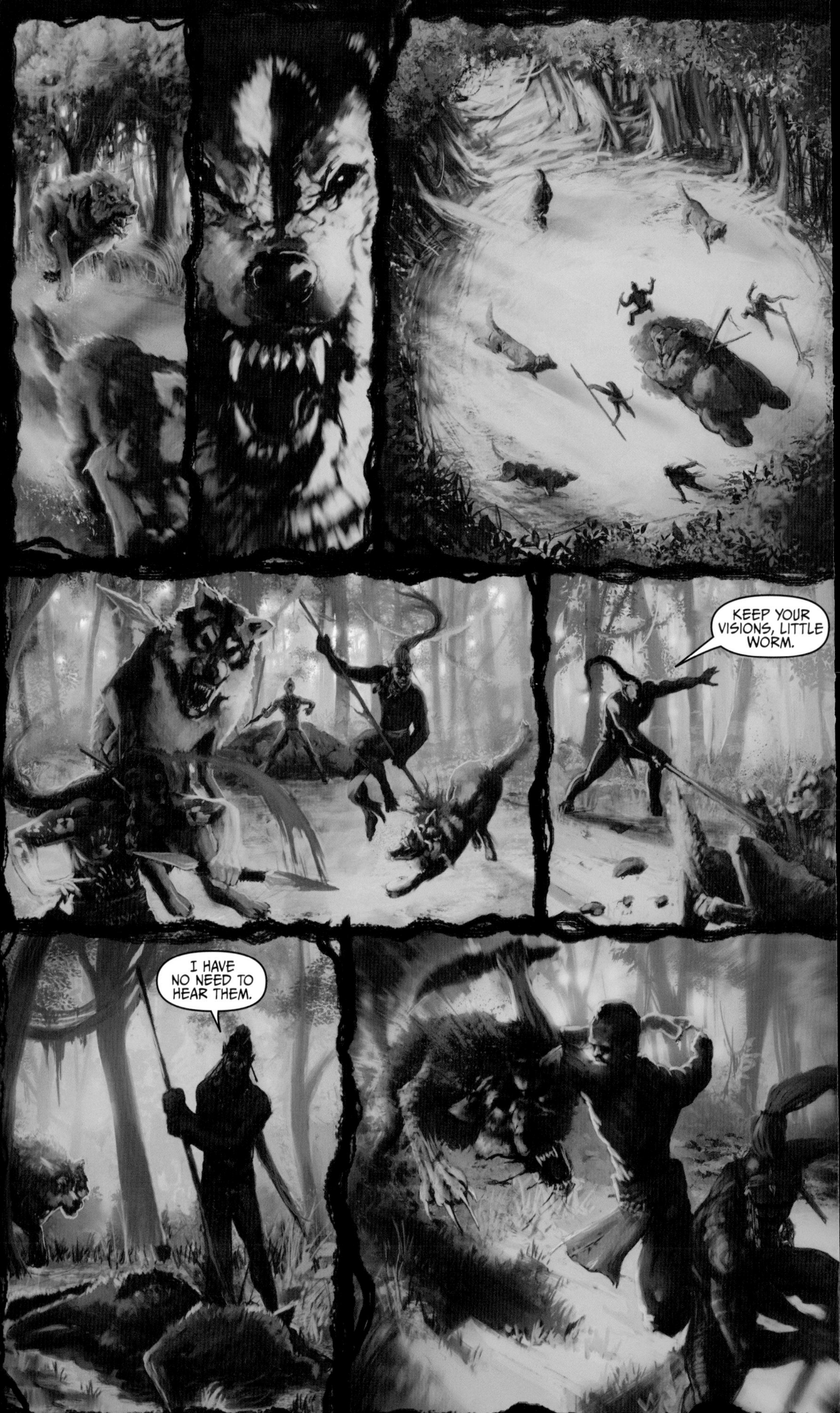
KEEP YOUR VISIONS, LITTLE WORM.
I HAVE NO NEED TO HEAR THEM.

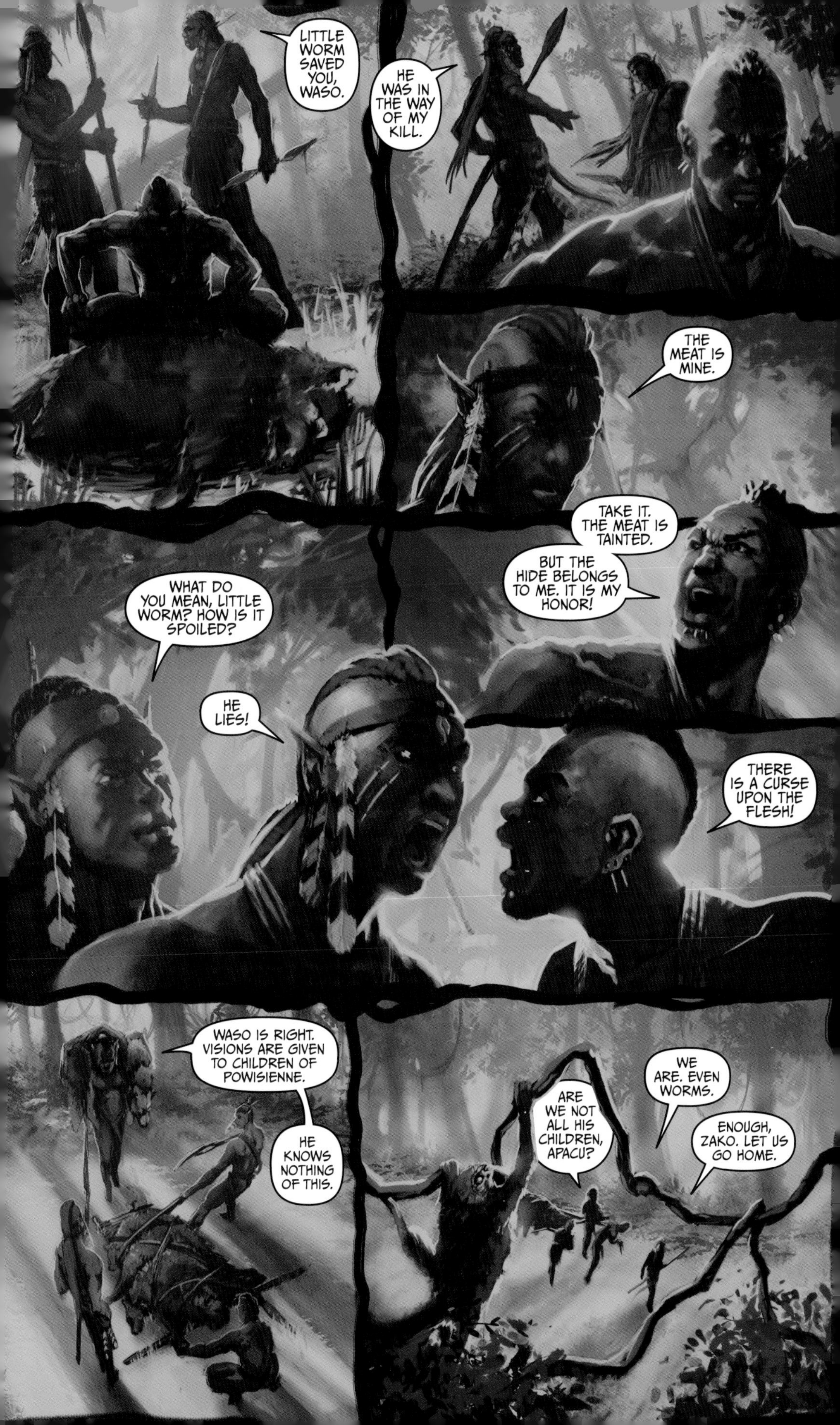
LITTLE WORM SAVED YOU, WASO.
HE WAS IN THE WAY OF MY KILL.
THE MEAT IS MINE.
TAKE IT. THE MEAT IS TAINTED.
BUT THE HIDE BELONGS TO ME. IT IS MY HONOR!
WHAT DO YOU MEAN, LITTLE WORM? HOW IS IT SPOILED?
HE LIES!
THERE IS A CURSE UPON THE FLESH!
WASO IS RIGHT. VISIONS ARE GIVEN TO CHILDREN OF POWISIENNE.
HE KNOWS NOTHING OF THIS.
ARE WE NOT ALL HIS CHILDREN, APACU?
WE ARE. EVEN WORMS.
ENOUGH, ZAKO. LET US GO HOME.

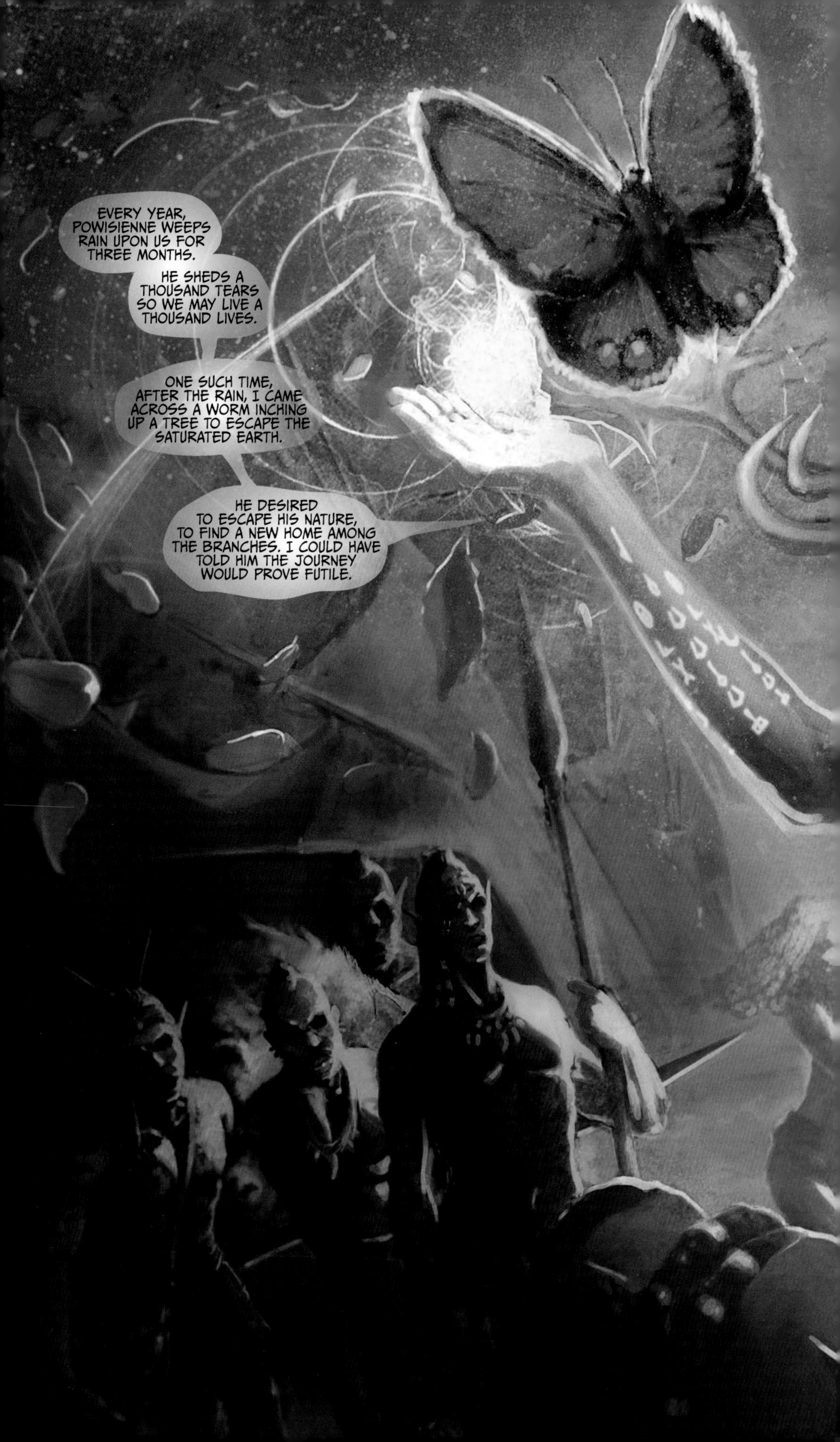
EVERY YEAR, POWISIENNE WEEPS RAIN UPON US FOR THREE MONTHS.
HE SHEDS A THOUSAND TEARS SO WE MAY LIVE A THOUSAND LIVES.
ONE SUCH TIME, AFTER THE RAIN, I CAME ACROSS A WORM INCHING UP A TREE TO ESCAPE THE SATURATED EARTH.
HE DESIRED TO ESCAPE HIS NATURE, TO FIND A NEW HOME AMONG THE BRANCHES. I COULD HAVE TOLD HIM THE JOURNEY WOULD PROVE FUTILE.

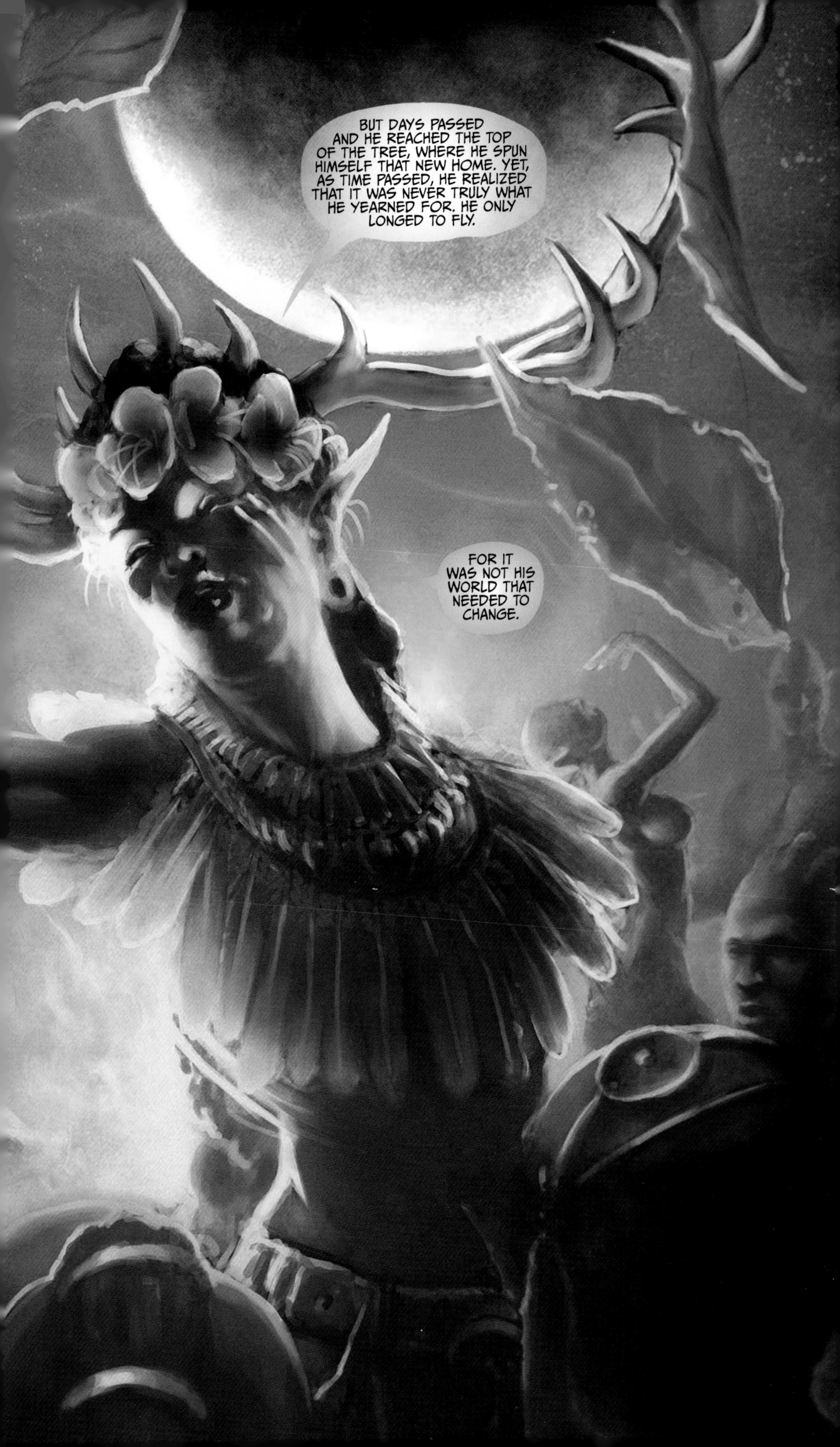
BUT DAYS PASSED AND HE REACHED THE TOP OF THE TREE, WHERE HE SPUN HIMSELF THAT NEW HOME. YET, AS TIME PASSED, HE REALIZED THAT IT WAS NEVER TRULY WHAT HE YEARNED FOR. HE ONLY LONGED TO FLY.
FOR IT WAS NOT HIS WORLD THAT NEEDED TO CHANGE.

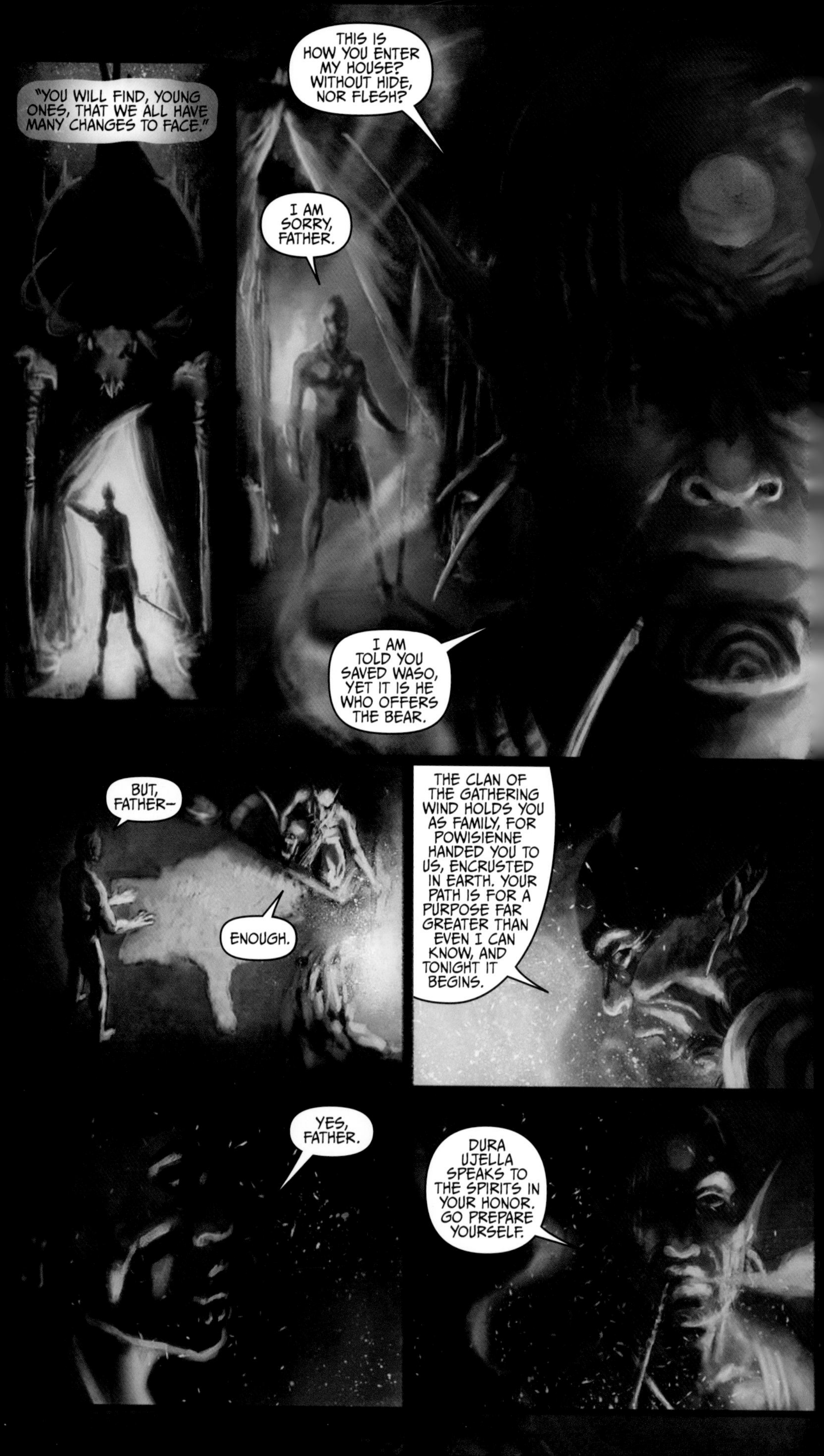
"YOU WILL FIND, YOUNG ONES, THAT WE ALL HAVE MANY CHANGES TO FACE."
THIS IS HOW YOU ENTER MY HOUSE? WITHOUT HIDE, NOR FLESH?
I AM SORRY, FATHER.
I AM TOLD YOU SAVED WASO, YET IT IS HE WHO OFFERS THE BEAR.
BUT, FATHER--
ENOUGH.
THE CLAN OF THE GATHERING WIND HOLDS YOU AS FAMILY, FOR POWISIENNE HANDED YOU TO US, ENCRUSTED IN EARTH. YOUR PATH IS FOR A PURPOSE FAR GREATER THAN EVEN I CAN KNOW, AND TONIGHT IT BEGINS.
YES, FATHER.
DURA UJELLA SPEAKS TO THE SPIRITS IN YOUR HONOR. GO PREPARE YOURSELF.

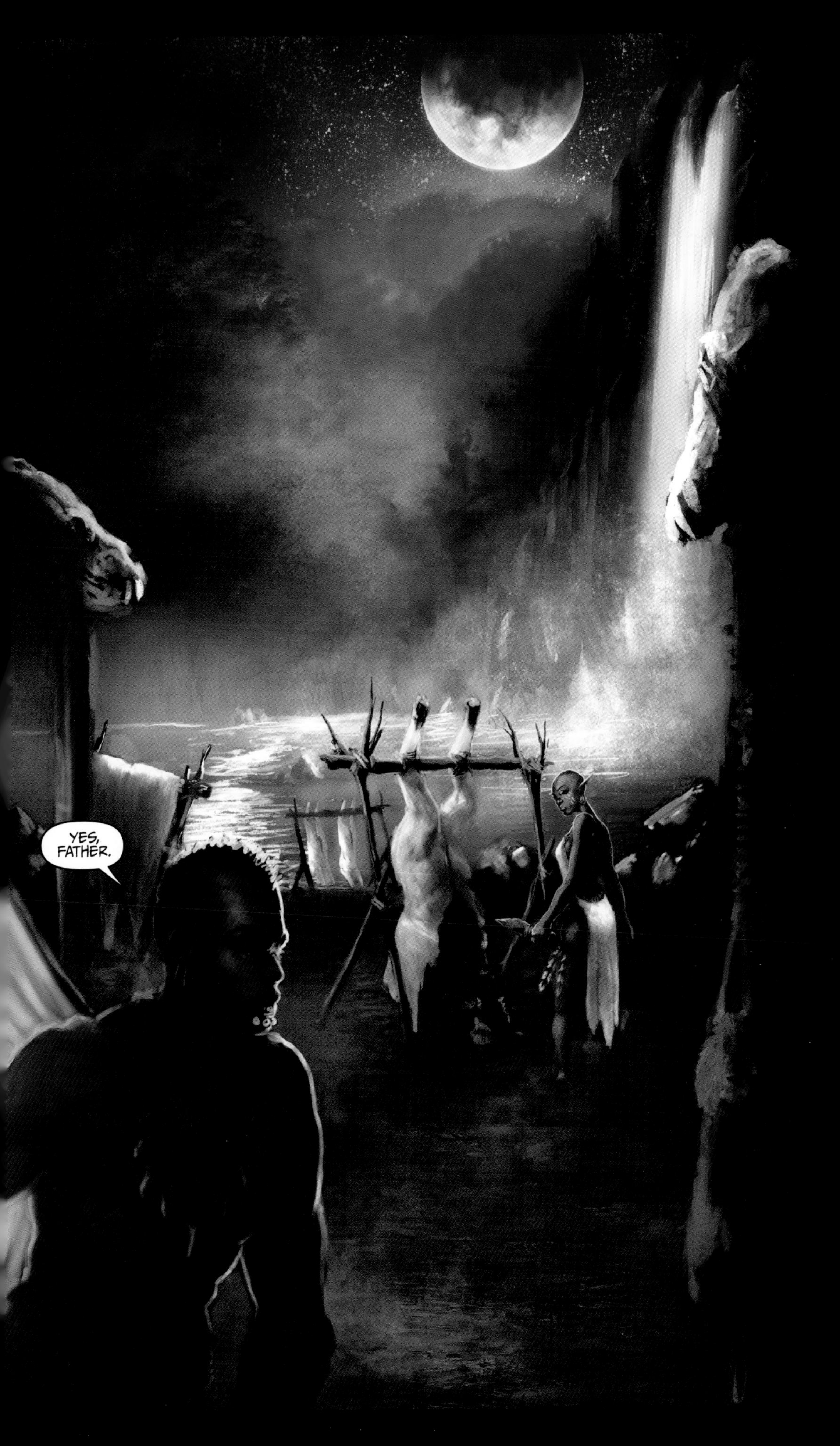
YES, FATHER.

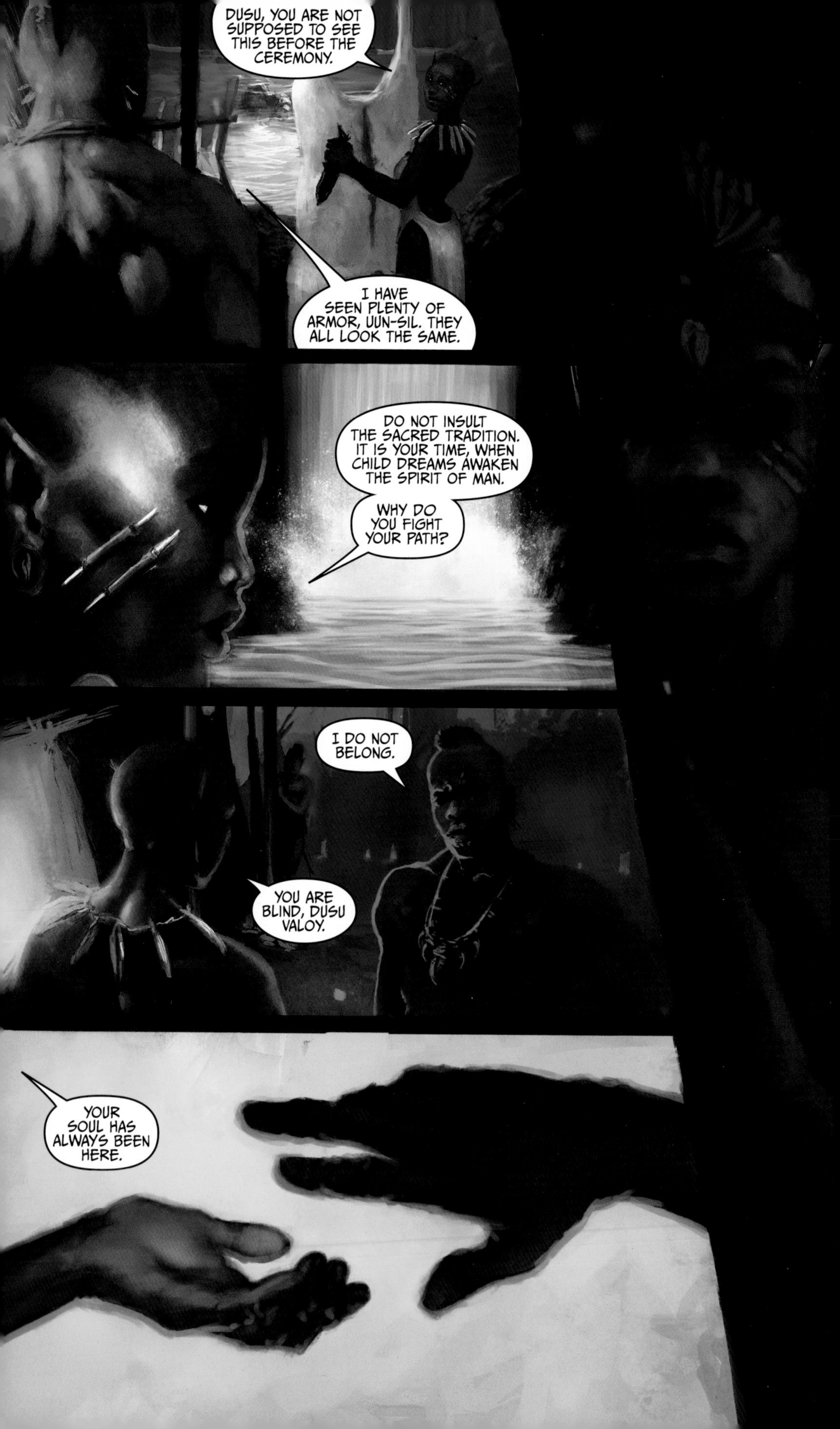
DUSU, YOU ARE NOT SUPPOSED TO SEE THIS BEFORE THE CEREMONY.
I HAVE SEEN PLENTY OF ARMOR, UUN-SIL. THEY ALL LOOK THE SAME.
DO NOT INSULT THE SACRED TRADITION. IT IS YOUR TIME, WHEN CHILD DREAMS AWAKEN THE SPIRIT OF MAN.
WHY DO YOU FIGHT YOUR PATH?
I DO NOT BELONG.
YOU ARE BLIND, DUSU VALOY.
YOUR SOUL HAS ALWAYS BEEN HERE.

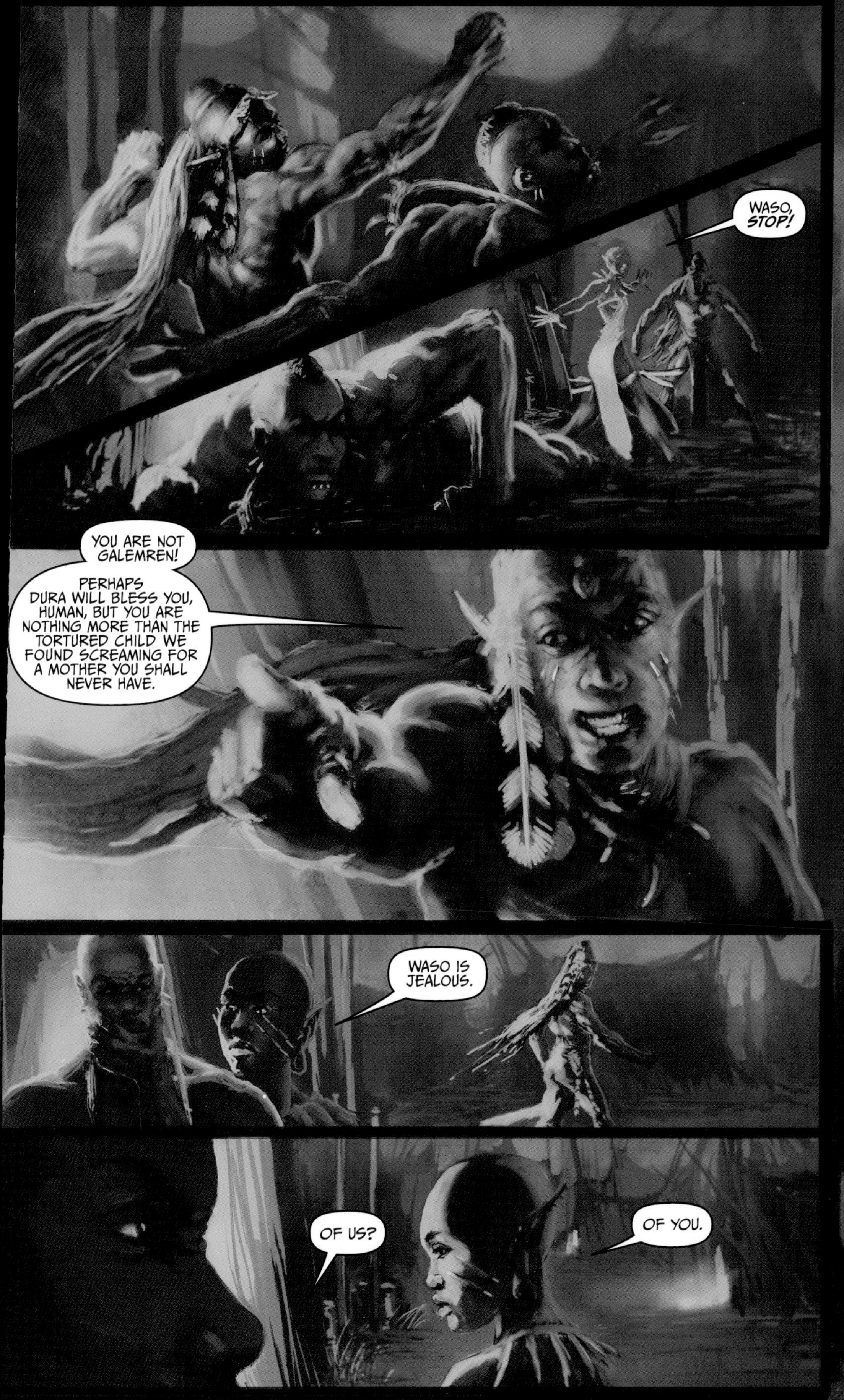

WASO, STOP!
YOU ARE NOT GALEMREN!
PERHAPS DURA WILL BLESS YOU, HUMAN, BUT YOU ARE NOTHING MORE THAN THE TORTURED CHILD WE FOUND SCREAMING FOR A MOTHER YOU SHALL NEVER HAVE.
WASO IS JEALOUS.
OF US?
OF YOU.

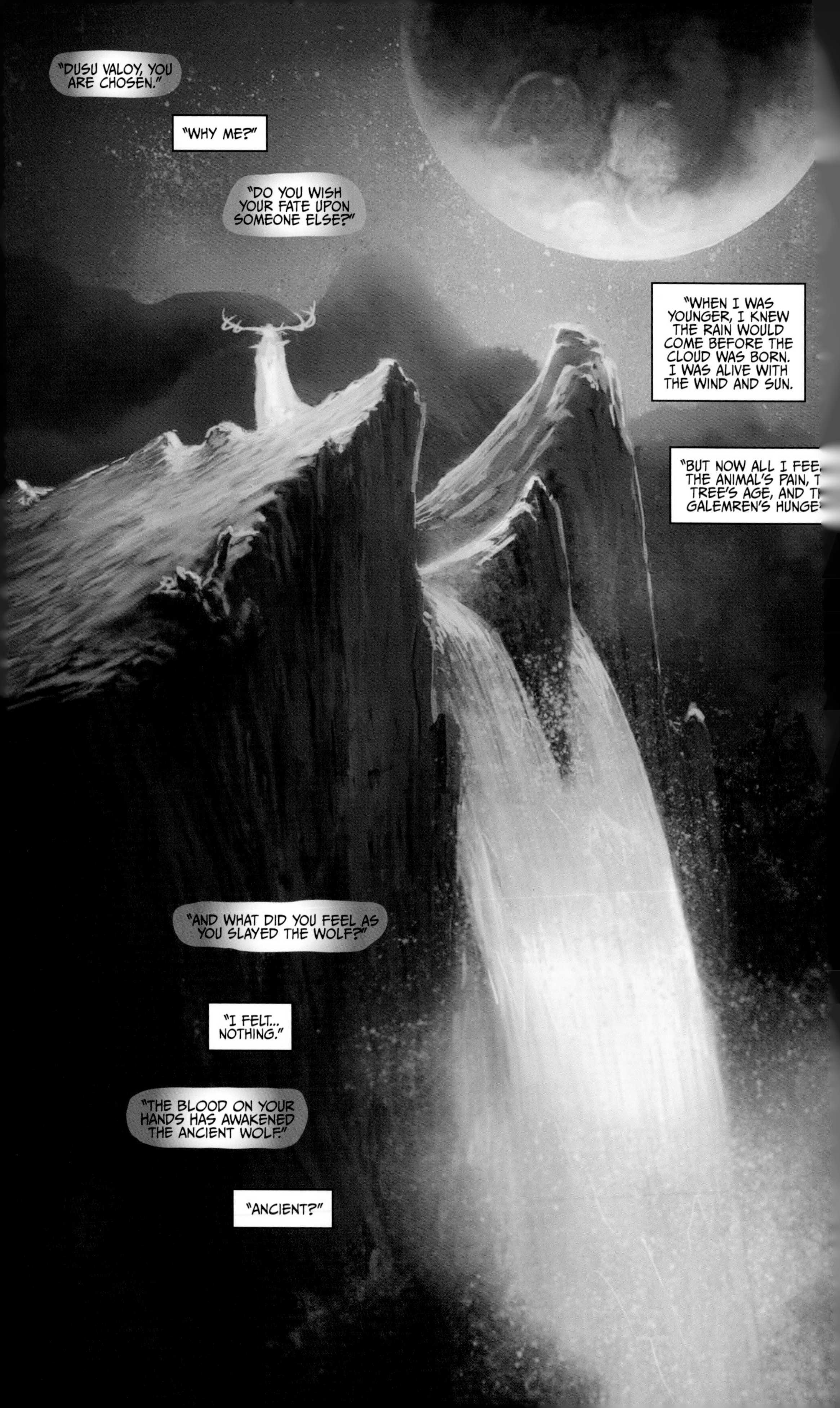
"DUSU VALOY, YOU ARE CHOSEN."
"WHY ME?"
"DO YOU WISH YOUR FATE UPON SOMEONE ELSE?"
"WHEN I WAS YOUNGER, I KNEW THE RAIN WOULD COME BEFORE THE CLOUD WAS BORN. I WAS ALIVE WITH THE WIND AND SUN.
"BUT NOW ALL I FEE THE ANIMAL'S PAIN, T TREE'S AGE, AND T GALEMREN'S HUNGE
"AND WHAT DID YOU FEEL AS YOU SLAYED THE WOLF?"
"I FELT... NOTHING."
"THE BLOOD ON YOUR HANDS HAS AWAKENED THE ANCIENT WOLF."
"ANCIENT?"

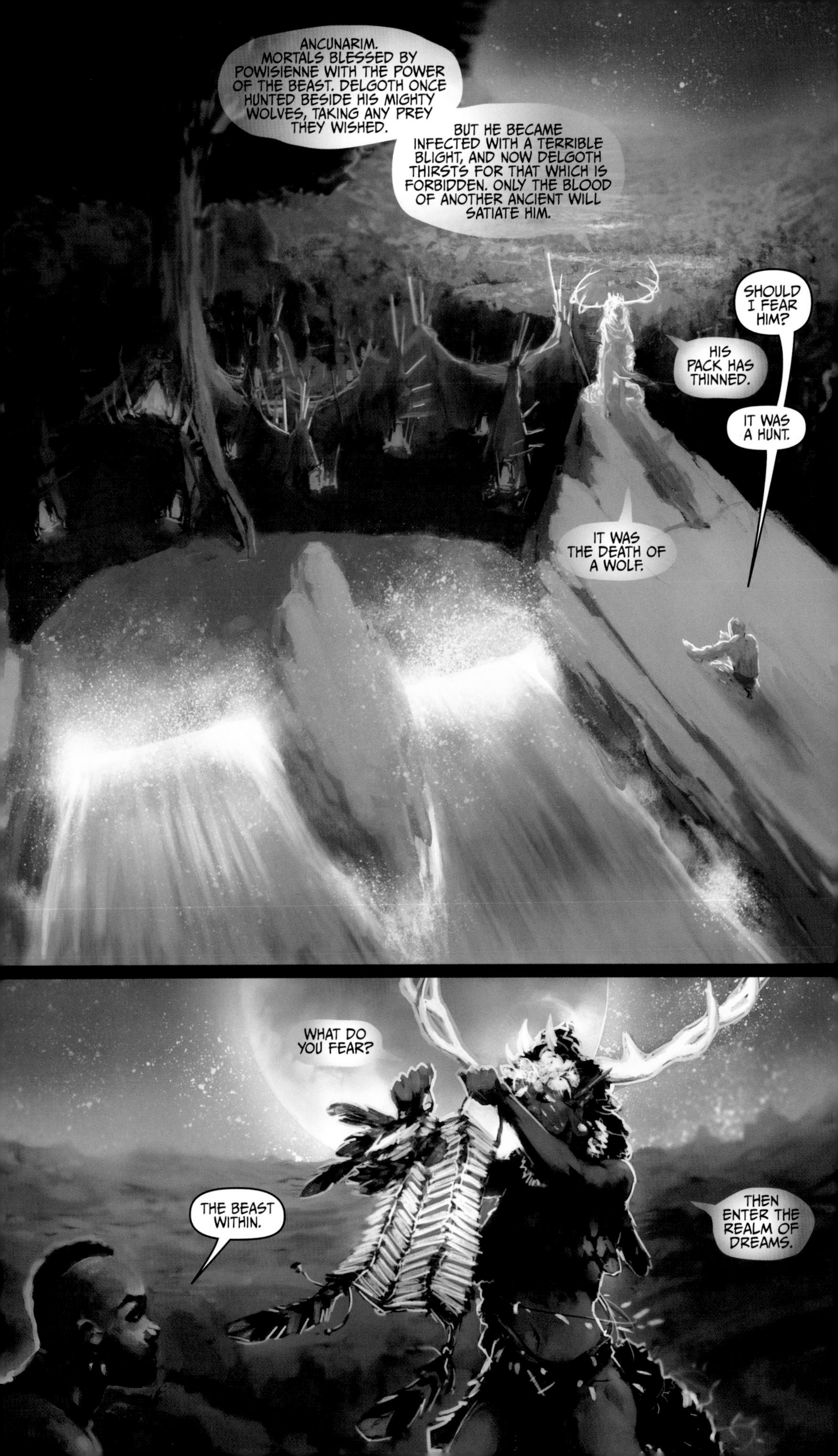
ANCUNARIM. MORTALS BLESSED BY POWISIENNE WITH THE POWER OF THE BEAST. DELGOTH ONCE HUNTED BESIDE HIS MIGHTY WOLVES, TAKING ANY PREY THEY WISHED.
BUT HE BECAME INFECTED WITH A TERRIBLE BLIGHT, AND NOW DELGOTH THIRSTS FOR THAT WHICH IS FORBIDDEN. ONLY THE BLOOD OF ANOTHER ANCIENT WILL SATIATE HIM.
SHOULD I FEAR HIM?
HIS PACK HAS THINNED.
IT WAS A HUNT.
IT WAS THE DEATH OF A WOLF.
WHAT DO YOU FEAR?
THE BEAST WITHIN.
THEN ENTER THE REALM OF DREAMS.

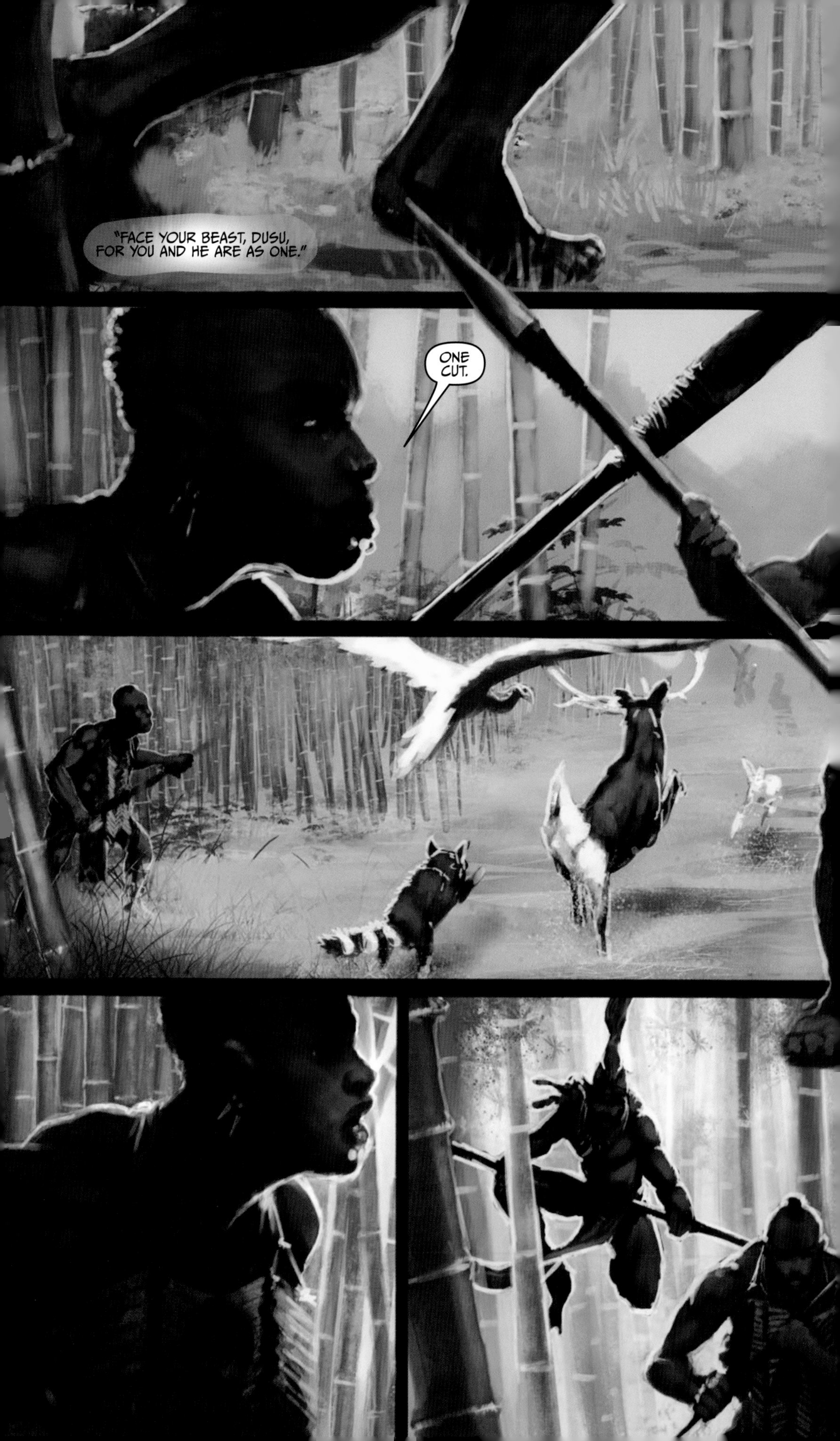
"FACE YOUR BEAST, DUSU, FOR YOU AND HE ARE AS ONE."
ONE CUT.

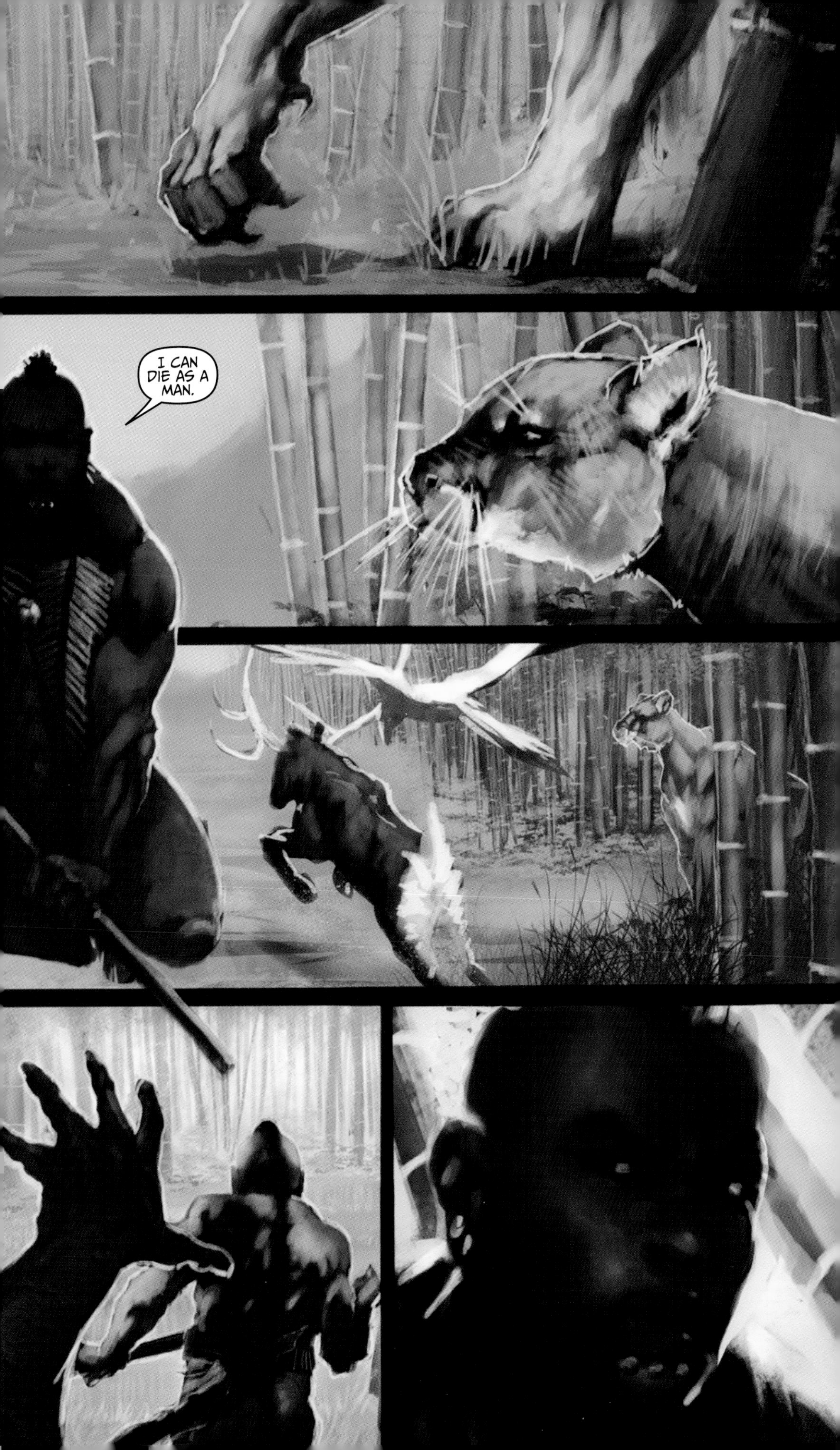
I CAN DIE AS A MAN.

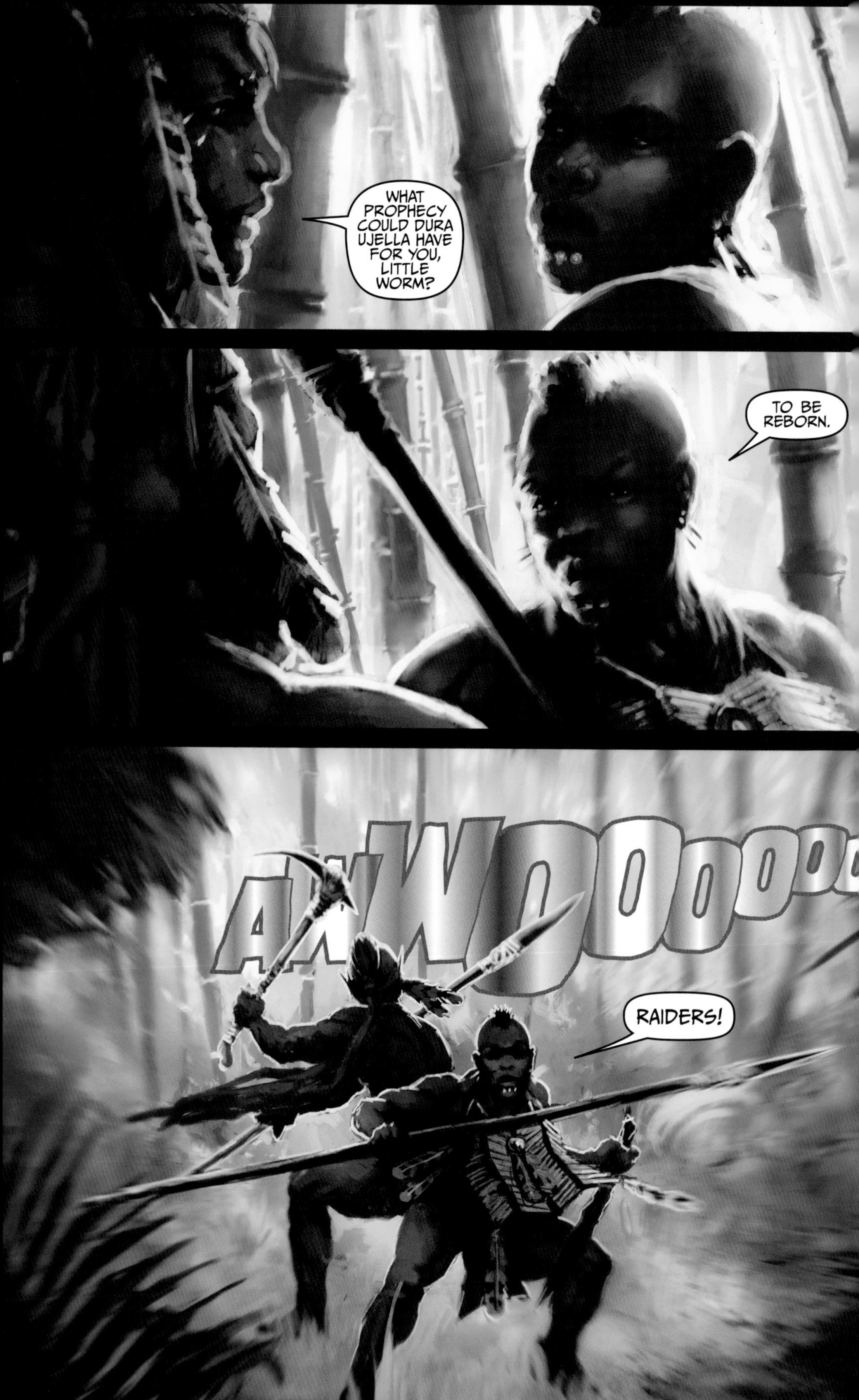
WHAT PROPHECY COULD DURA UJELLA HAVE FOR YOU, LITTLE WORM?
TO BE REBORN.
RAIDERS!

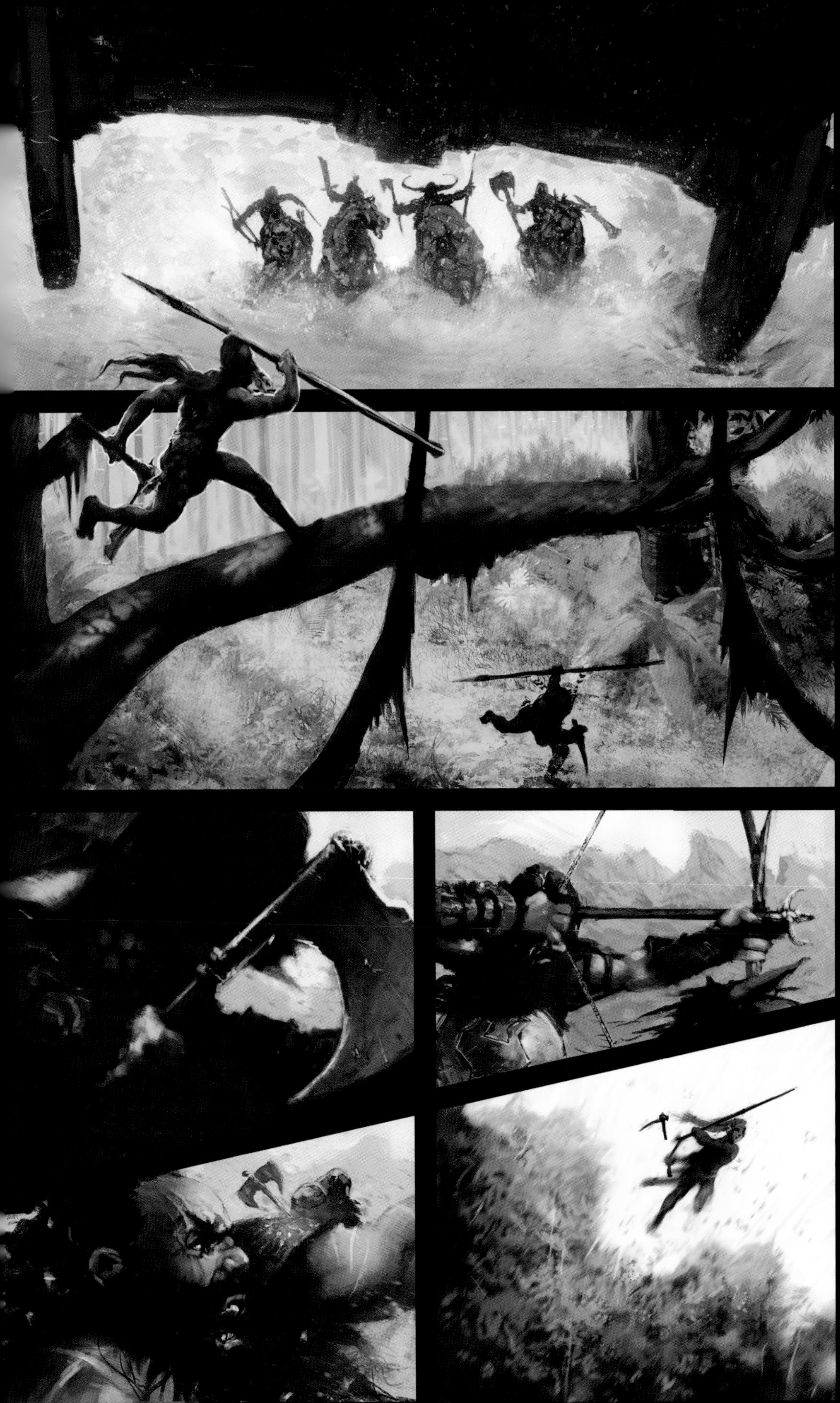

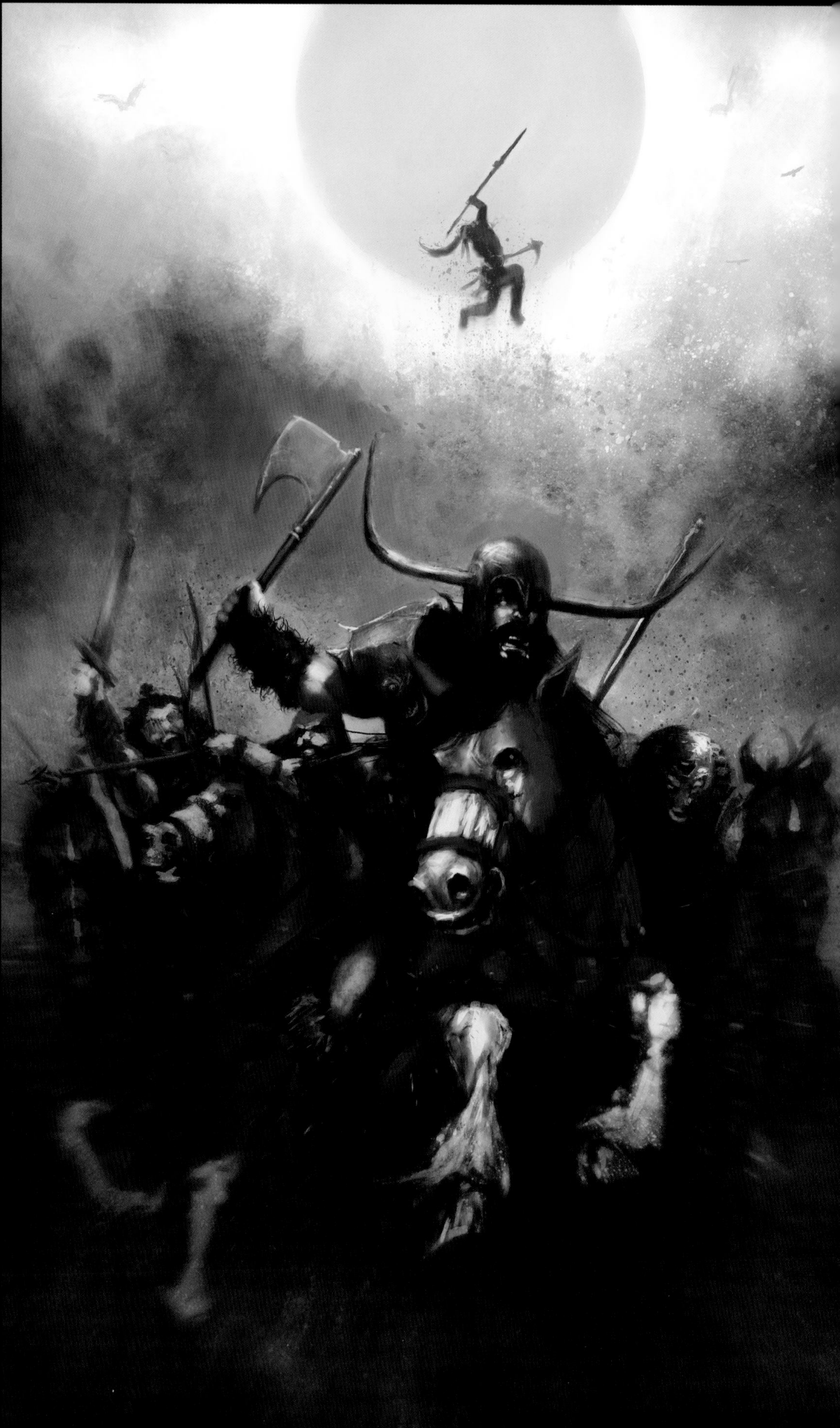

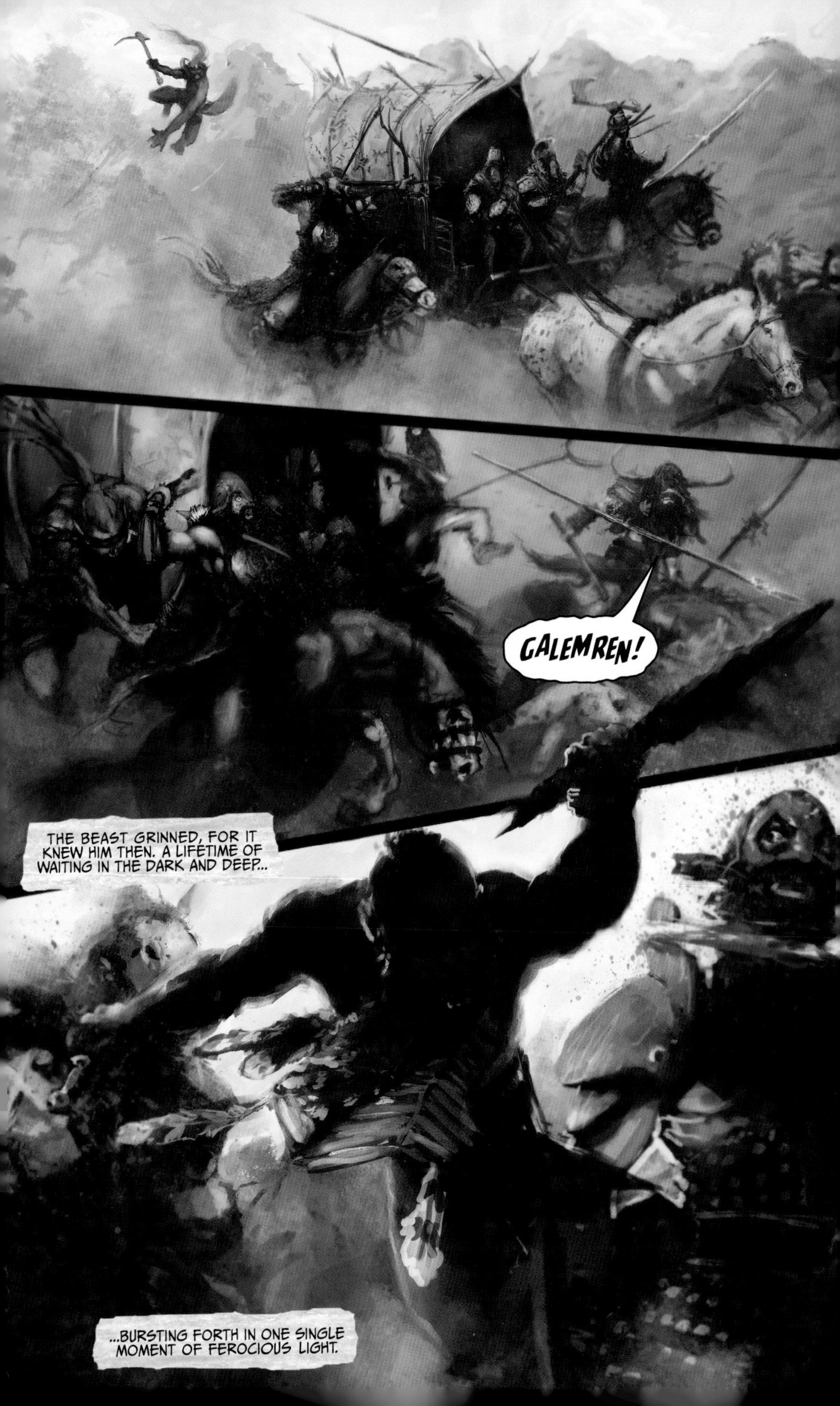
GALEMREN!
THE BEAST GRINNED, FOR IT KNEW HIM THEN. A LIFETIME OF WAITING IN THE DARK AND DEEP...
...BURSTING FORTH IN ONE SINGLE MOMENT OF FEROCIOUS LIGHT.

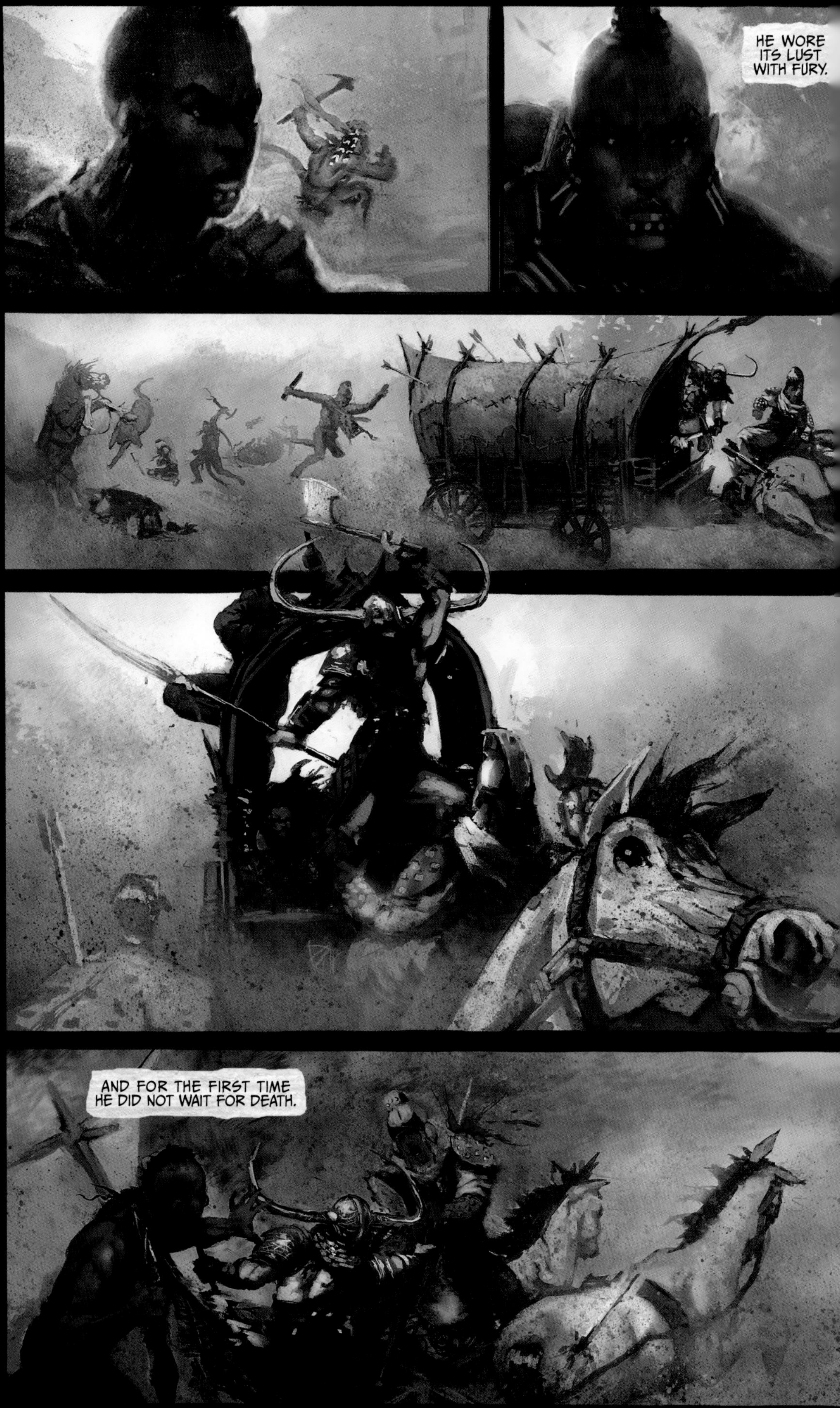
HE WORE ITS LUST WITH FURY.
AND FOR THE FIRST TIME HE DID NOT WAIT FOR DEATH.

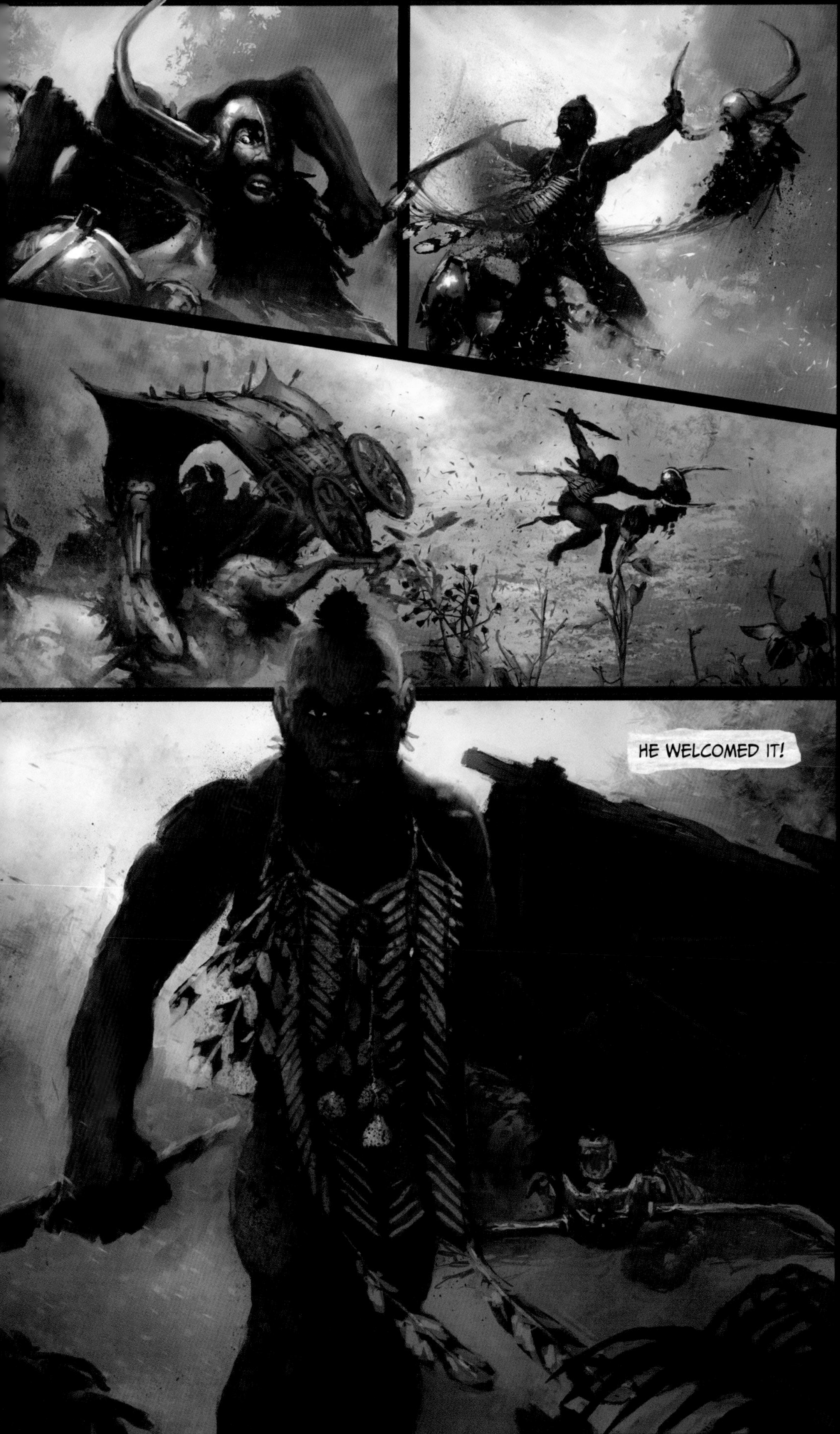
HE WELCOMED IT!

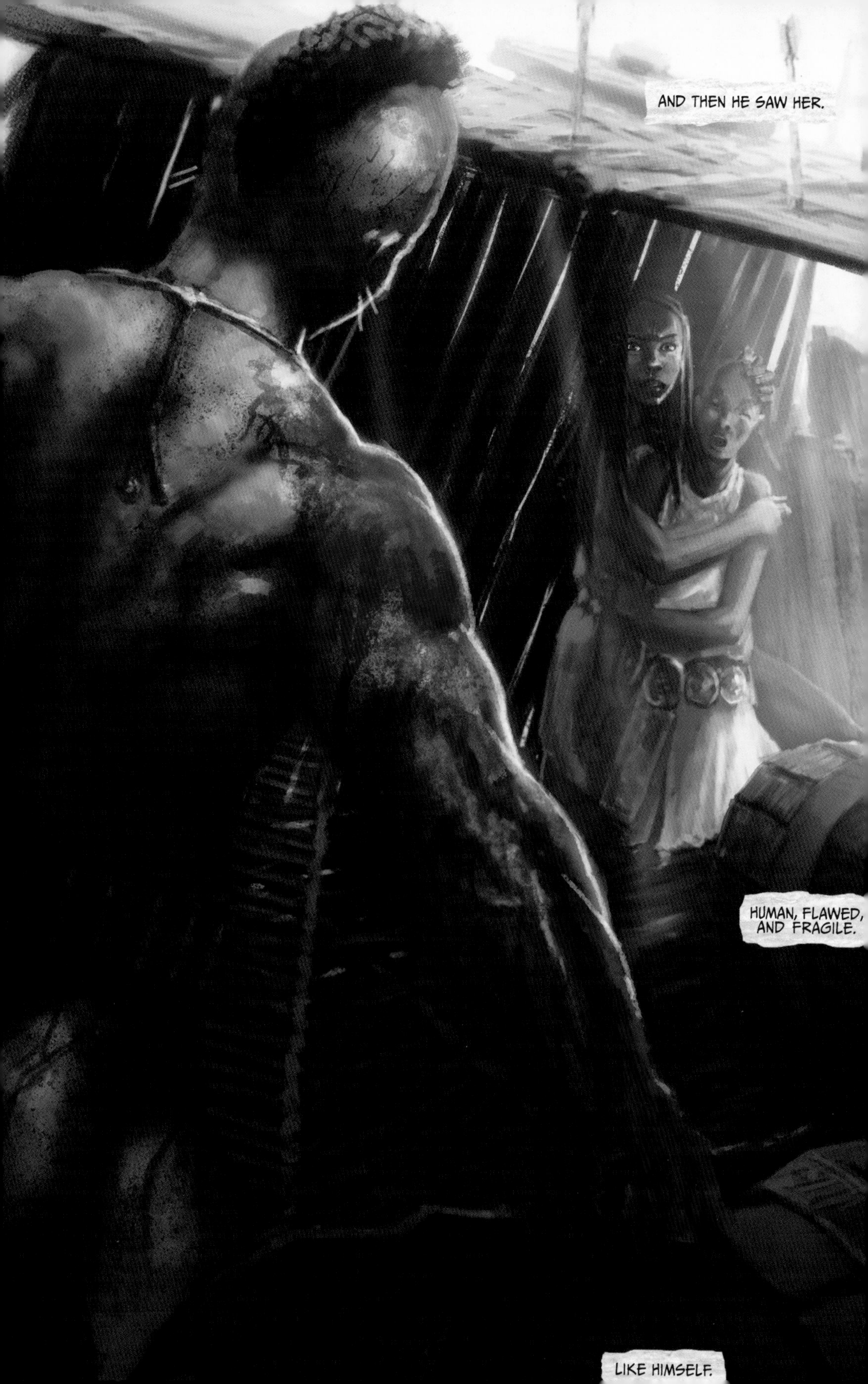
AND THEN HE SAW HER.
HUMAN, FLAWED, AND FRAGILE.
LIKE HIMSELF.

Hello Stranger,

Tales of love and loss are kin to life and death, and for those who are sired in such and turmoil, they must either look for answers, hide within, or seek the ruin of those they would blame. Such is the fable of Powisienne, The Shepherd God, Su, The First Born, and their Isinniel offspring, the Elves of Asunda.

When the world was first born, Powisienne, The Woodweaver, was sculpting the forests of Frivanna when he saw Su, the first Fey Child of Esu, The Mother Dragon of Creation. They fell in love, and Su bore the God many children. Some took after their Mother and attuned to the world's essence of mana, whereas others followed their spirit father's love of flora and fauna and became guardians of nature, allowing Powisienne to work with Mithiriel, The Maker, on the carving of mountains.

It was upon a wet, overcast day that Mithiriel bade Powisienne rest while The Maker slept deep within the mountain realm of Turanghem. As Powisienne looked out upon all he had wrought, Su came to visit her husband, and they made love. But the God was deceived. It was not Su, but Magga, The Silver Moon Dragon, in her guise. Soon Magga bore children of her own deep within the cavernous bowels of Morrok, children so like their half-siblings but with the unmistakable touch of their silver mother. These Silver Elves were to be called the Morkai, the most feared and hated race on Asunda. Upon learning of this trickery, Su became so consumed with grief that she passed away. Her magical essence rippled across Asunda, waking her kin and all others who slumbered. Powisienne wept, and his tears fell from the heavens, swelling rivers and crumbling cliffs.

The Morkai cling to a very different belief, that they were the first born, but that is a tale for another day. Whichever you believe, the Isinniel were broken. The high-minded Quellya, who were closest to their mother, shut themselves in hidden cities and tall towers, refusing to trust the outside world. The woodland Selvanu pitied their father and continued to till the earth and tend the trees. And the Galemren, they would embody Powisienne's free spirit and righteous anger, proclaiming an oath to annihilate their Morkai cousins and anyone who would tamper with the balance of things. These tribal elves, harnessing the soul of the land, roam as warrior nomads with wrath and furious vengeance across the vast and volatile world of…

Chapter 2

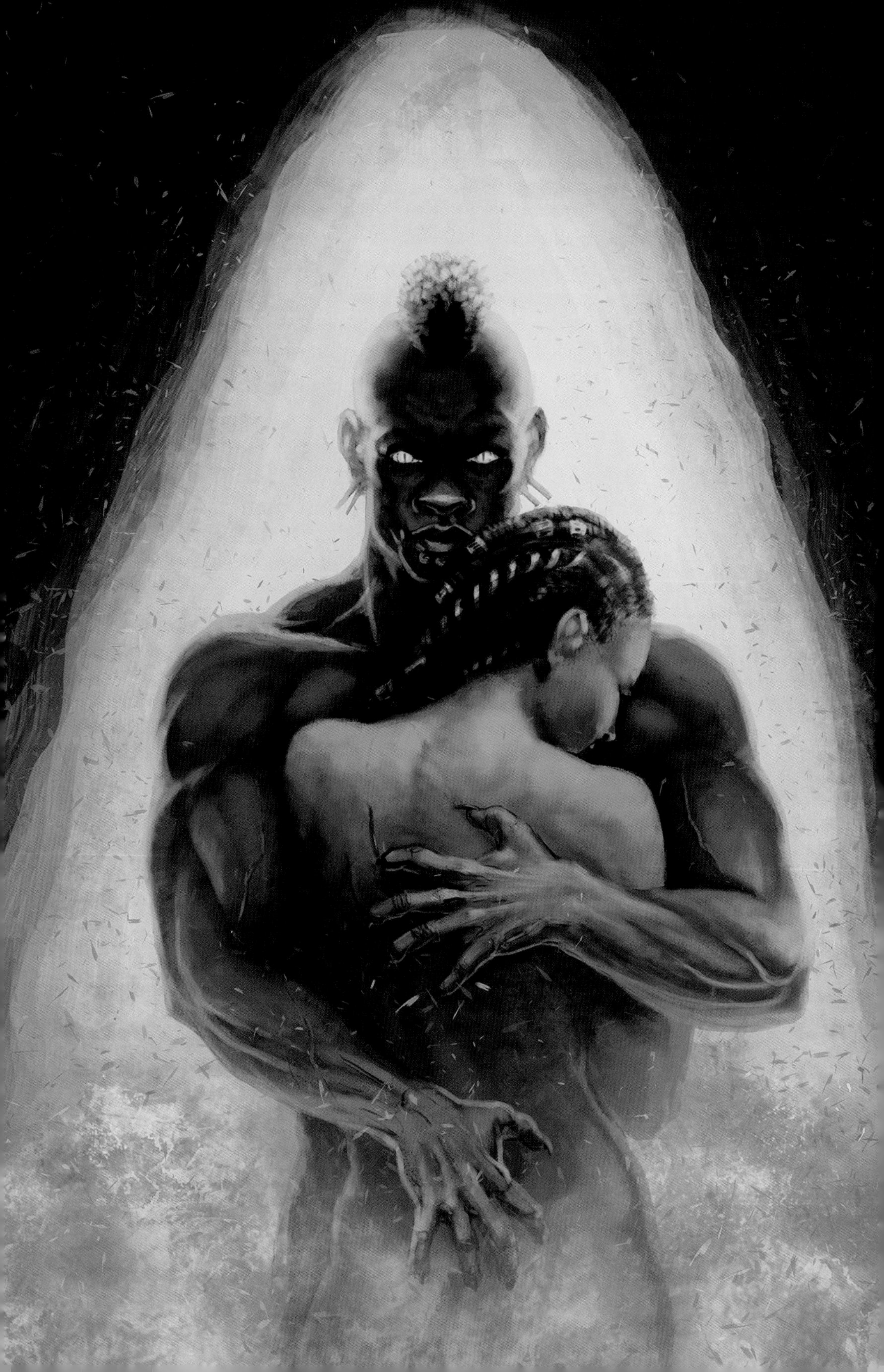

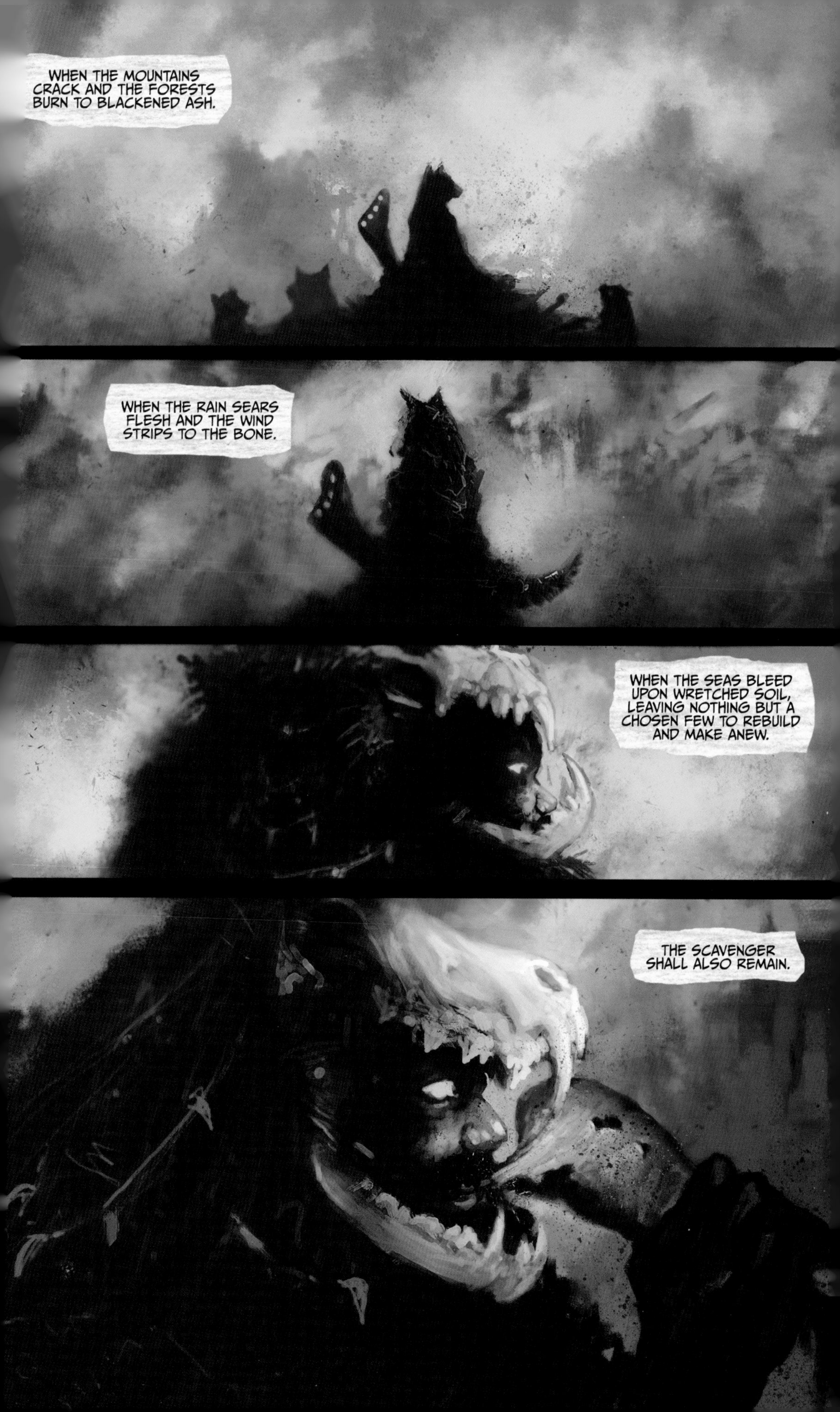

WHEN THE MOUNTAINS CRACK AND THE FORESTS BURN TO BLACKENED ASH.
WHEN THE RAIN SEARS FLESH AND THE WIND STRIPS TO THE BONE.
WHEN THE SEAS BLEED UPON WRETCHED SOIL, LEAVING NOTHING BUT A CHOSEN FEW TO REBUILD AND MAKE ANEW.
THE SCAVENGER SHALL ALSO REMAIN.

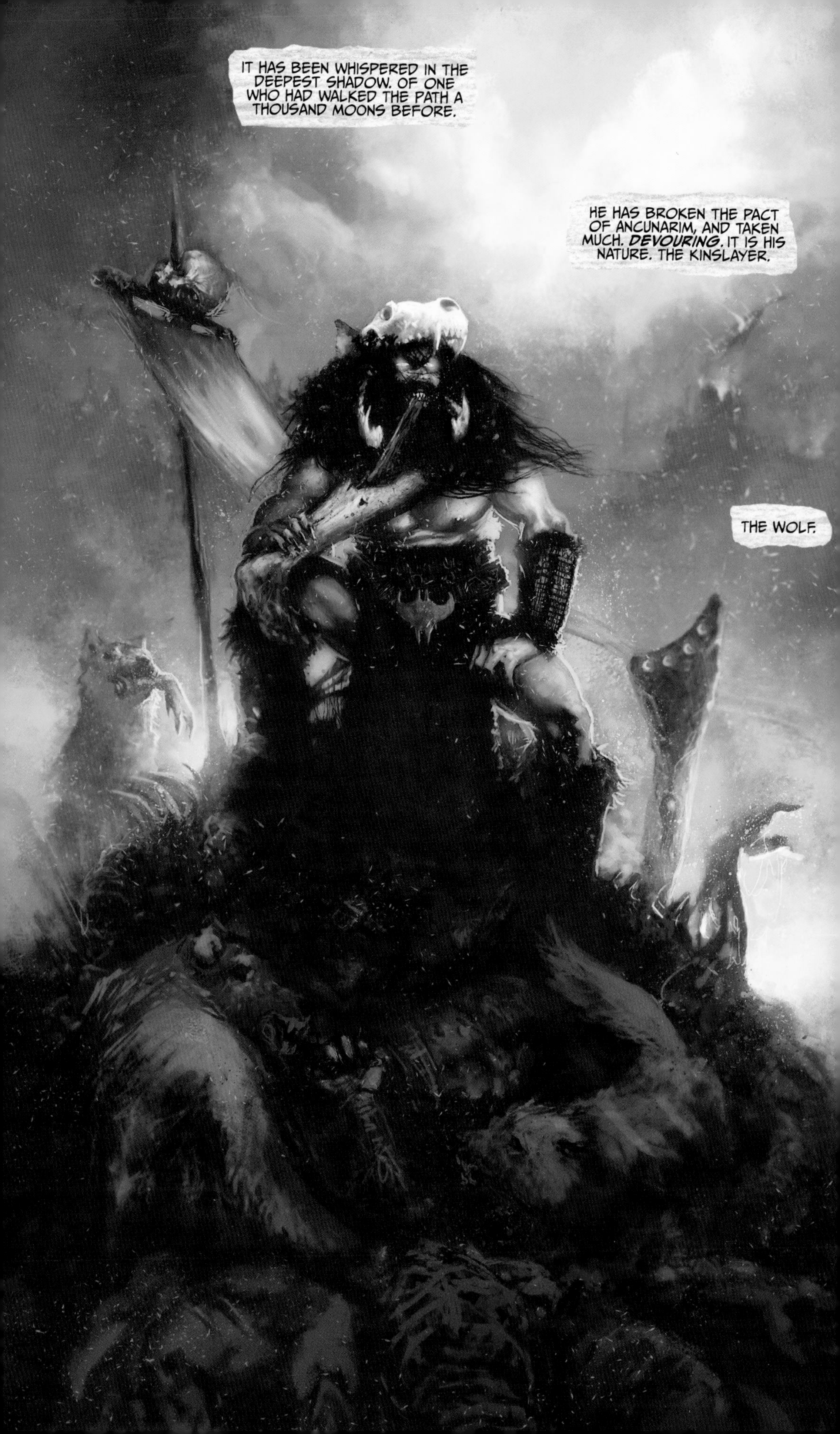
IT HAS BEEN WHISPERED IN THE DEEPEST SHADOW. OF ONE WHO HAD WALKED THE PATH A THOUSAND MOONS BEFORE.
HE HAS BROKEN THE PACT OF ANCUNARIM, AND TAKEN MUCH. *DEVOURING.* IT IS HIS NATURE. THE KINSLAYER.
THE WOLF.

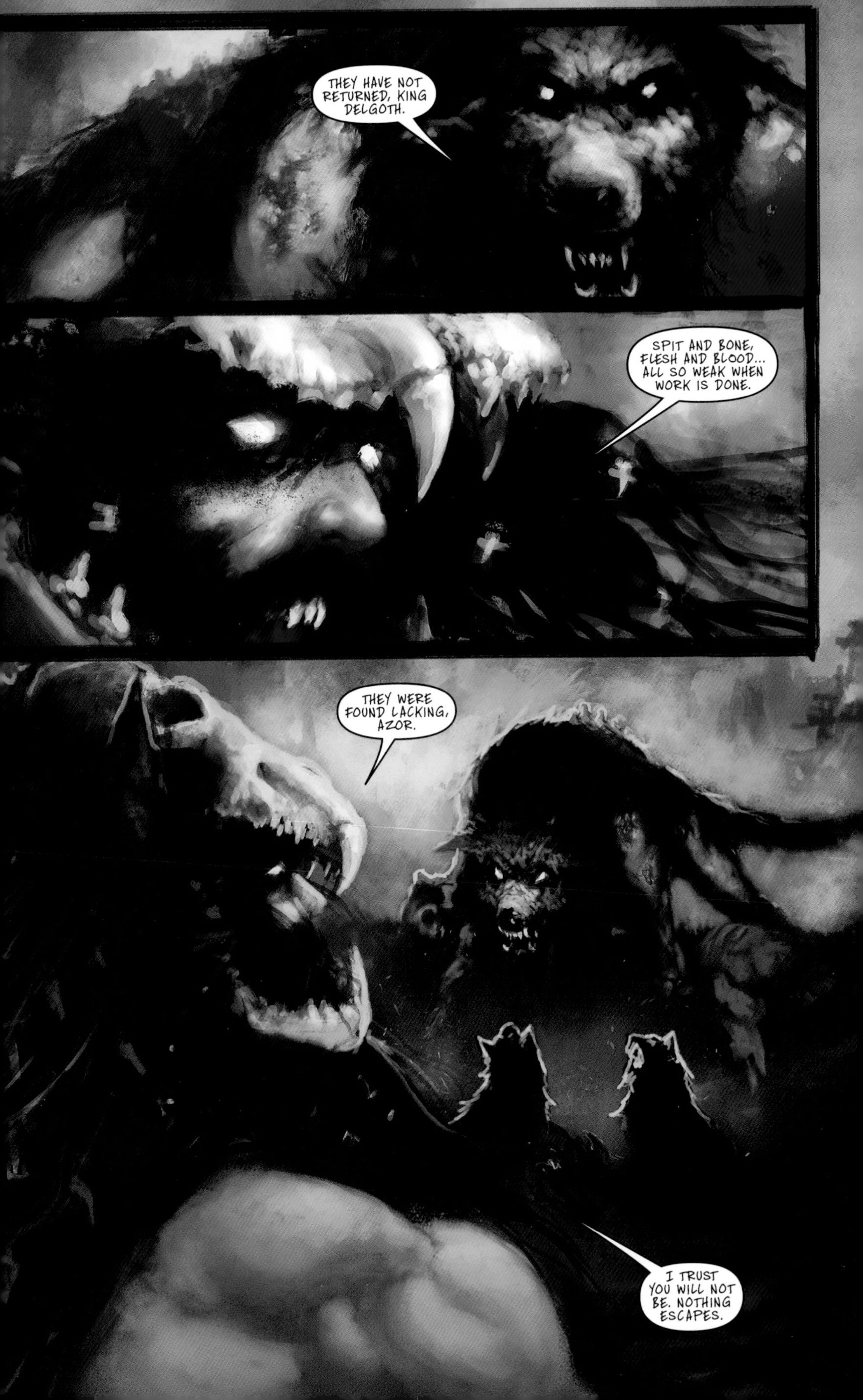
THEY HAVE NOT RETURNED, KING DELGOTH.
SPIT AND BONE, FLESH AND BLOOD... ALL SO WEAK WHEN WORK IS DONE.
THEY WERE FOUND LACKING, AZOR.
I TRUST YOU WILL NOT BE. NOTHING ESCAPES.

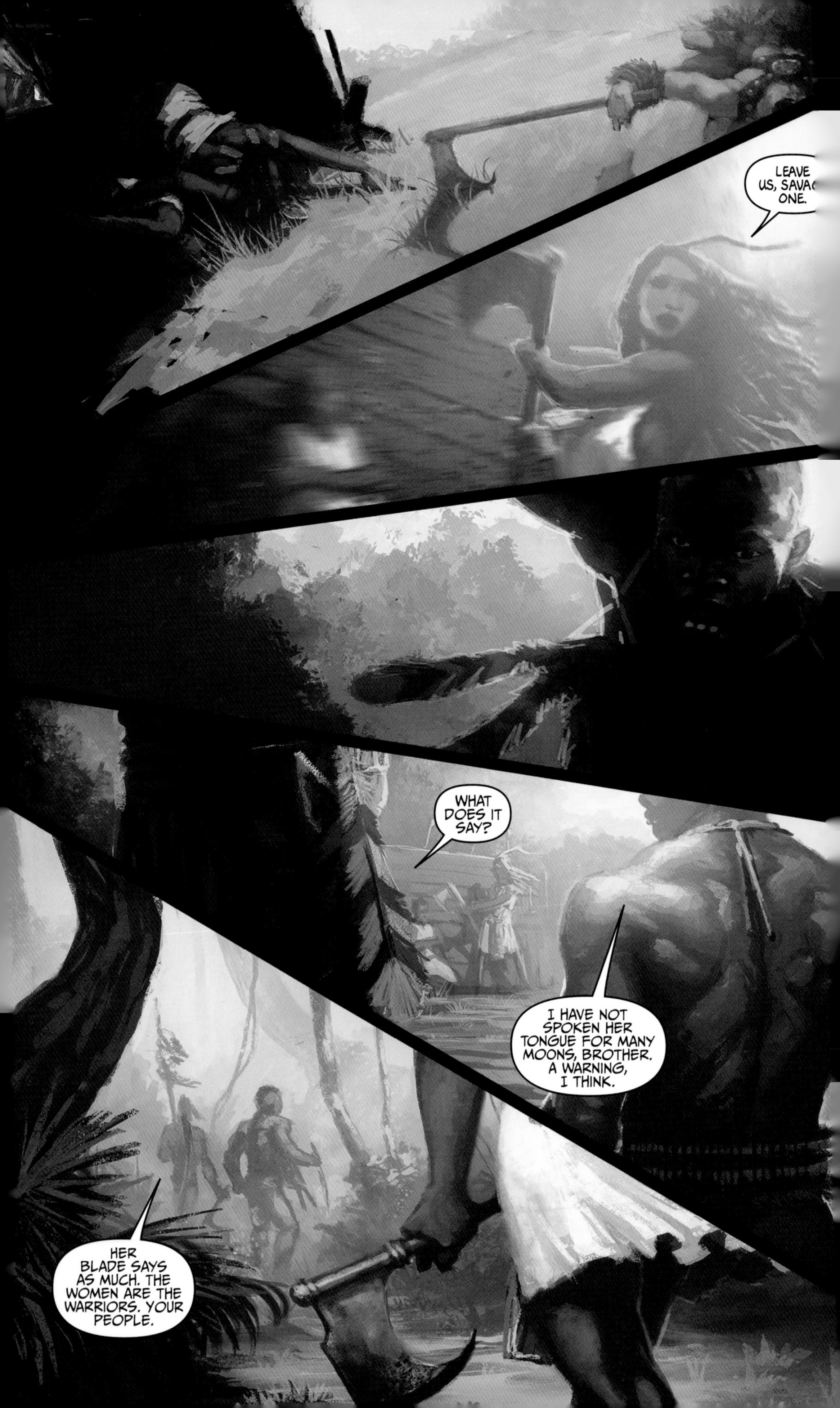
LEAVE US, SAVAG ONE.
WHAT DOES IT SAY?
I HAVE NOT SPOKEN HER TONGUE FOR MANY MOONS, BROTHER. A WARNING, I THINK.
HER BLADE SAYS AS MUCH. THE WOMEN ARE THE WARRIORS. YOUR PEOPLE.

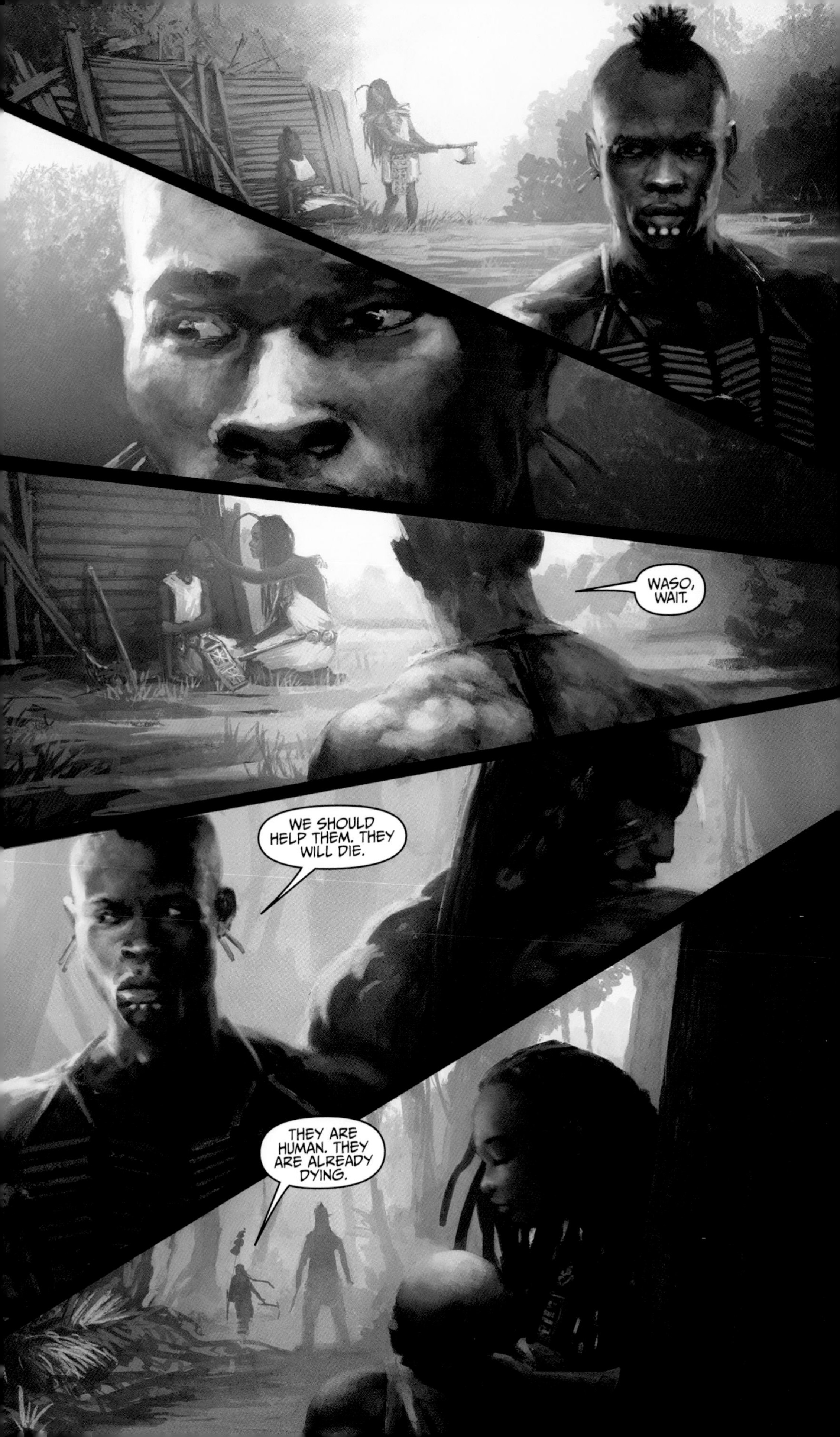
WASO, WAIT.
WE SHOULD HELP THEM. THEY WILL DIE.
THEY ARE HUMAN. THEY ARE ALREADY DYING.

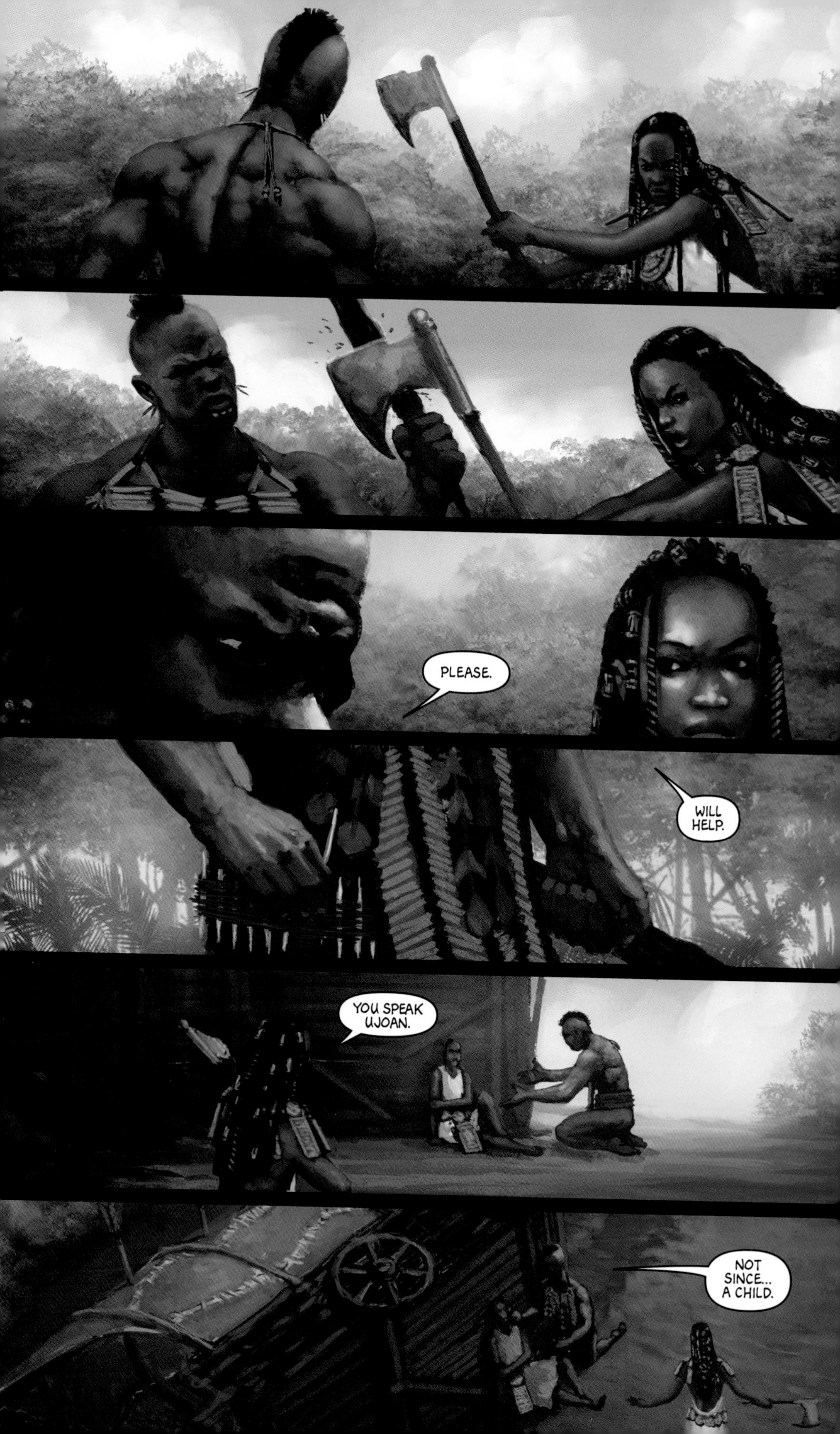
PLEASE.
WILL HELP.
YOU SPEAK UJOAN.
NOT SINCE... A CHILD.

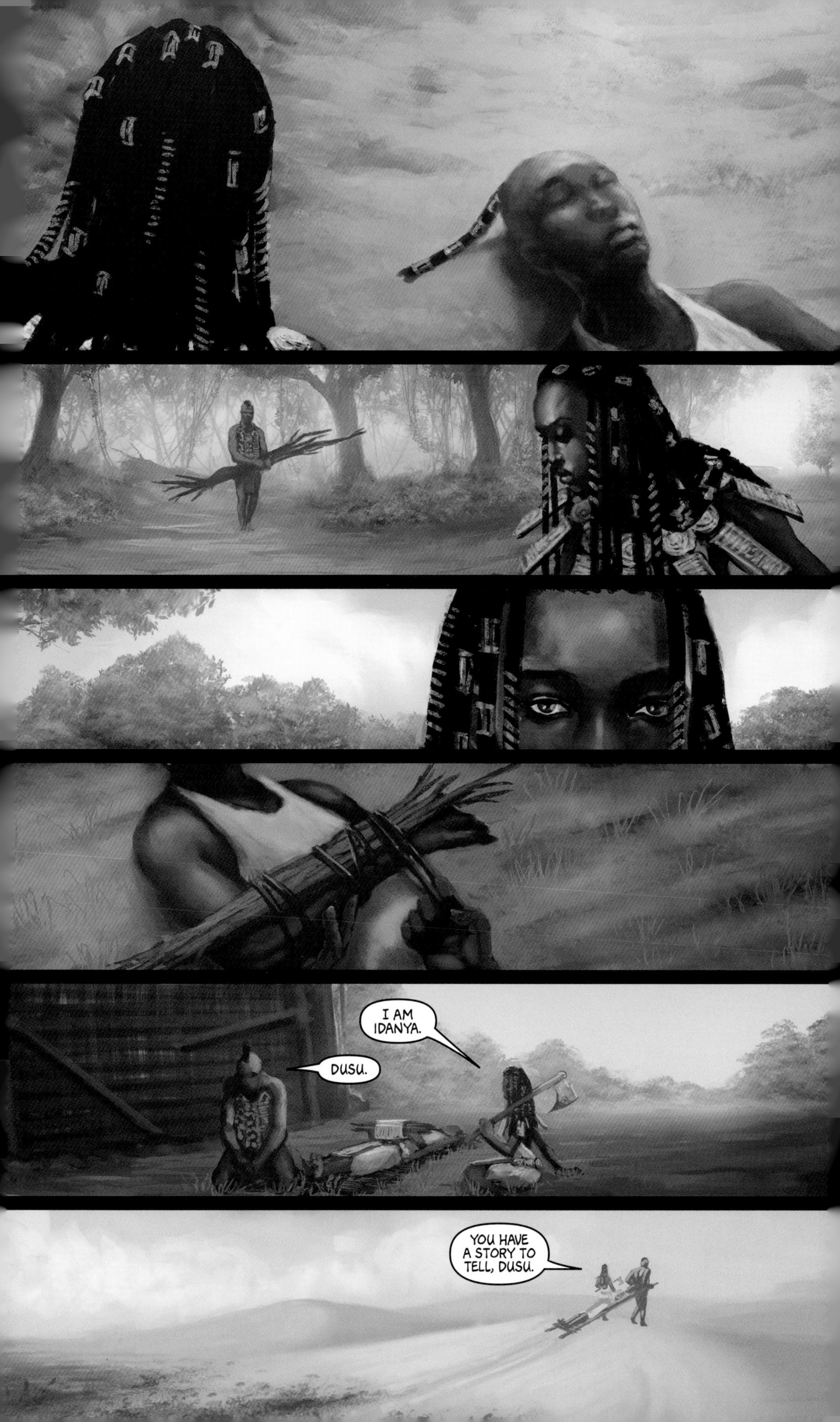
I AM IDANYA.
DUSU.
YOU HAVE A STORY TO TELL, DUSU.

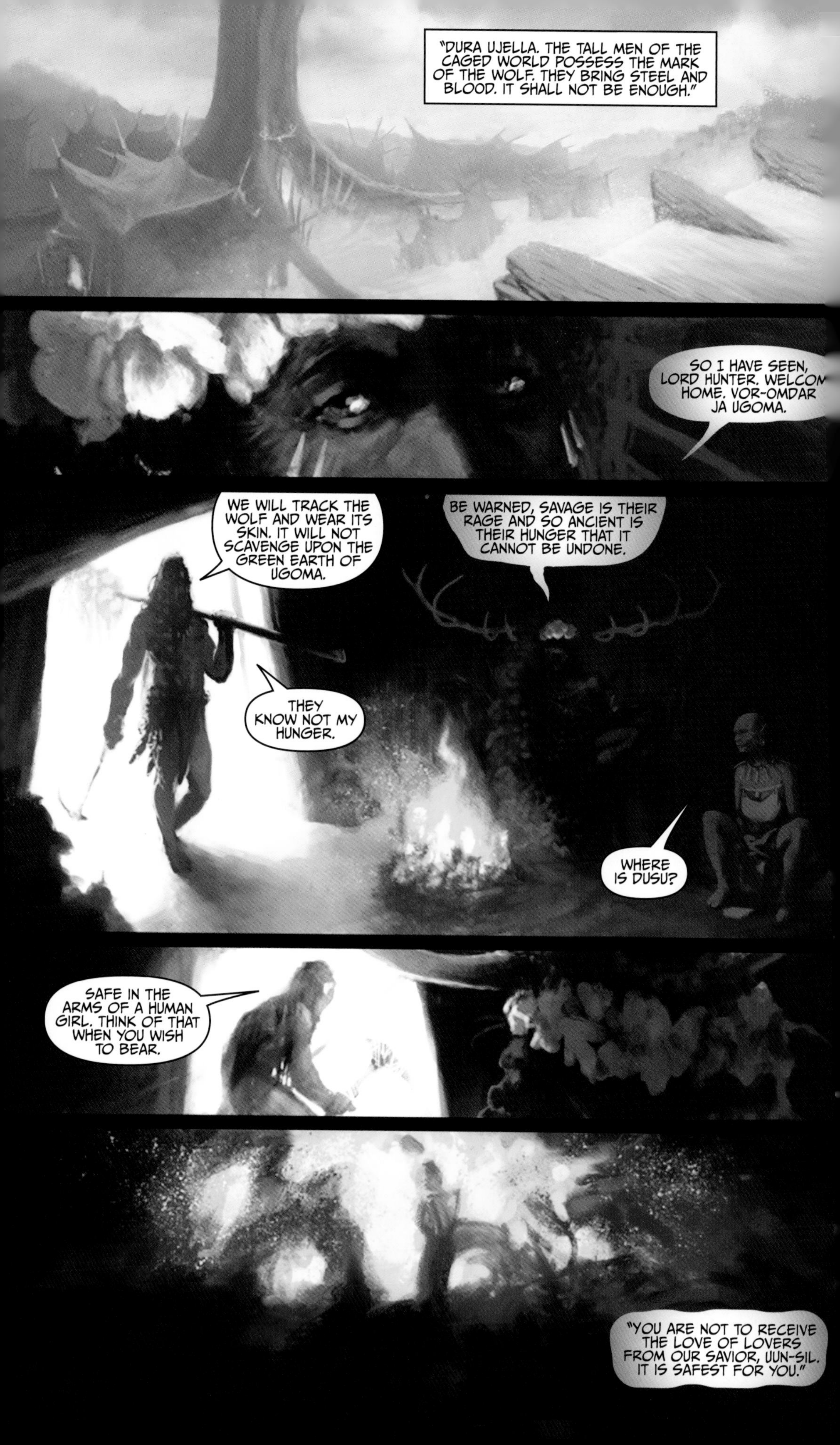
"DURA UJELLA. THE TALL MEN OF THE CAGED WORLD POSSESS THE MARK OF THE WOLF. THEY BRING STEEL AND BLOOD. IT SHALL NOT BE ENOUGH."
SO I HAVE SEEN, LORD HUNTER. WELCOM HOME. VOR-OMDAR JA UGOMA.
WE WILL TRACK THE WOLF AND WEAR ITS SKIN. IT WILL NOT SCAVENGE UPON THE GREEN EARTH OF UGOMA.
BE WARNED, SAVAGE IS THEIR RAGE AND SO ANCIENT IS THEIR HUNGER THAT IT CANNOT BE UNDONE.
THEY KNOW NOT MY HUNGER.
WHERE IS DUSU?
SAFE IN THE ARMS OF A HUMAN GIRL. THINK OF THAT WHEN YOU WISH TO BEAR.
"YOU ARE NOT TO RECEIVE THE LOVE OF LOVERS FROM OUR SAVIOR, UUN-SIL. IT IS SAFEST FOR YOU."

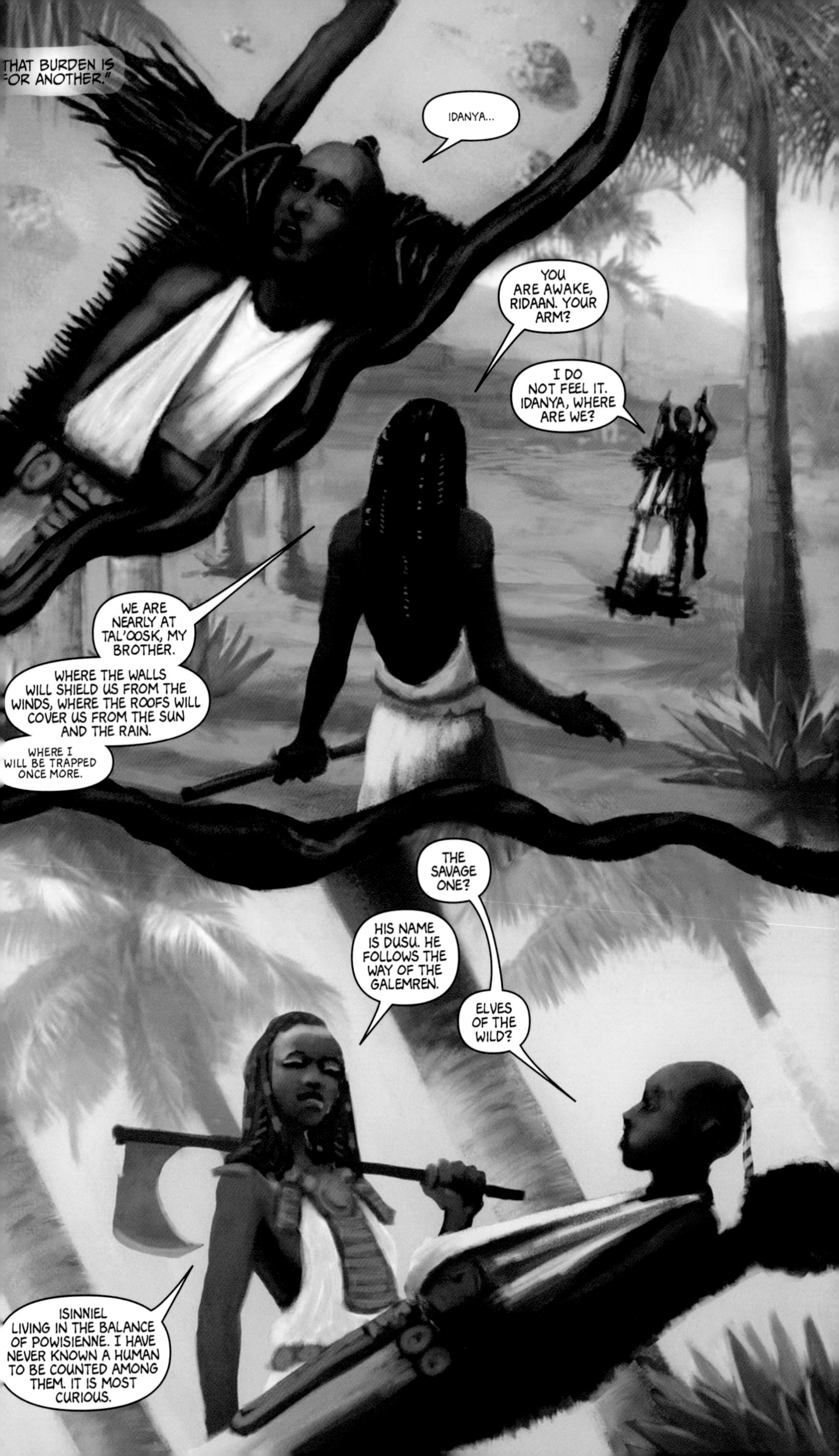
THAT BURDEN IS FOR ANOTHER."
IDANYA...
YOU ARE AWAKE, RIDAAN. YOUR ARM?
I DO NOT FEEL IT. IDANYA, WHERE ARE WE?
WE ARE NEARLY AT TAL'OOSK, MY BROTHER.
WHERE THE WALLS WILL SHIELD US FROM THE WINDS, WHERE THE ROOFS WILL COVER US FROM THE SUN AND THE RAIN.
WHERE I WILL BE TRAPPED ONCE MORE.
THE SAVAGE ONE?
HIS NAME IS DUSU. HE FOLLOWS THE WAY OF THE GALEMREN.
ELVES OF THE WILD?
ISINNIEL LIVING IN THE BALANCE OF POWISIENNE. I HAVE NEVER KNOWN A HUMAN TO BE COUNTED AMONG THEM. IT IS MOST CURIOUS.

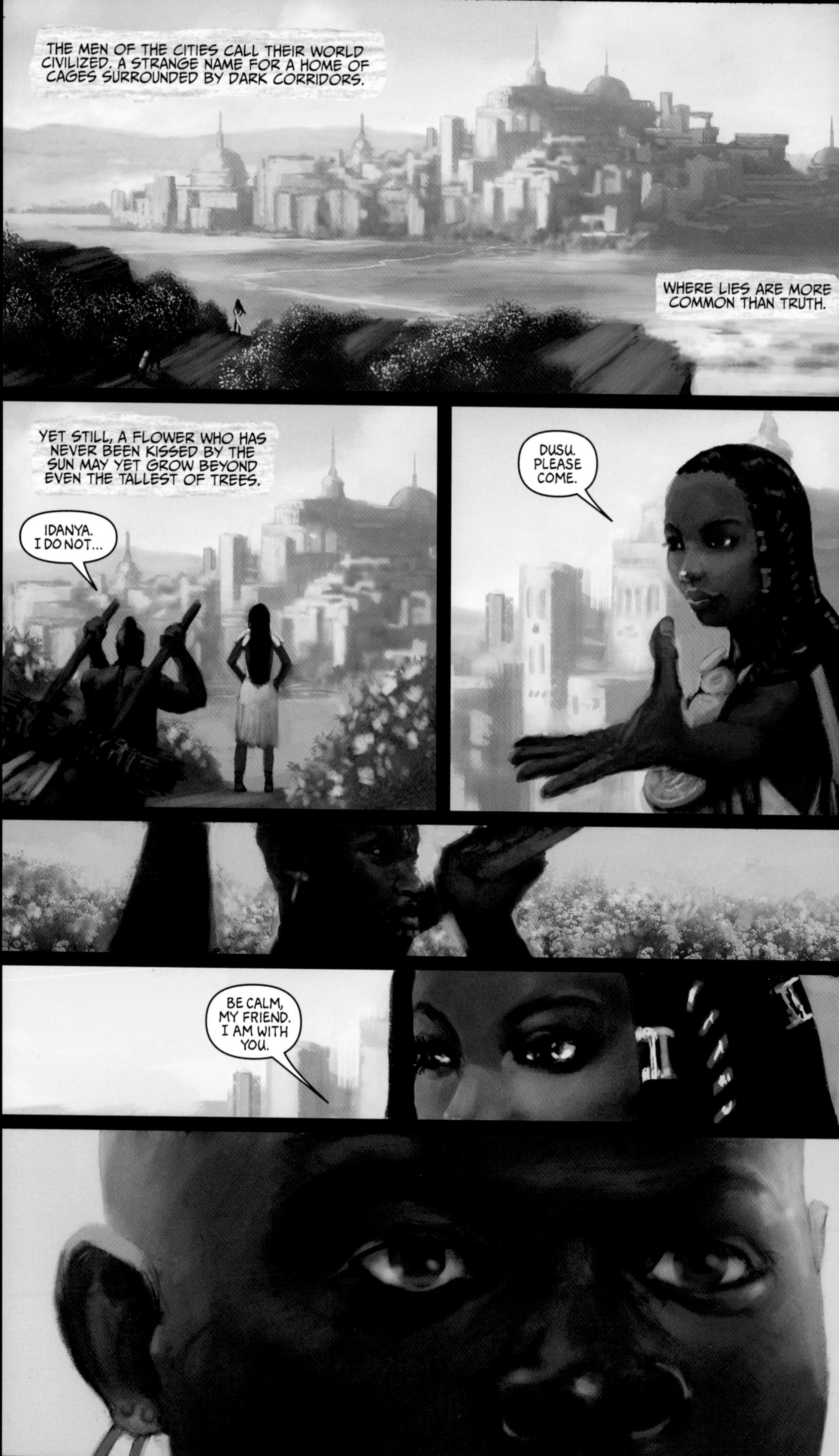
THE MEN OF THE CITIES CALL THEIR WORLD CIVILIZED. A STRANGE NAME FOR A HOME OF CAGES SURROUNDED BY DARK CORRIDORS.
WHERE LIES ARE MORE COMMON THAN TRUTH.
YET STILL, A FLOWER WHO HAS NEVER BEEN KISSED BY THE SUN MAY YET GROW BEYOND EVEN THE TALLEST OF TREES.
IDANYA. I DO NOT...
DUSU. PLEASE COME.
BE CALM, MY FRIEND. I AM WITH YOU.

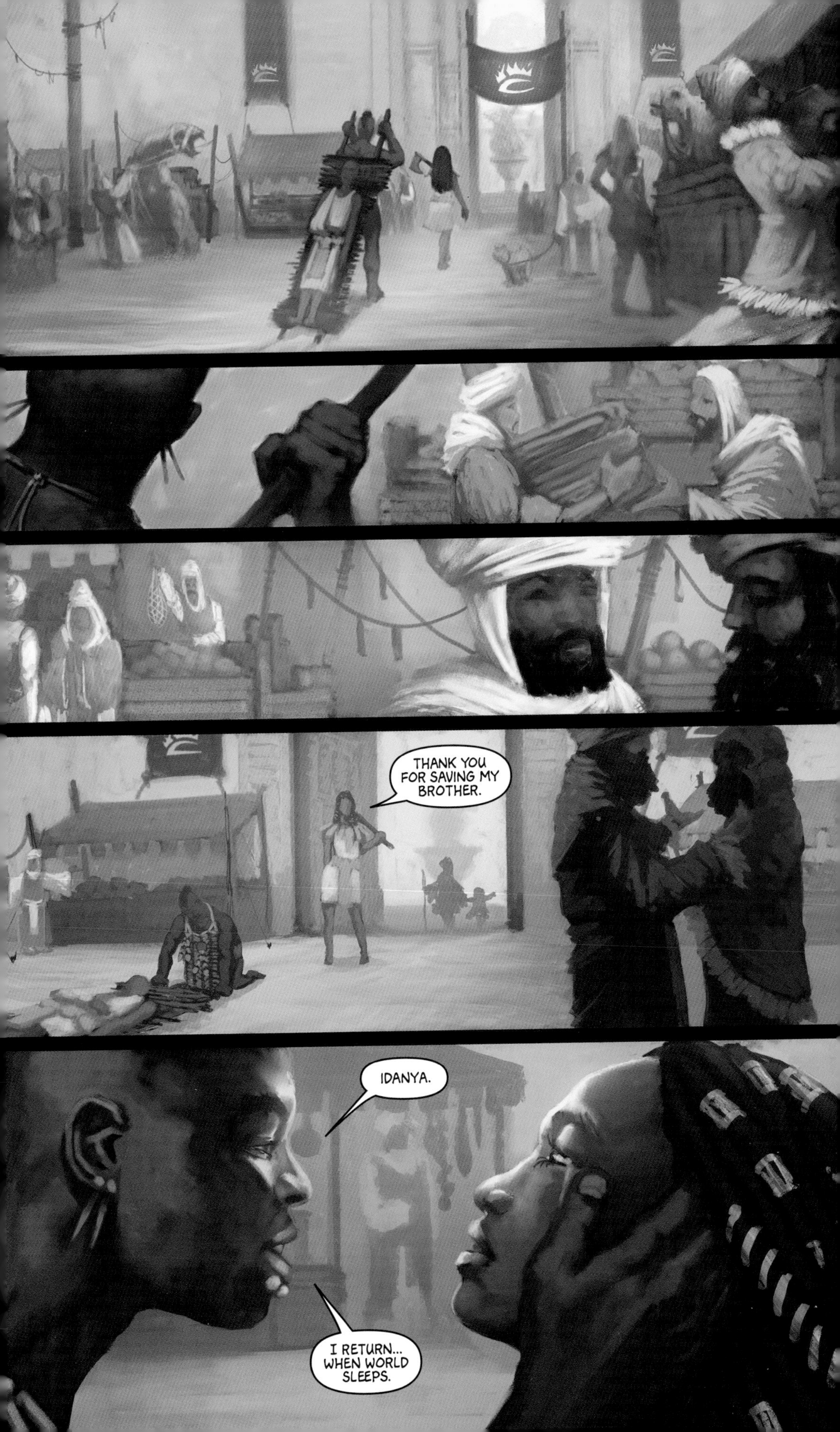
THANK YOU FOR SAVING MY BROTHER.
IDANYA.
I RETURN... WHEN WORLD SLEEPS.

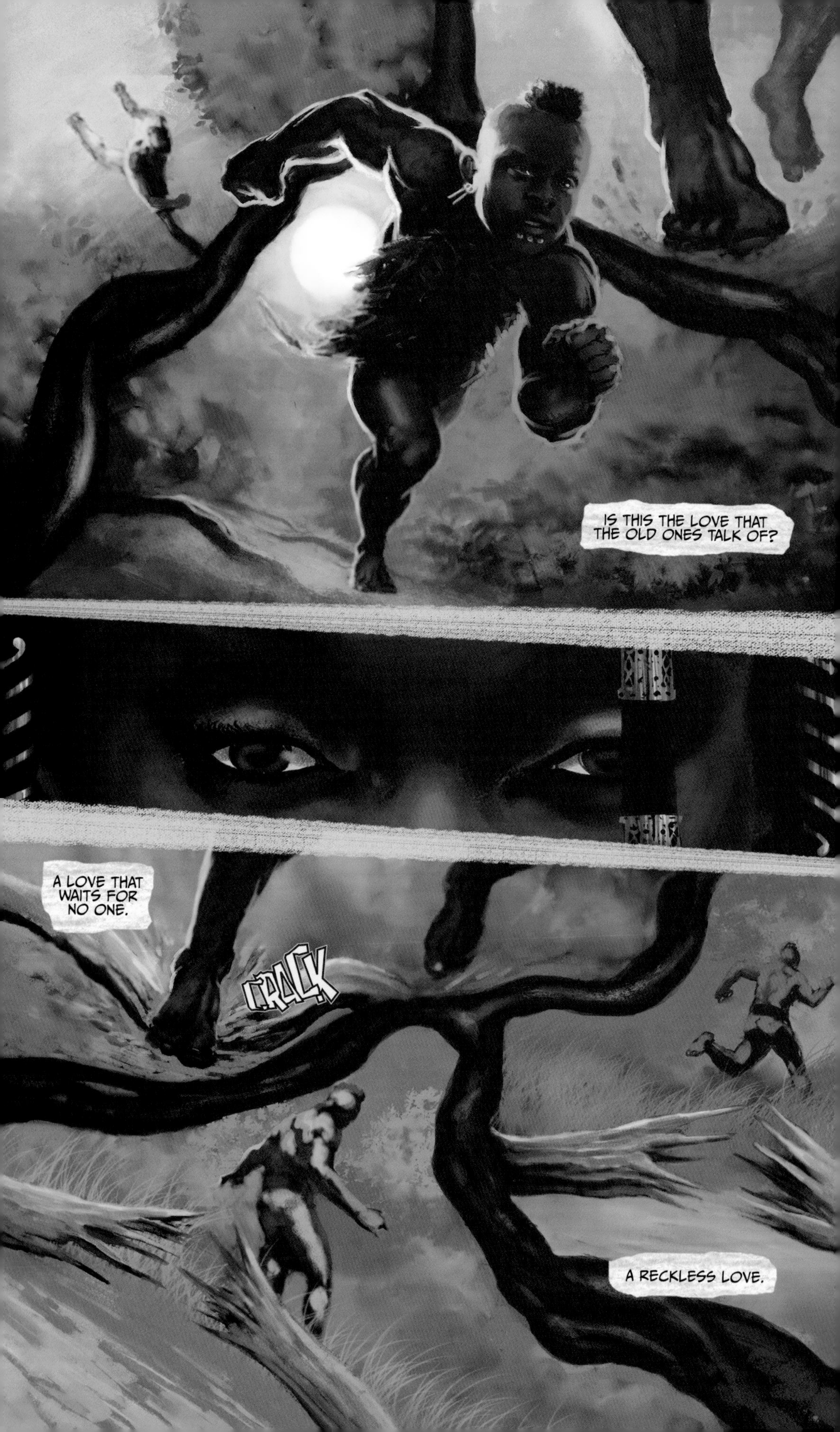
IS THIS THE LOVE THAT THE OLD ONES TALK OF?
A LOVE THAT WAITS FOR NO ONE.
CRACK
A RECKLESS LOVE.

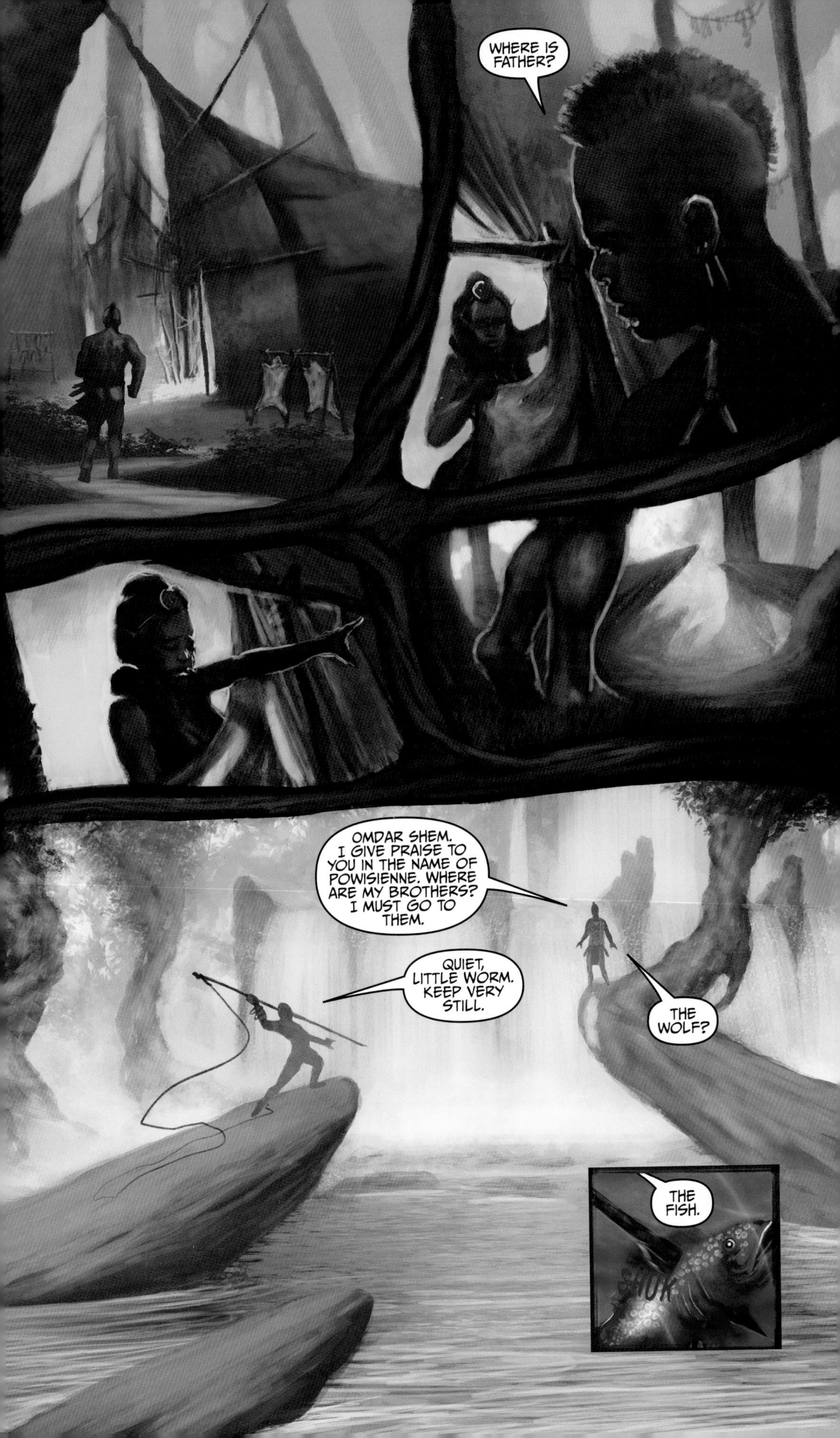
WHERE IS FATHER?
OMDAR SHEM. I GIVE PRAISE TO YOU IN THE NAME OF POWISIENNE. WHERE ARE MY BROTHERS? I MUST GO TO THEM.
QUIET, LITTLE WORM. KEEP VERY STILL.
THE WOLF?
THE FISH.
SHUK

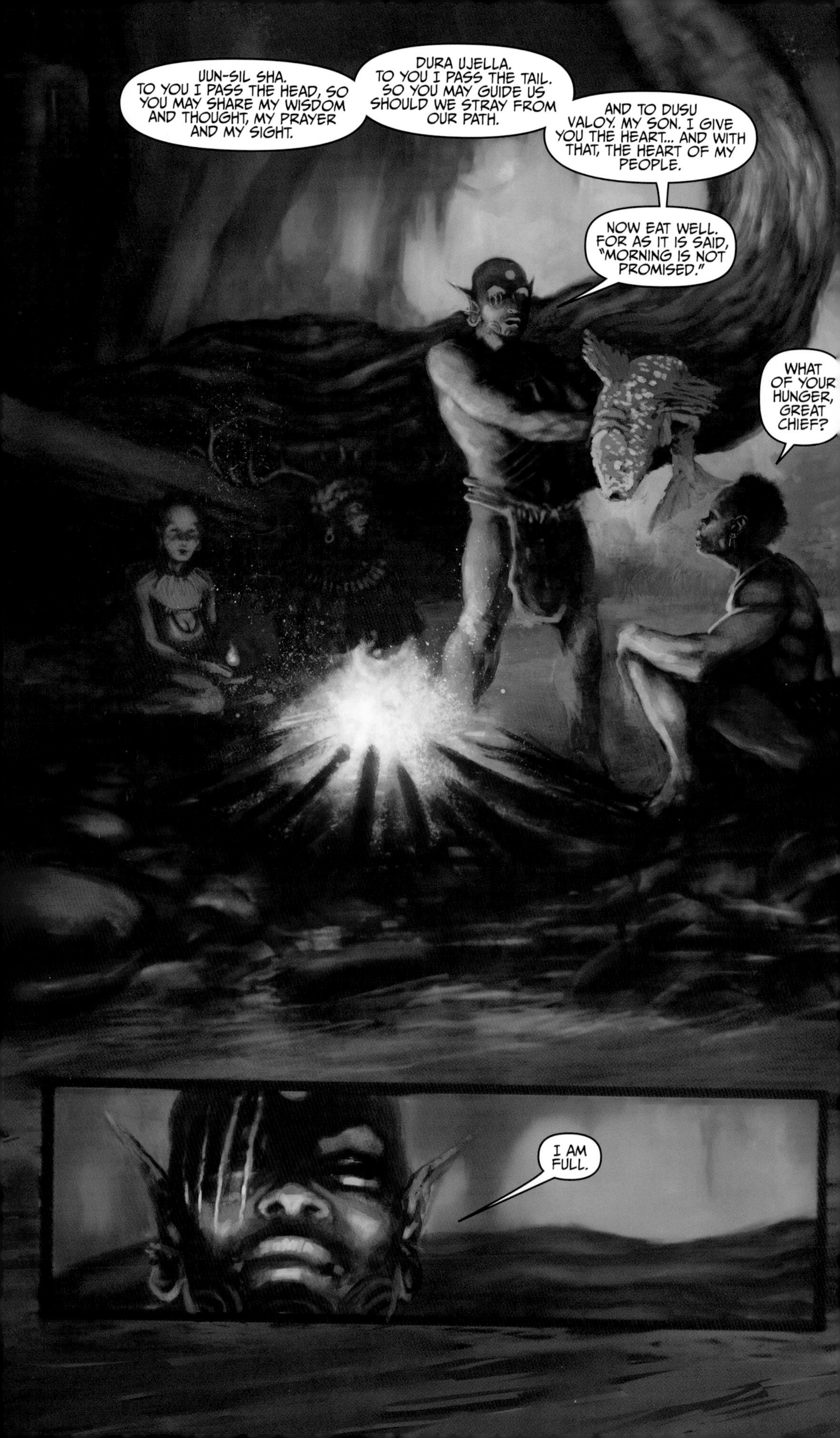
UUN-SIL SHA. TO YOU I PASS THE HEAD, SO YOU MAY SHARE MY WISDOM AND THOUGHT, MY PRAYER AND MY SIGHT.
DURA UJELLA. TO YOU I PASS THE TAIL. SO YOU MAY GUIDE US SHOULD WE STRAY FROM OUR PATH.
AND TO DUSU VALOY. MY SON. I GIVE YOU THE HEART... AND WITH THAT, THE HEART OF MY PEOPLE.
NOW EAT WELL. FOR AS IT IS SAID, "MORNING IS NOT PROMISED."
WHAT OF YOUR HUNGER, GREAT CHIEF?
I AM FULL.

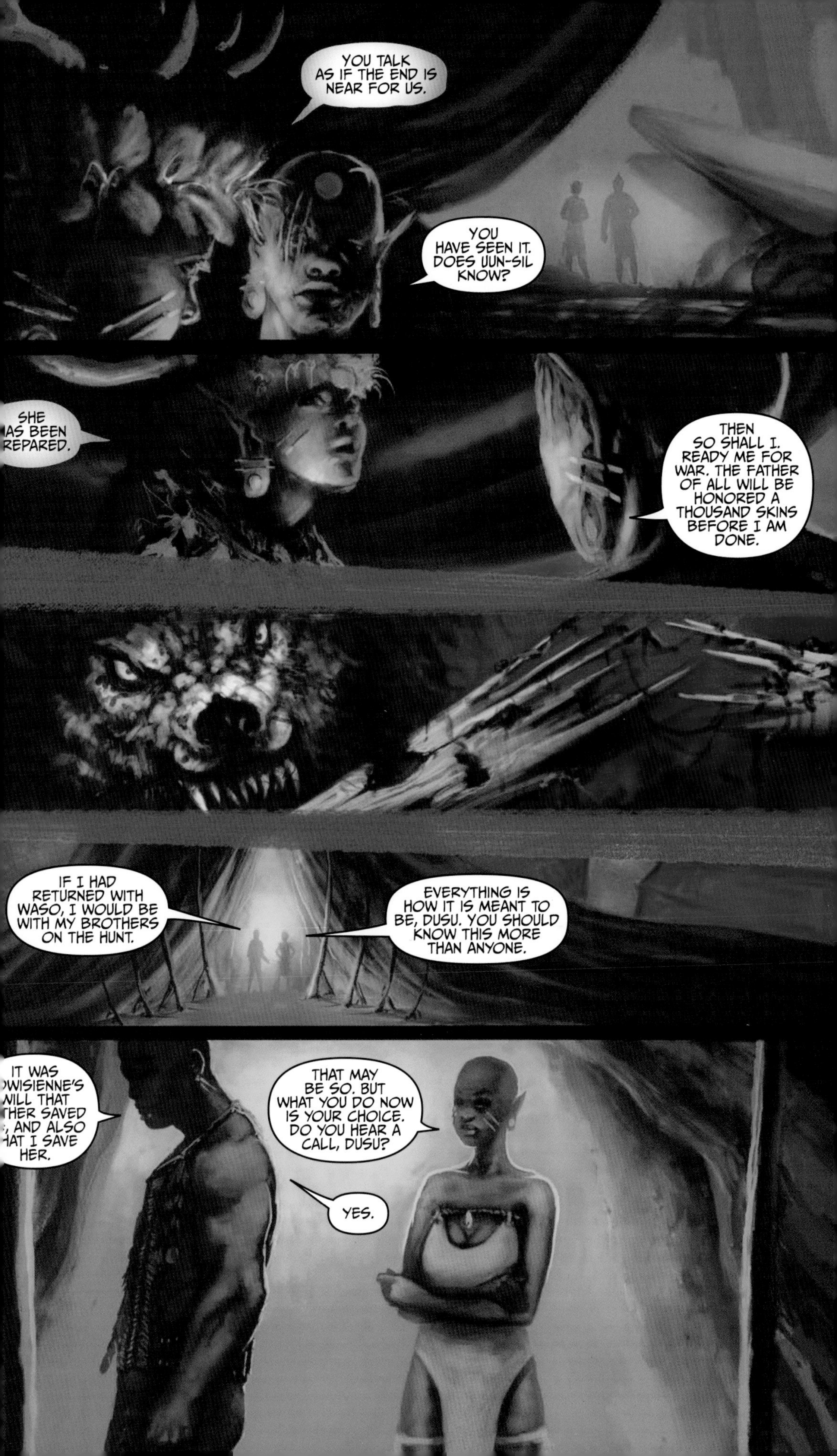

YOU TALK AS IF THE END IS NEAR FOR US.
YOU HAVE SEEN IT. DOES UUN-SIL KNOW?
SHE AS BEEN REPARED.
THEN SO SHALL I. READY ME FOR WAR. THE FATHER OF ALL WILL BE HONORED A THOUSAND SKINS BEFORE I AM DONE.
IF I HAD RETURNED WITH WASO, I WOULD BE WITH MY BROTHERS ON THE HUNT.
EVERYTHING IS HOW IT IS MEANT TO BE, DUSU. YOU SHOULD KNOW THIS MORE THAN ANYONE.
IT WAS WISIENNE'S WILL THAT THER SAVED , AND ALSO AT I SAVE HER.
THAT MAY BE SO. BUT WHAT YOU DO NOW IS YOUR CHOICE. DO YOU HEAR A CALL, DUSU?
YES.

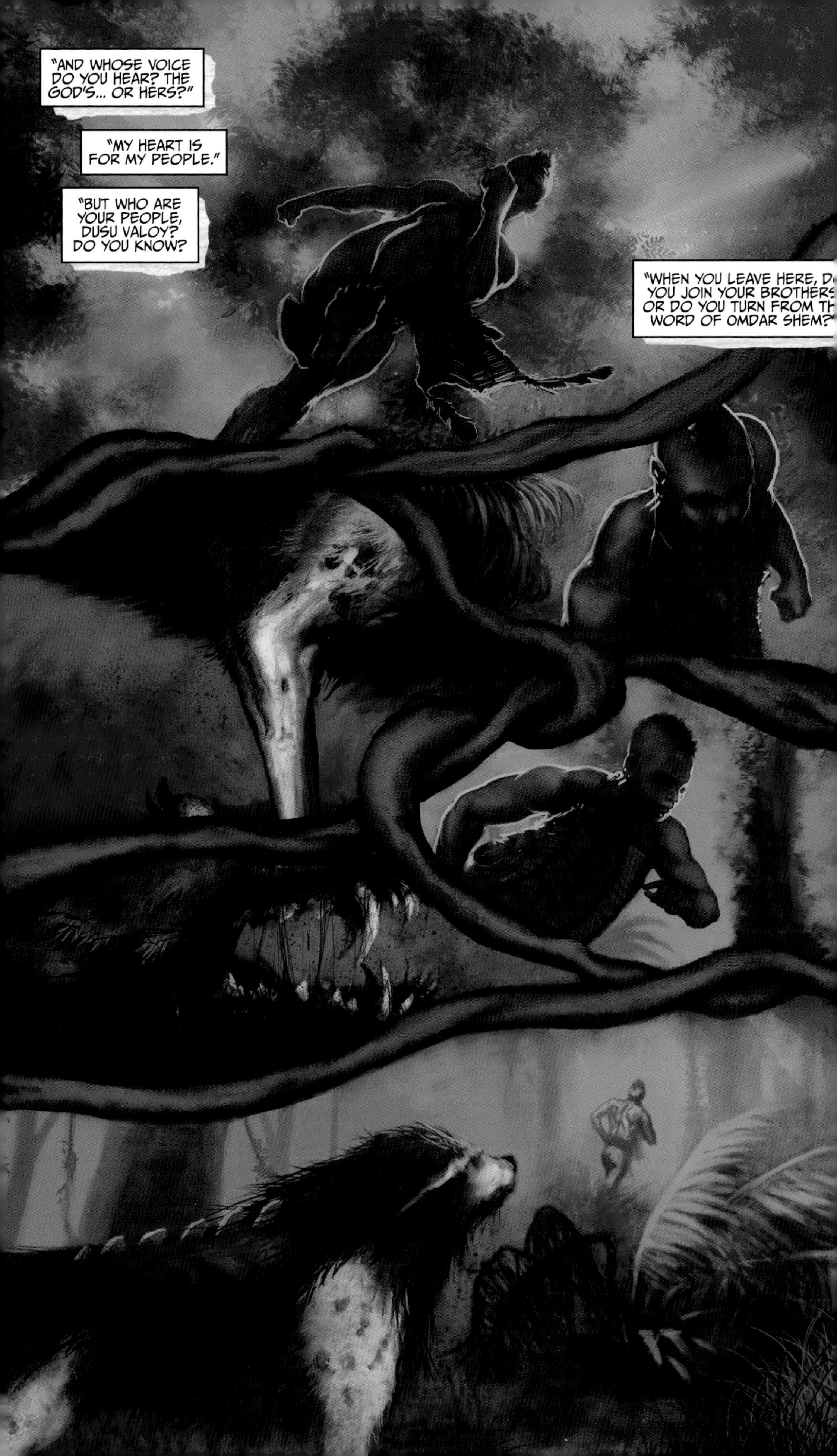
"AND WHOSE VOICE DO YOU HEAR? THE GOD'S... OR HERS?"
"MY HEART IS FOR MY PEOPLE."
"BUT WHO ARE YOUR PEOPLE, DUSU VALOY? DO YOU KNOW?
"WHEN YOU LEAVE HERE, D YOU JOIN YOUR BROTHERS OR DO YOU TURN FROM TH WORD OF OMDAR SHEM?"

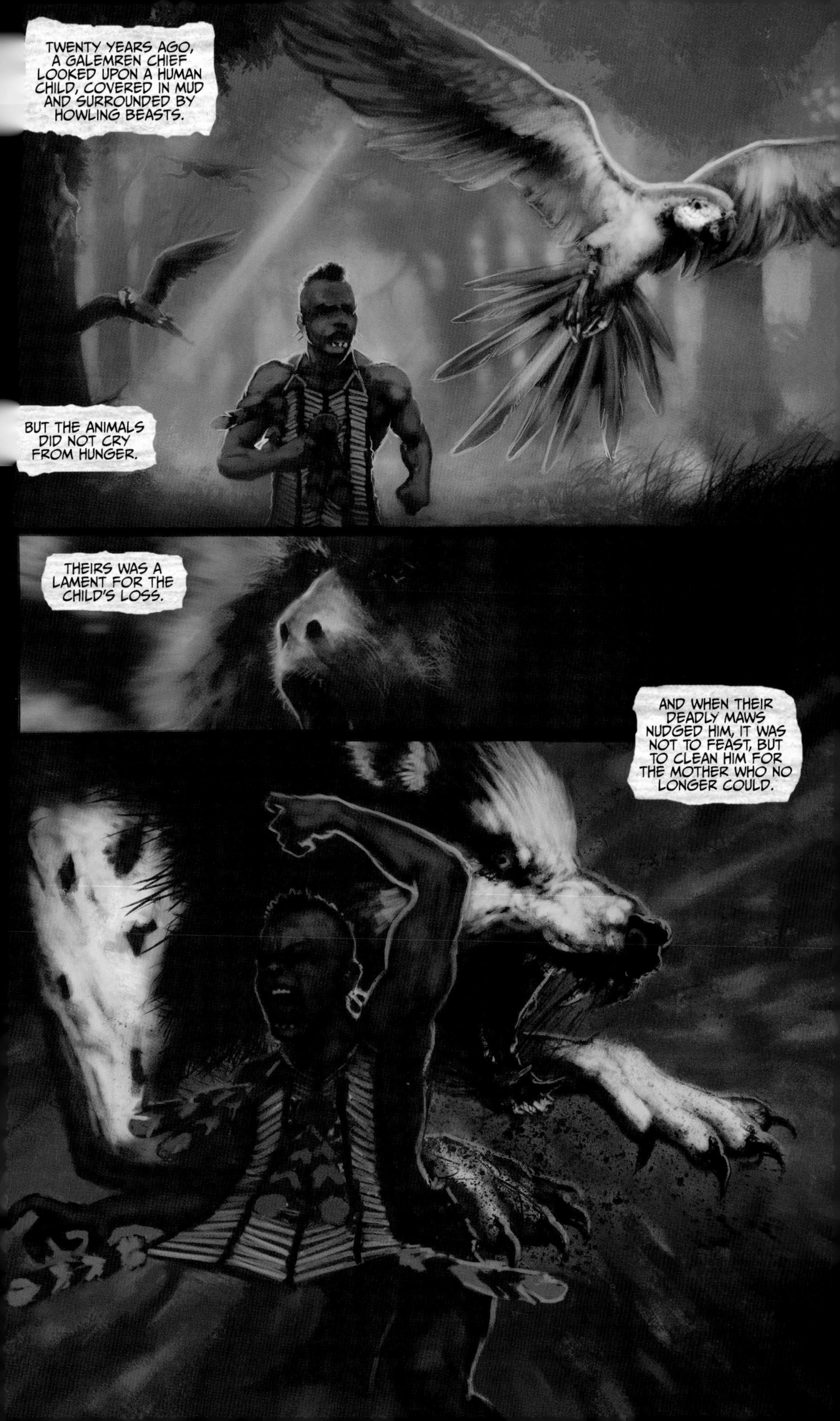
TWENTY YEARS AGO, A GALEMREN CHIEF LOOKED UPON A HUMAN CHILD, COVERED IN MUD AND SURROUNDED BY HOWLING BEASTS.
BUT THE ANIMALS DID NOT CRY FROM HUNGER.
THEIRS WAS A LAMENT FOR THE CHILD'S LOSS.
AND WHEN THEIR DEADLY MAWS NUDGED HIM, IT WAS NOT TO FEAST, BUT TO CLEAN HIM FOR THE MOTHER WHO NO LONGER COULD.

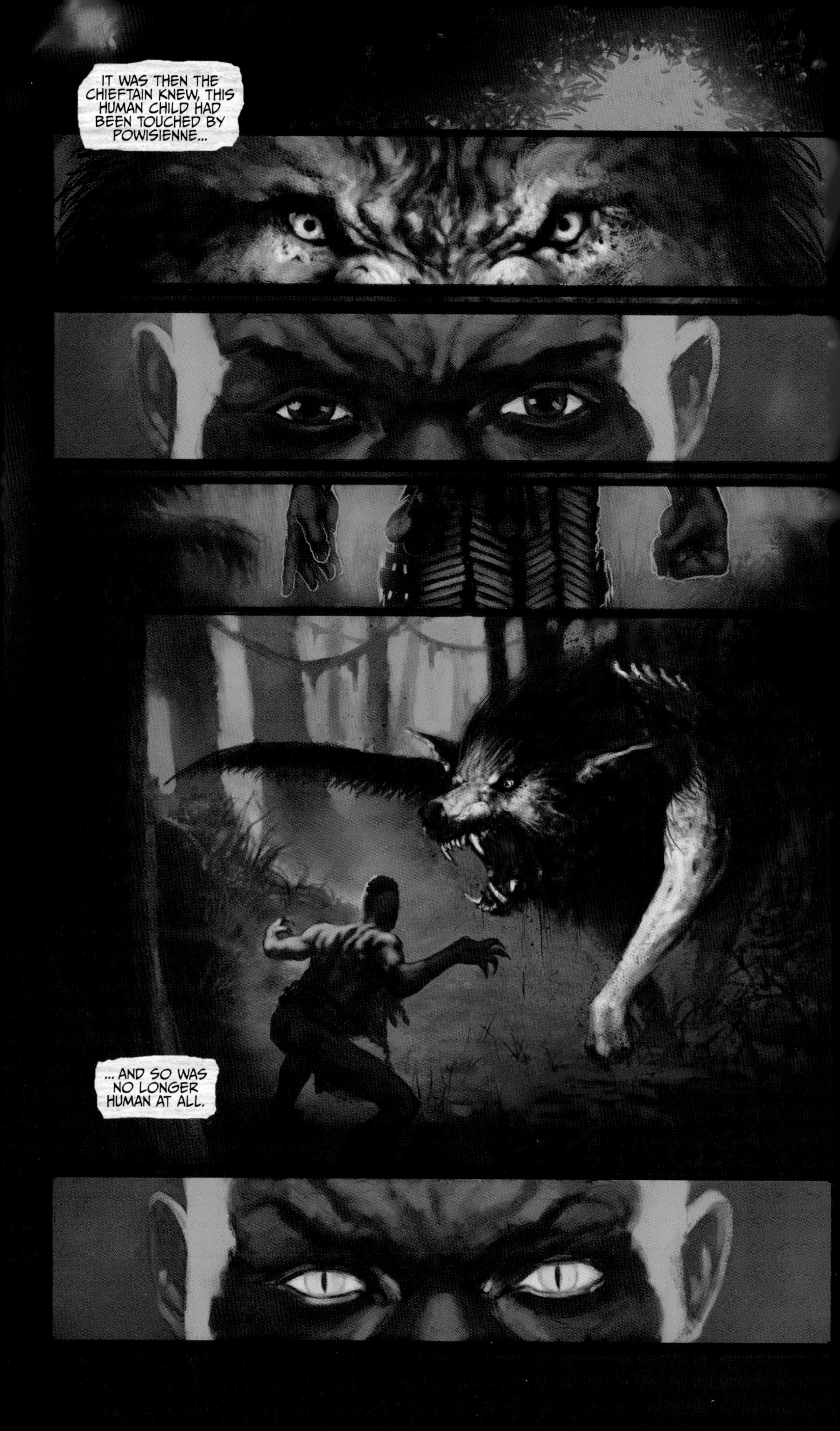
IT WAS THEN THE CHIEFTAIN KNEW, THIS HUMAN CHILD HAD BEEN TOUCHED BY POWISIENNE...
... AND SO WAS NO LONGER HUMAN AT ALL.

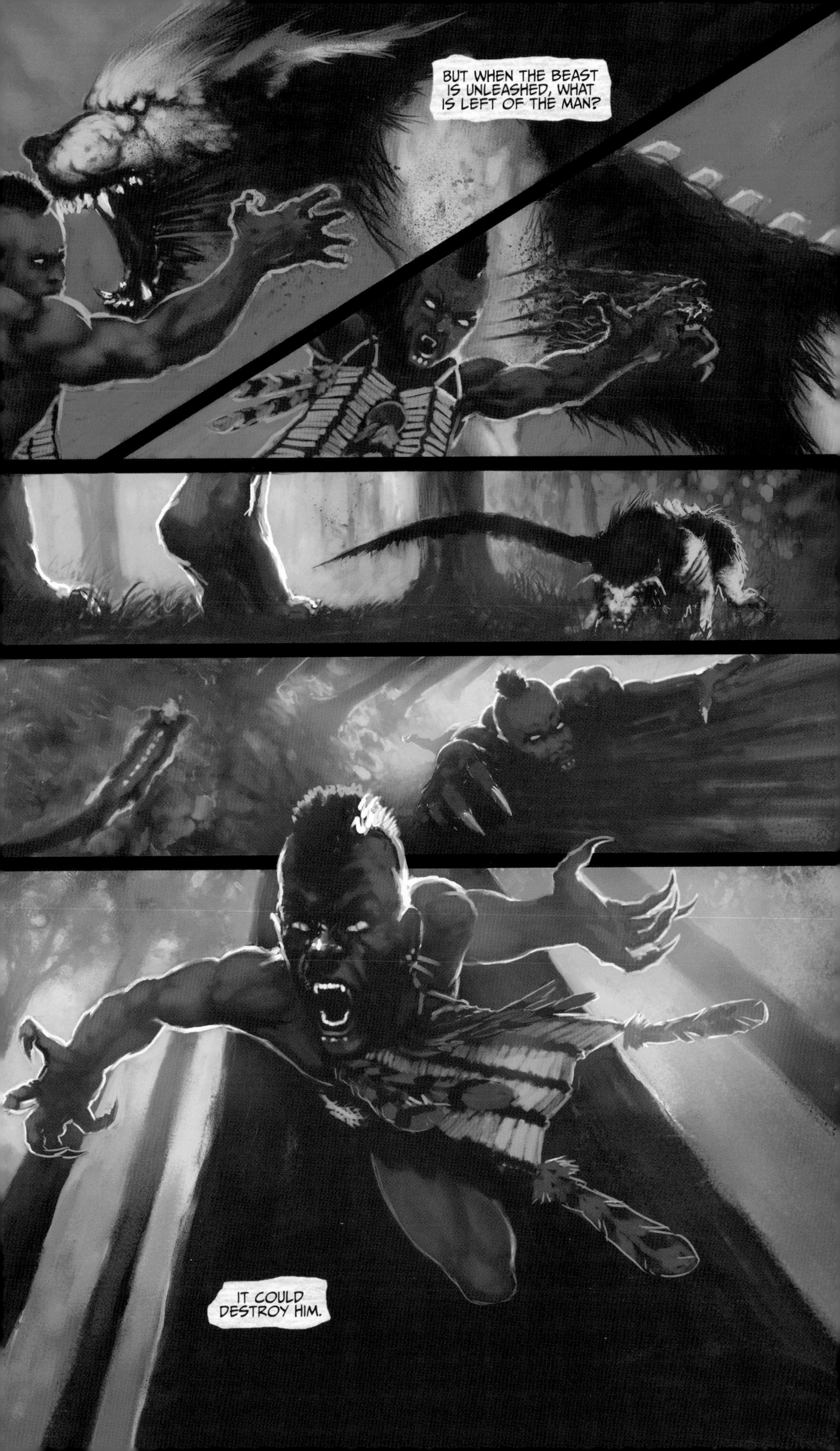
BUT WHEN THE BEAST IS UNLEASHED, WHAT IS LEFT OF THE MAN?
IT COULD DESTROY HIM.

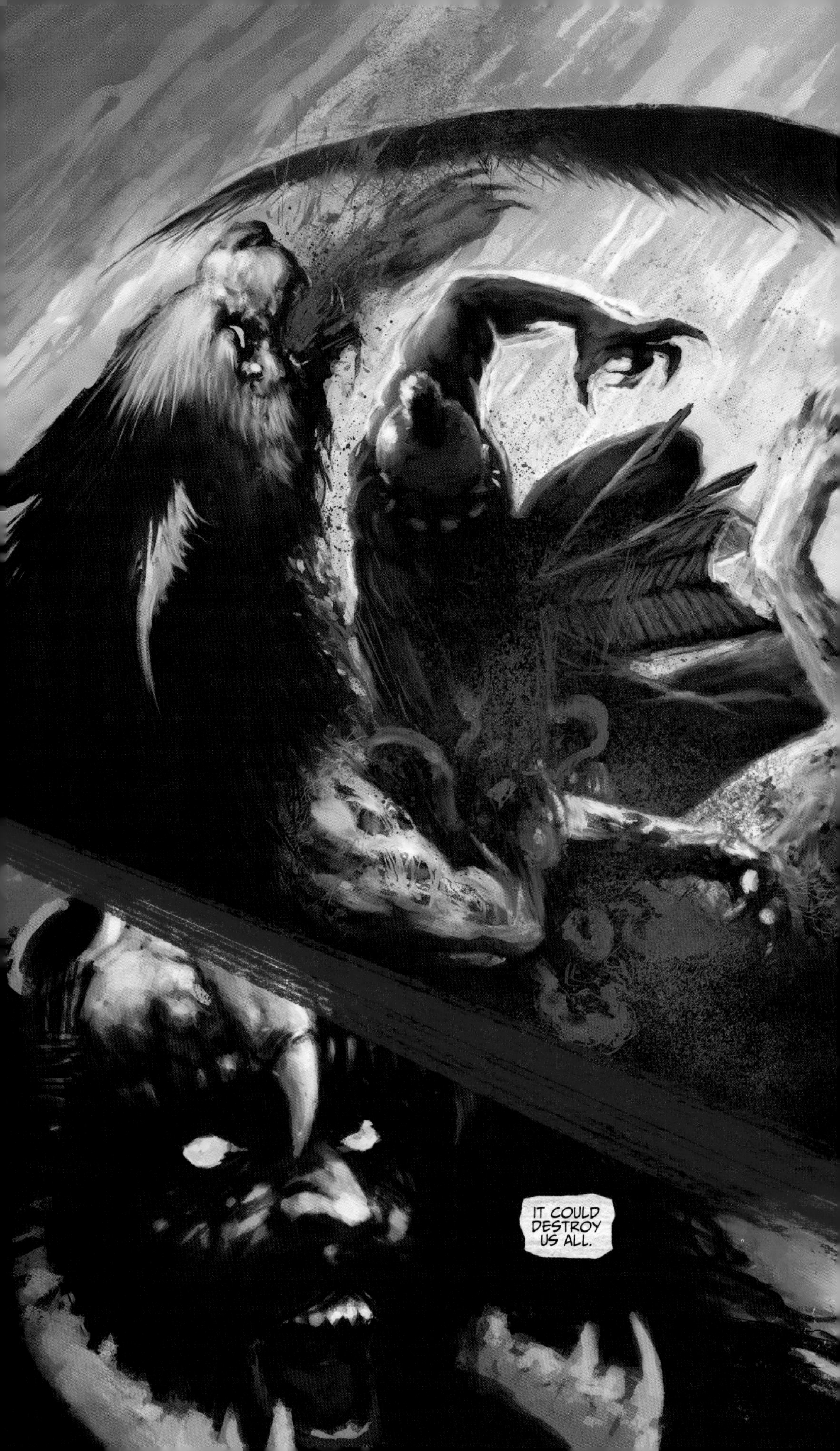
IT COULD DESTROY US ALL.

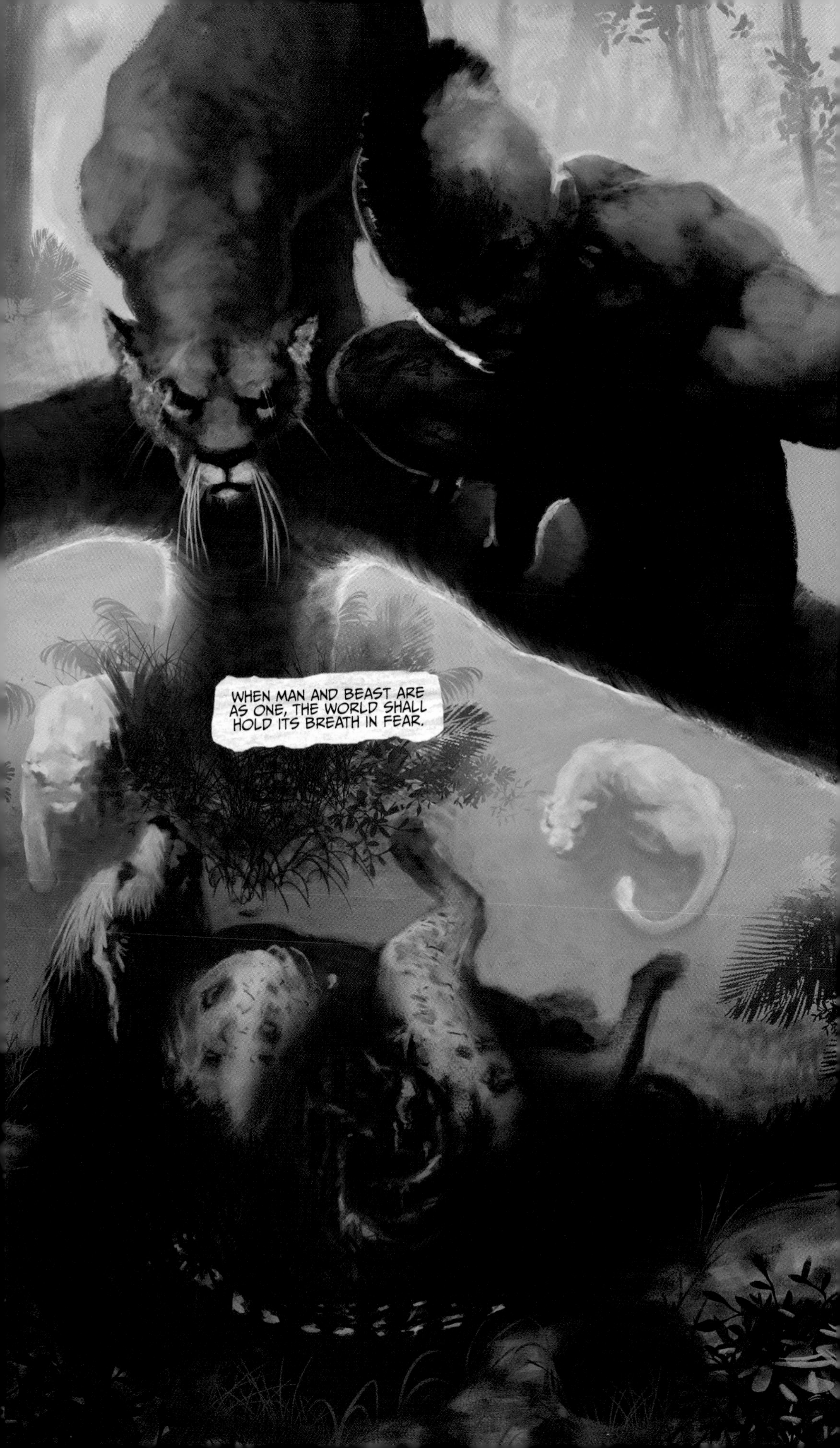
WHEN MAN AND BEAST ARE AS ONE, THE WORLD SHALL HOLD ITS BREATH IN FEAR.

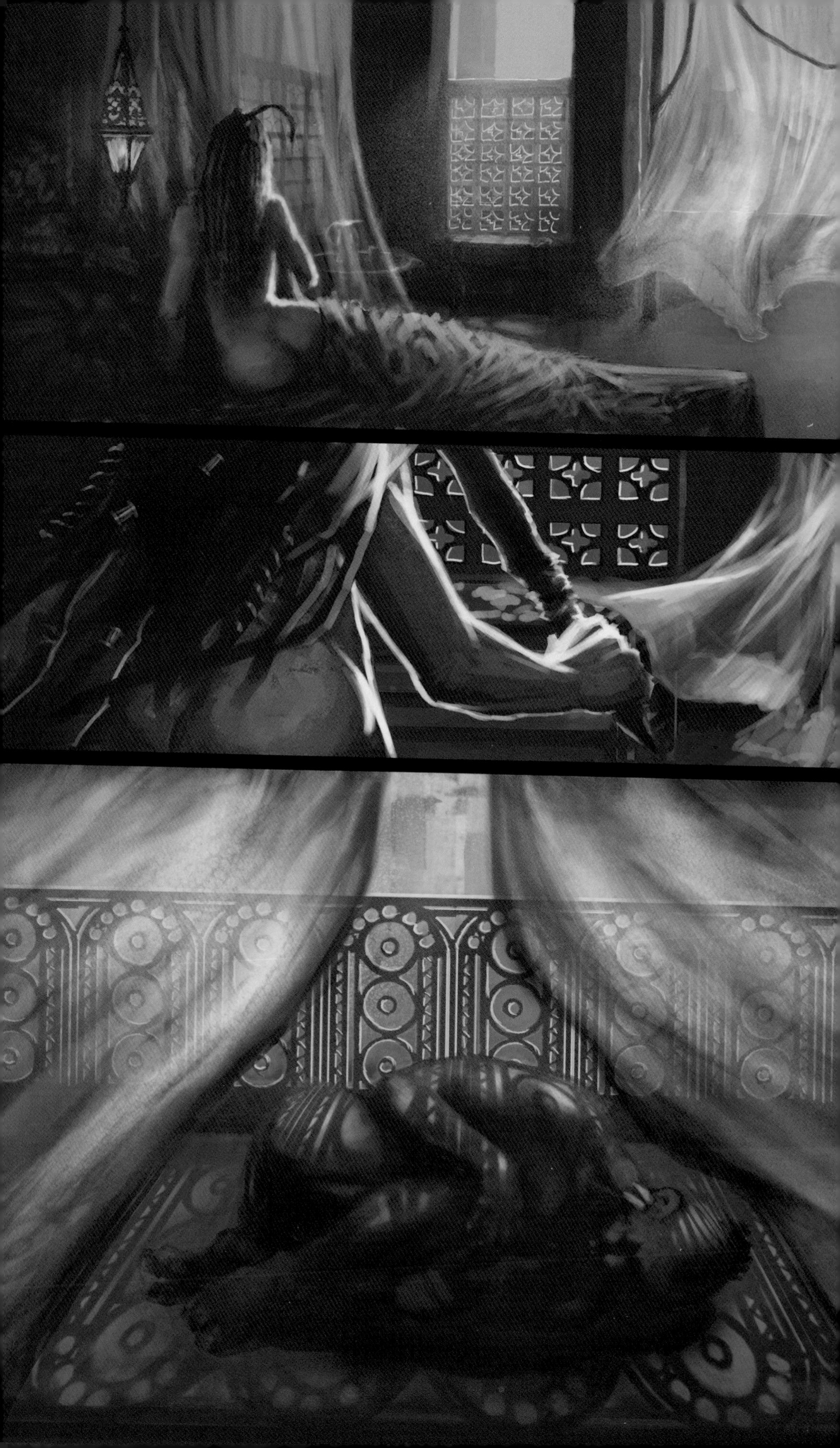

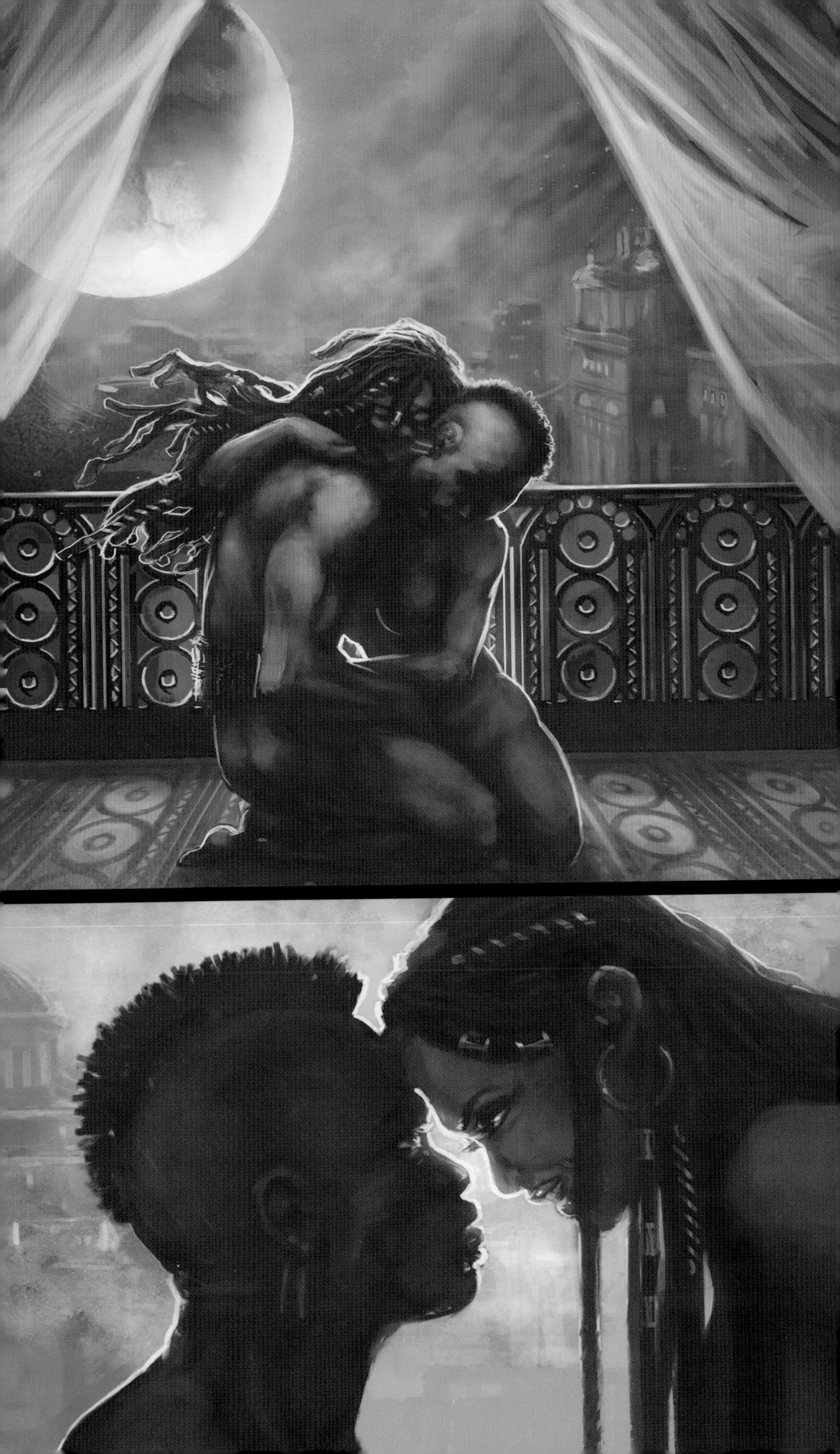

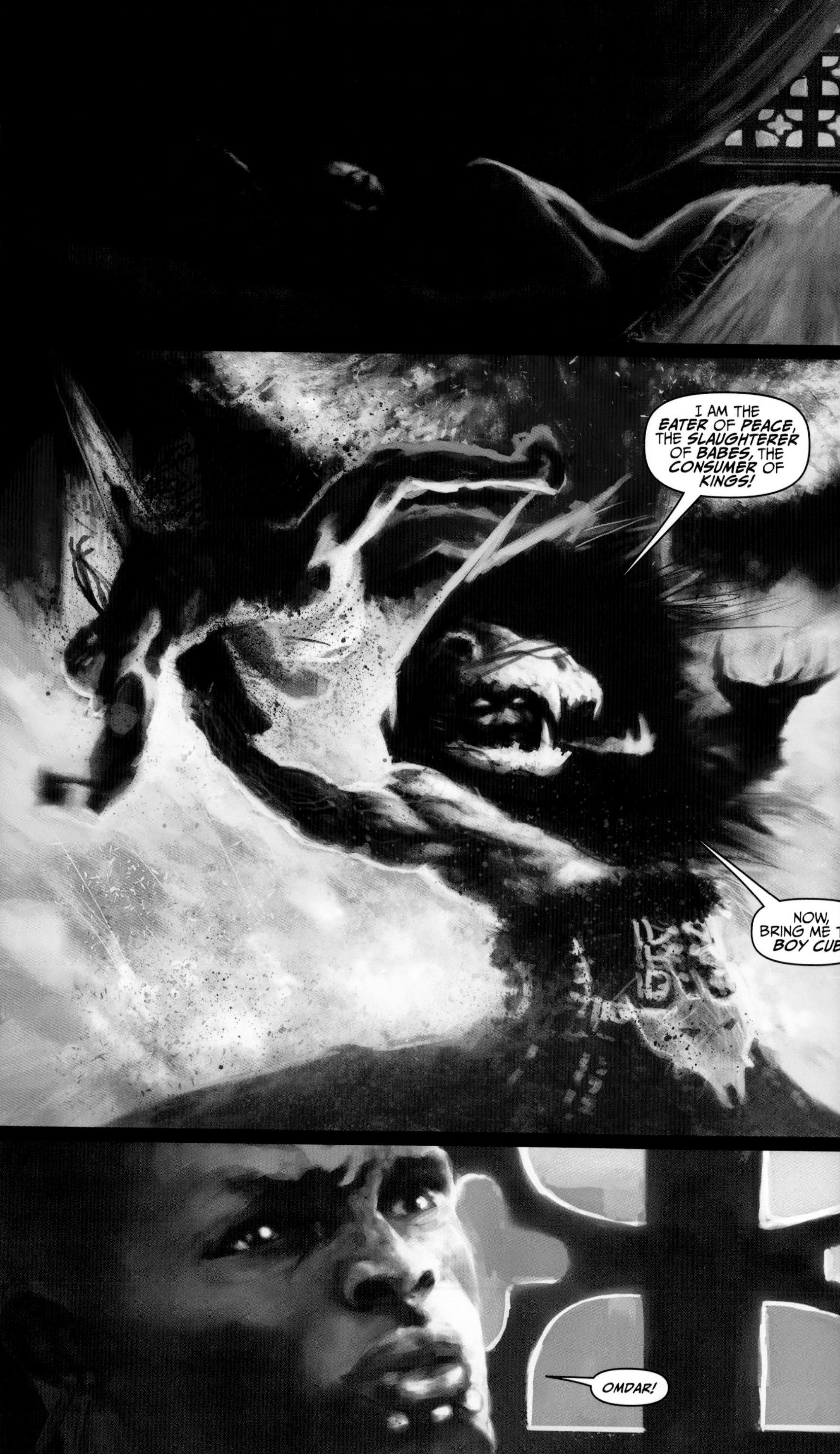
I AM THE EATER OF PEACE, THE SLAUGHTERER OF BABES, THE CONSUMER OF KINGS!
NOW, BRING ME T
BOY CUB
OMDAR!

Hello Stranger,

"*And still they come with iron and grinning rage, spitting blood and drinking souls. All a man can do is wait to die or head into the storm knowing the end is near. It is hard for a warrior to fight against history, when the enemy is just in his wrath. We are simply at the time when evil deeds are punished. We pay for the sins of our forefathers. Andrek II betrayed our Urzoth ancestors and they have finally united under Kenga. Soon all those who dwell within walled cities will no longer sleep safely.*"

– Taken from the journal of soldier Menka Andren before the slaughter at the gates of Endulan by the beserking hordes of Sil-Sakramoor (Durka – 156)

At the dawn of the age of spirit, when the Gods bore the races to cultivate the lands, the tribal children of Urzog (God of War) took to the rich and natural splendor within the realms. Then the tenth tribe was born, so much like their older brethren, but smaller and untrusting. They followed a different calling. They became known as the humans, creatures who dwelled within tall cities, hiding and plotting, yet with a lust for growth that is unmatched. The others remained Urzoth, fierce in their beliefs and customs, which their human cousins had renounced.

The Urzoth, the true men born of Urzog himself, were viewed as savages... BARBARIANS! These nomadic people roam across the more remote areas in Asunda, keeping to themselves and their cultural roots. And although their love for battle remains fierce, these proud people relish in the natural wonders of life, and when war is called for, they fight with the honor expected by their god.

However, not all remain content with the hand that has been dealt them. Some pervert the wishes of Urzog, following a darker calling as raiders and marauders, plundering and conquering with a hateful might and savage abandon across the vast and volatile world of…

Chapter 3

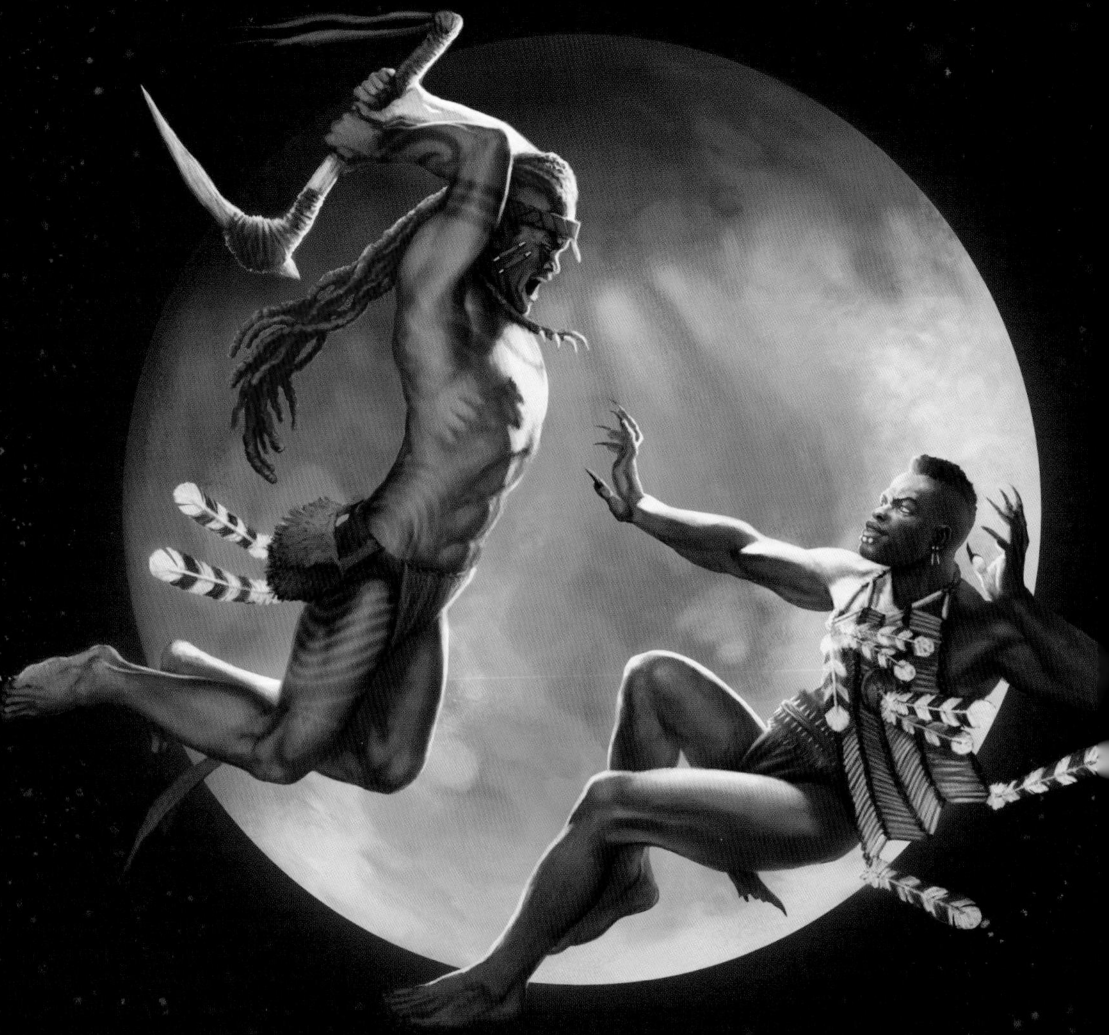

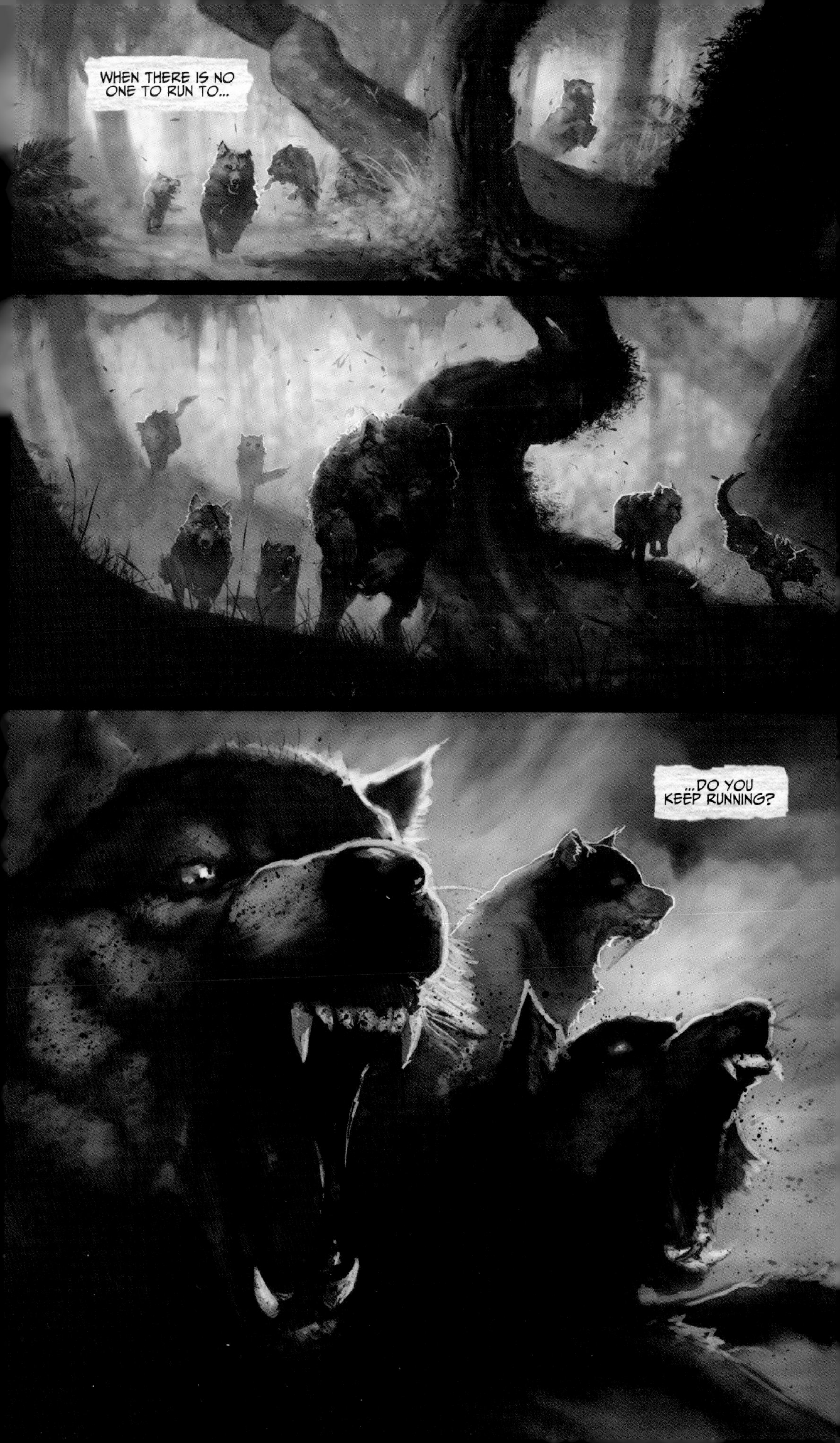
WHEN THERE IS NO ONE TO RUN TO...
...DO YOU KEEP RUNNING?

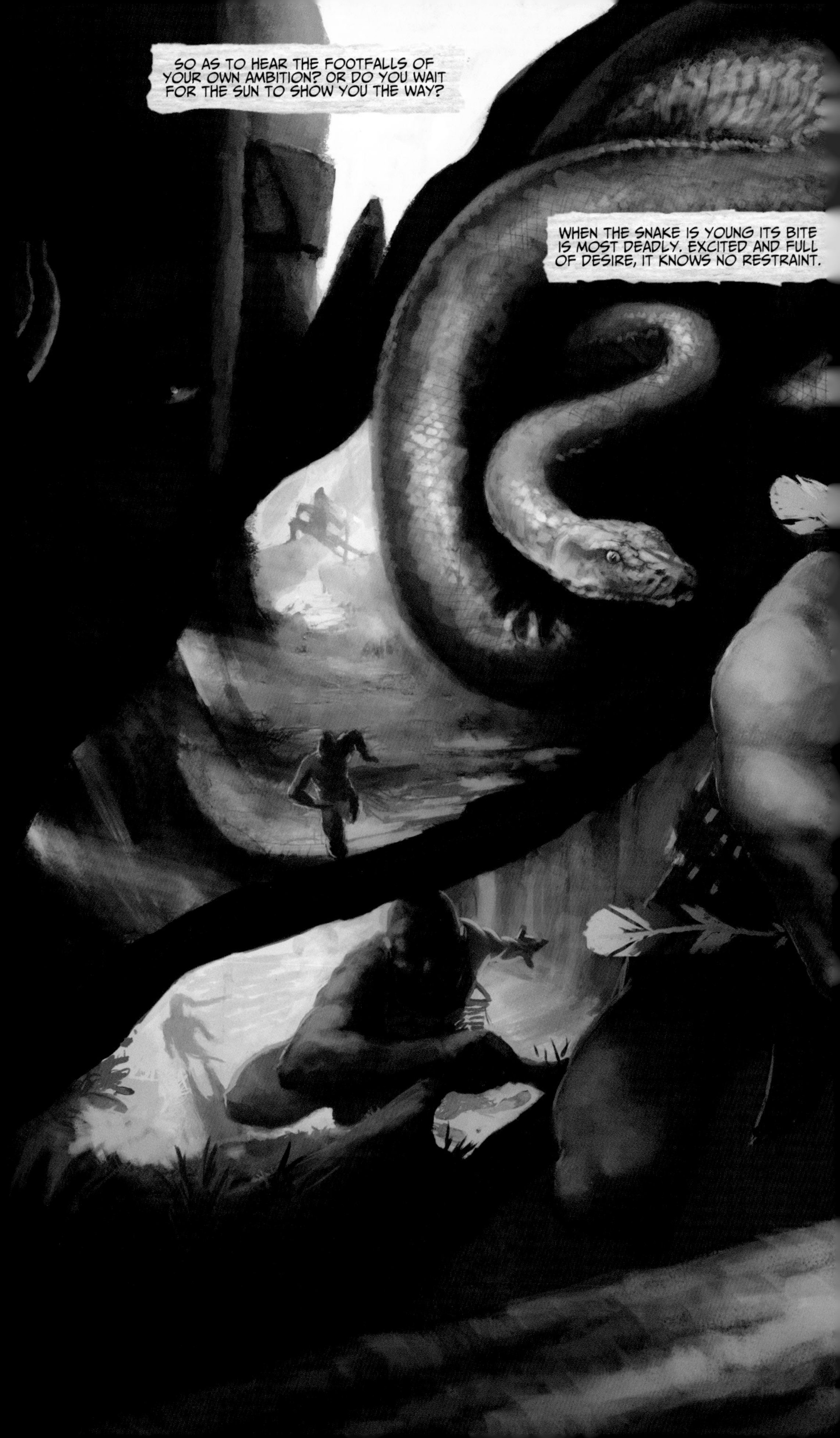
SO AS TO HEAR THE FOOTFALLS OF YOUR OWN AMBITION? OR DO YOU WAIT FOR THE SUN TO SHOW YOU THE WAY?
WHEN THE SNAKE IS YOUNG ITS BITE IS MOST DEADLY. EXCITED AND FULL OF DESIRE, IT KNOWS NO RESTRAINT.

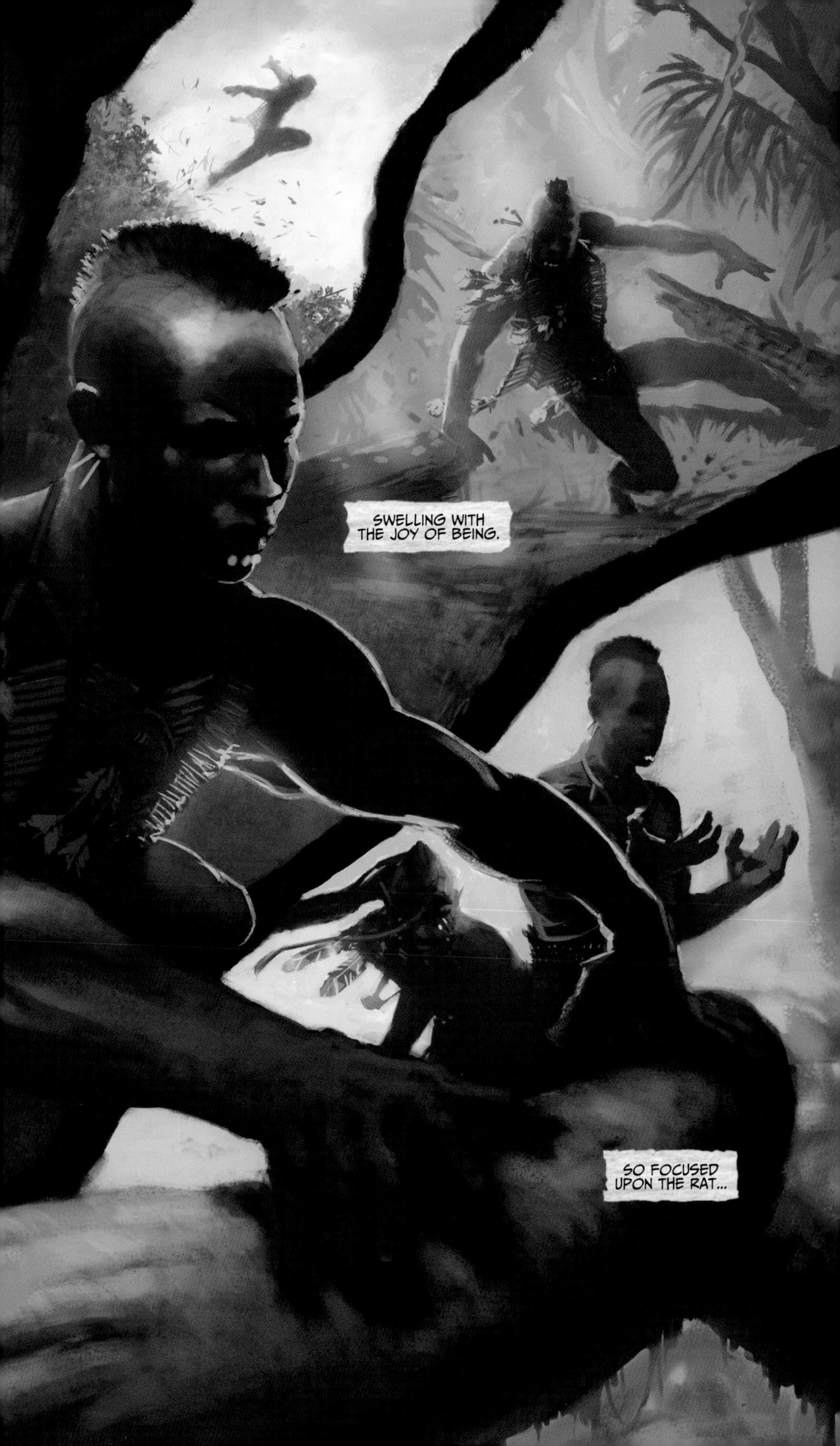
SWELLING WITH THE JOY OF BEING.
SO FOCUSED UPON THE RAT...

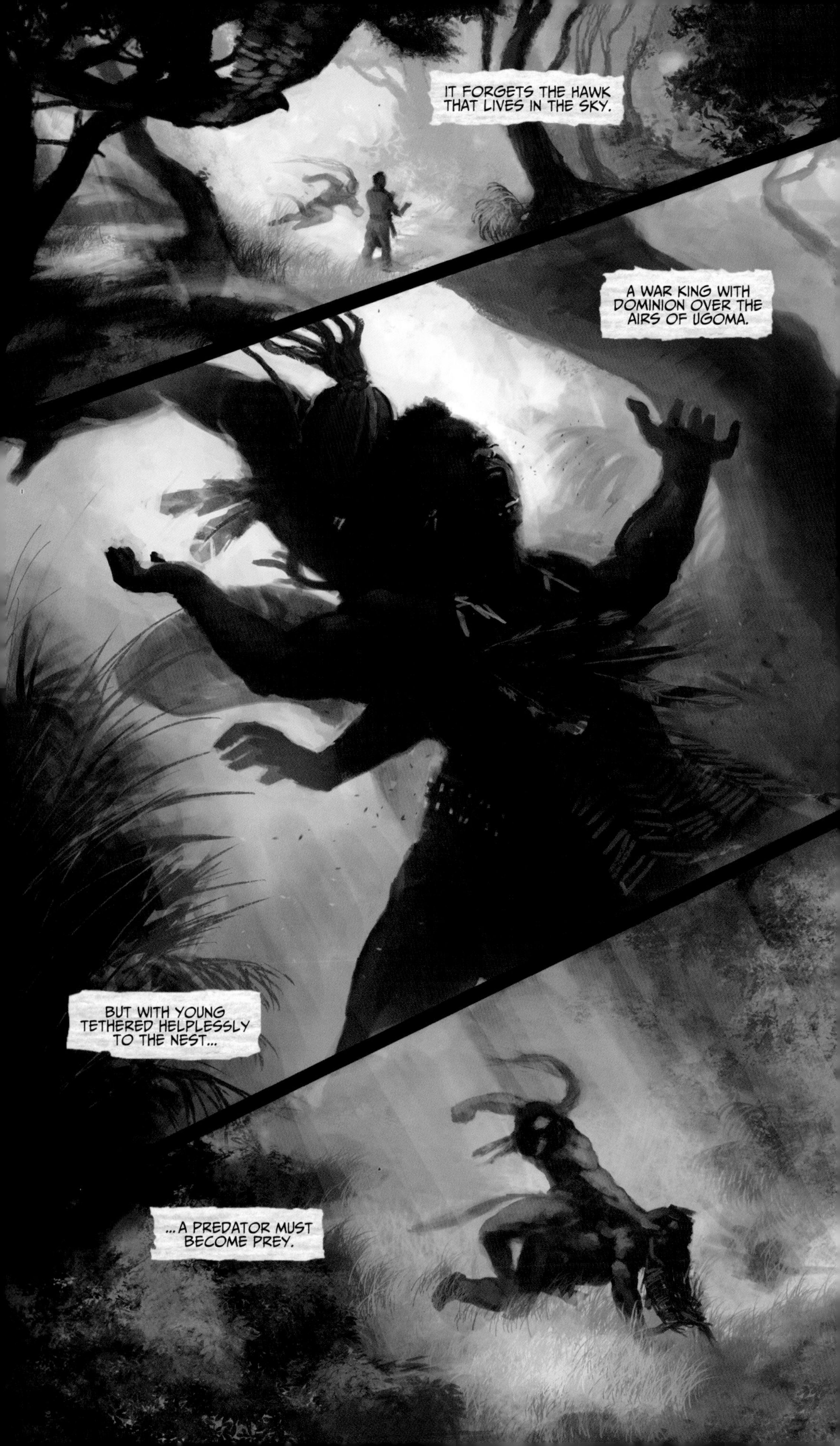
IT FORGETS THE HAWK THAT LIVES IN THE SKY.
A WAR KING WITH DOMINION OVER THE AIRS OF UGOMA.
BUT WITH YOUNG TETHERED HELPLESSLY TO THE NEST...
...A PREDATOR MUST BECOME PREY.

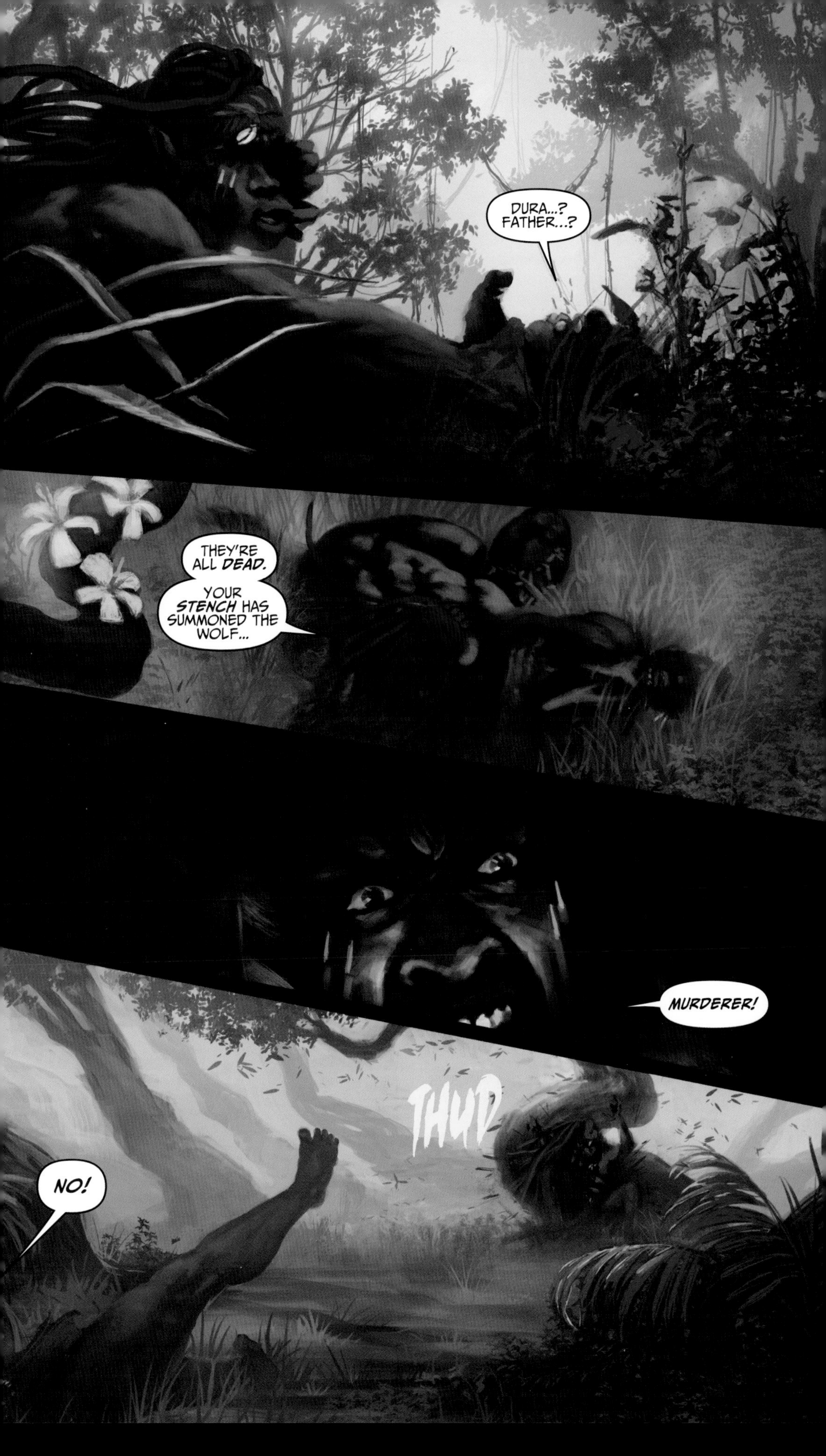
DURA...? FATHER...?
THEY'RE ALL DEAD.
YOUR STENCH HAS SUMMONED THE WOLF...
MURDERER!
THUD
NO!

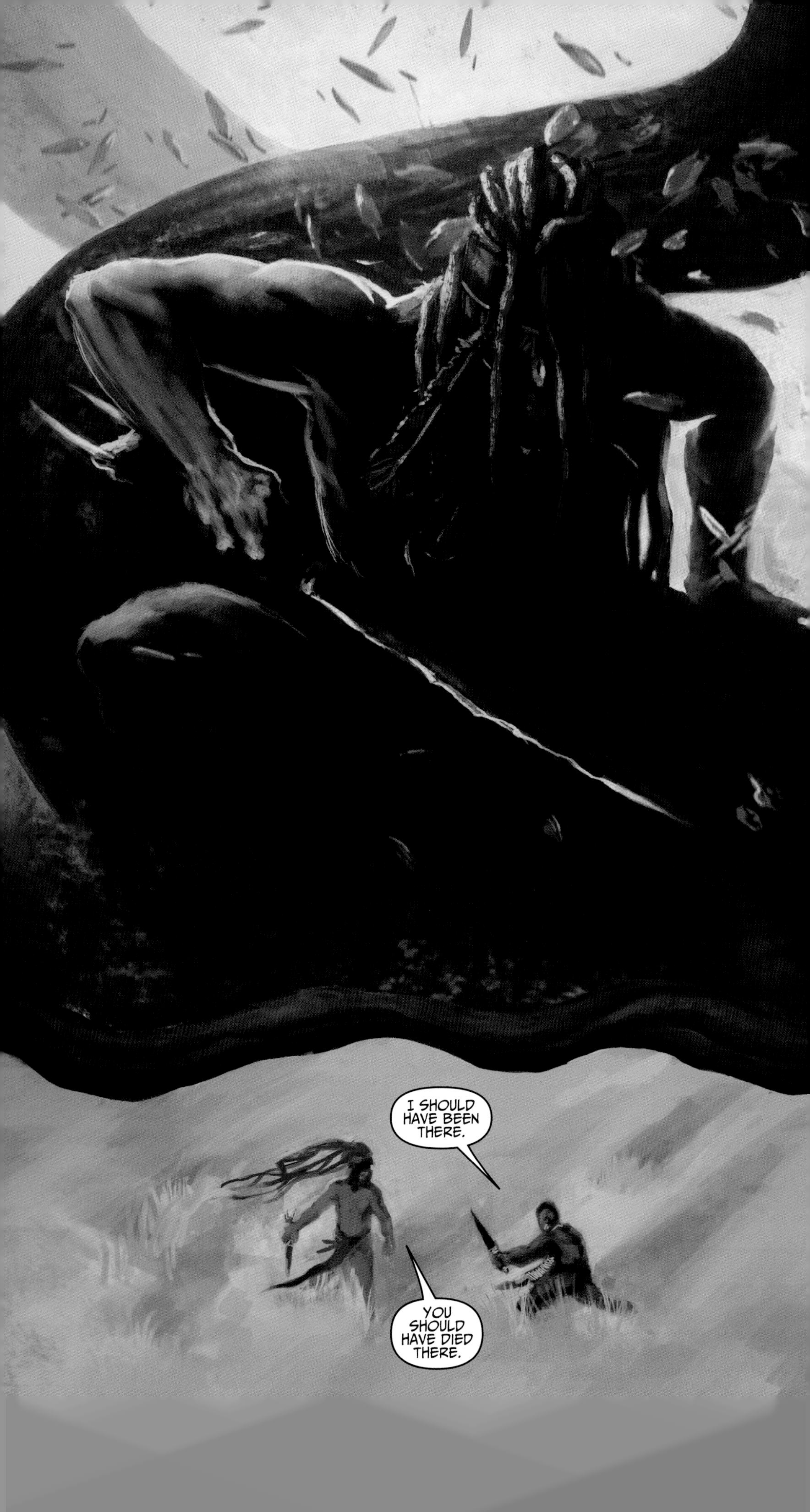
I SHOULD HAVE BEEN THERE.
YOU SHOULD HAVE DIED THERE.

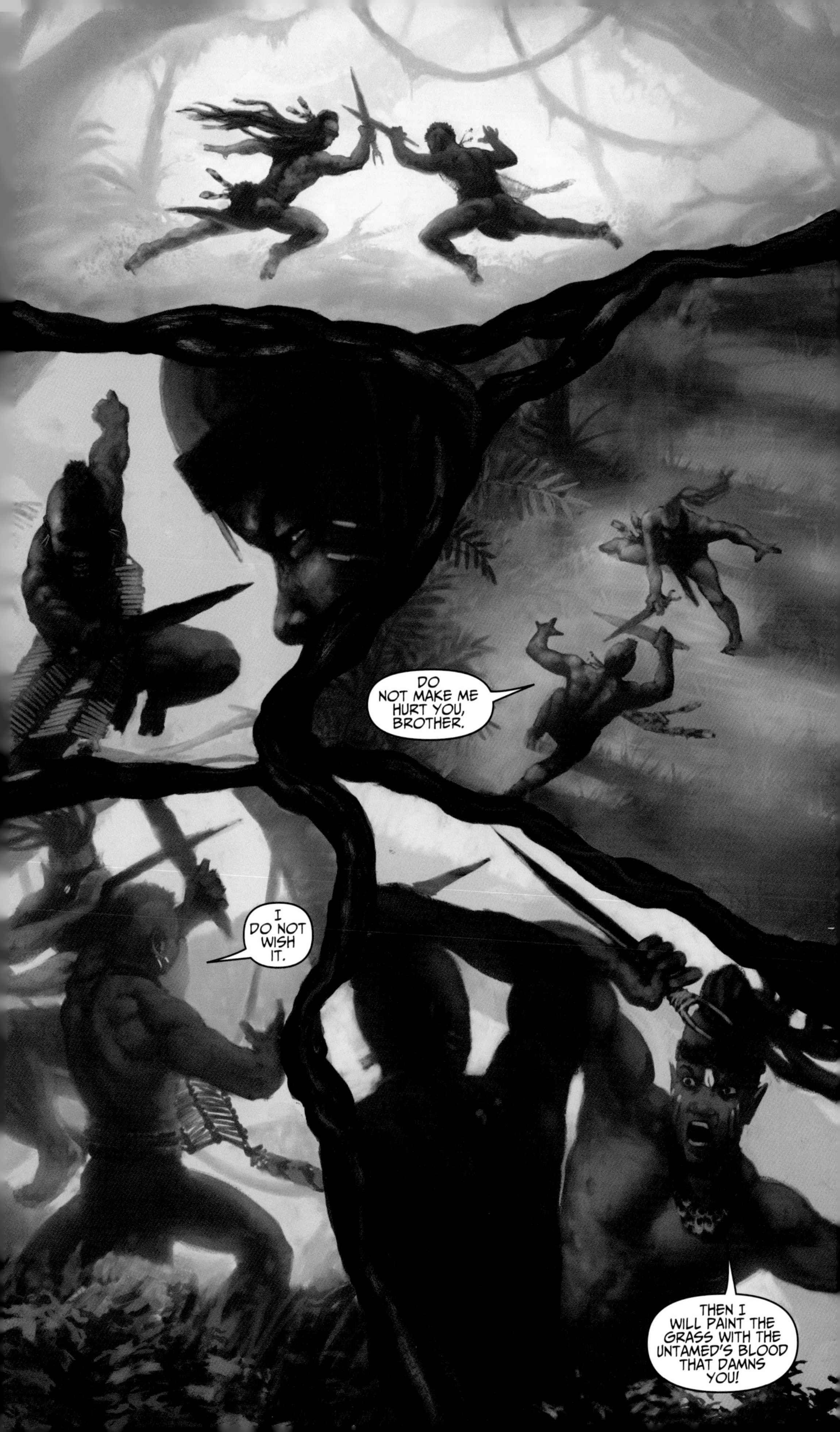
DO NOT MAKE ME HURT YOU, BROTHER.
I DO NOT WISH IT.
THEN I WILL PAINT THE GRASS WITH THE UNTAMED'S BLOOD THAT DAMNS YOU!

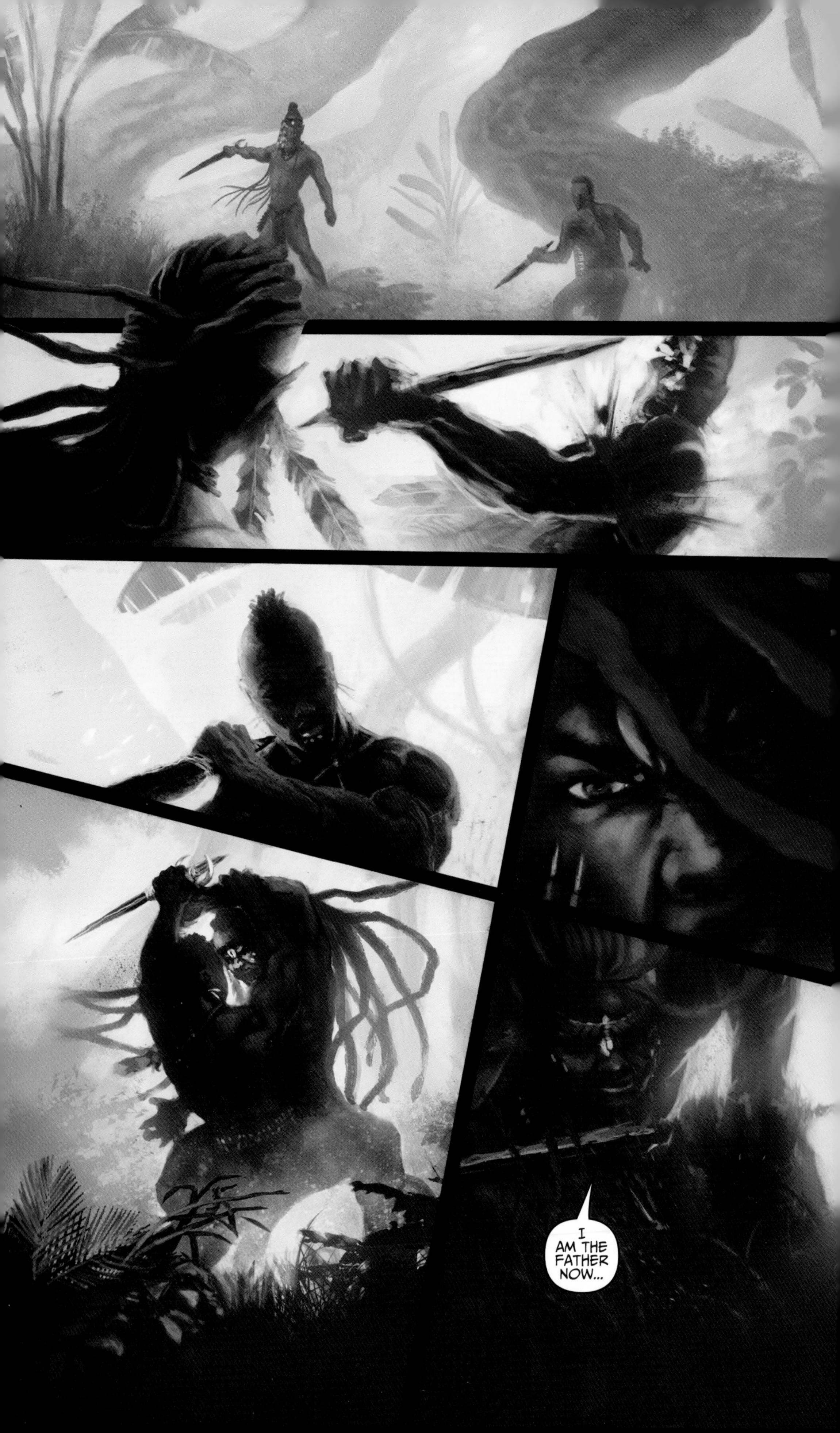
I AM THE FATHER NOW...

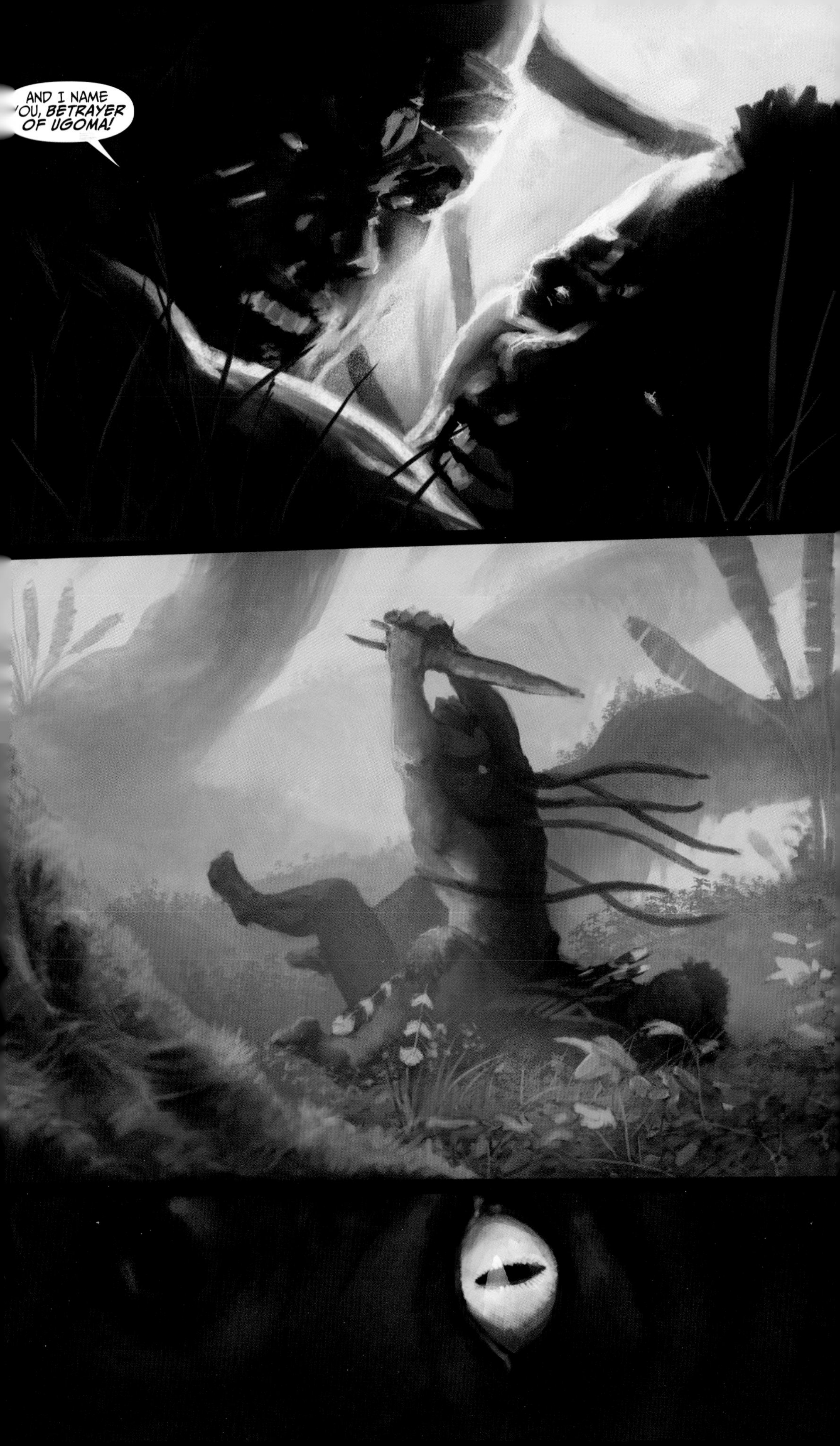
AND I NAME YOU, BETRAYER OF UGOMA!

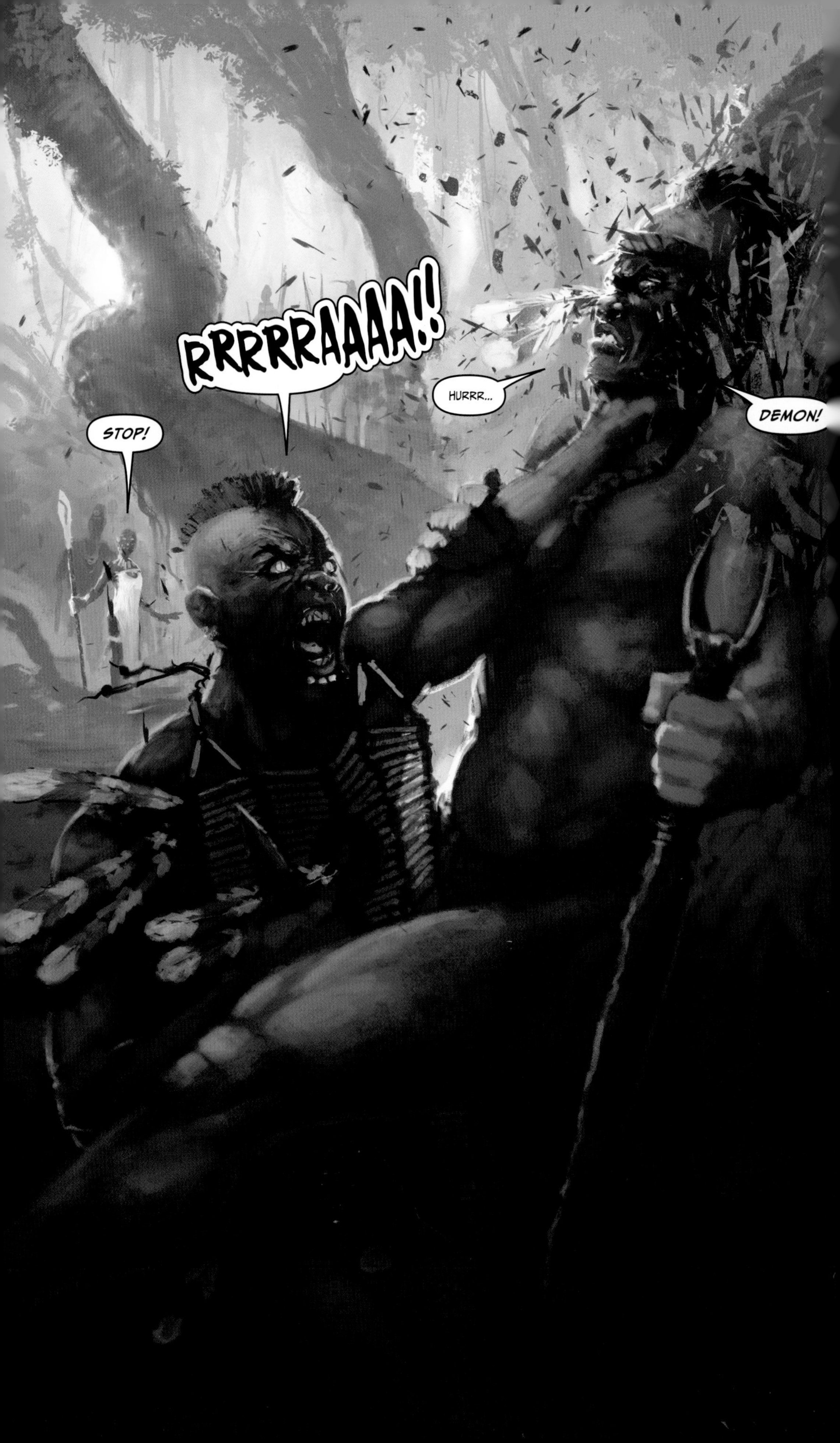
STOP!
RRRRRAAAA!!
HURRR...
DEMON!

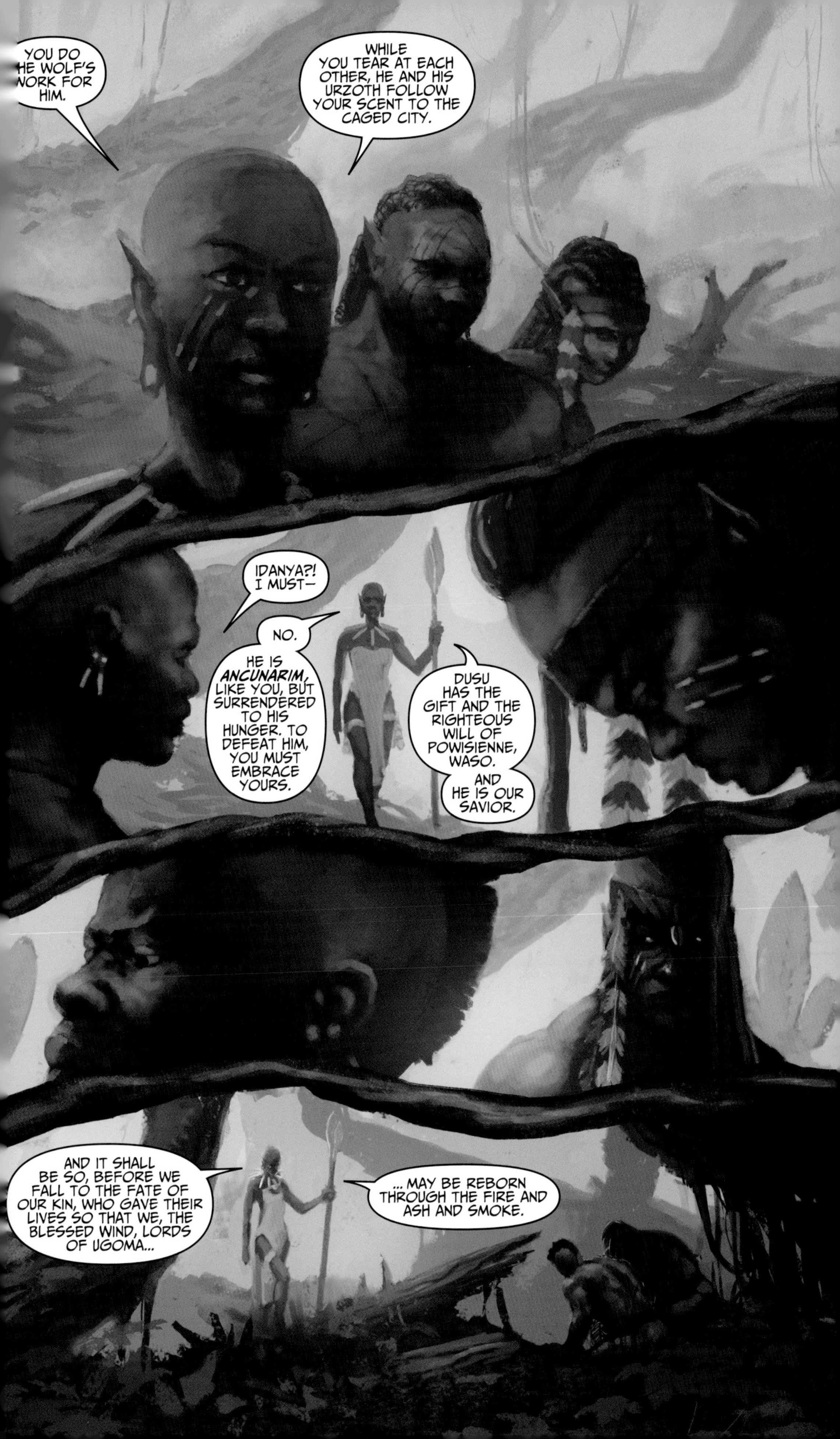
YOU DO THE WOLF'S WORK FOR HIM.
WHILE YOU TEAR AT EACH OTHER, HE AND HIS URZOTH FOLLOW YOUR SCENT TO THE CAGED CITY.
IDANYA?! I MUST—
NO.
HE IS ANCUNARIM, LIKE YOU, BUT SURRENDERED TO HIS HUNGER. TO DEFEAT HIM, YOU MUST EMBRACE YOURS.
DUSU HAS THE GIFT AND THE RIGHTEOUS WILL OF POWISIENNE, WASO.
AND HE IS OUR SAVIOR.
AND IT SHALL BE SO, BEFORE WE FALL TO THE FATE OF OUR KIN, WHO GAVE THEIR LIVES SO THAT WE, THE BLESSED WIND, LORDS OF UGOMA...
... MAY BE REBORN THROUGH THE FIRE AND ASH AND SMOKE.

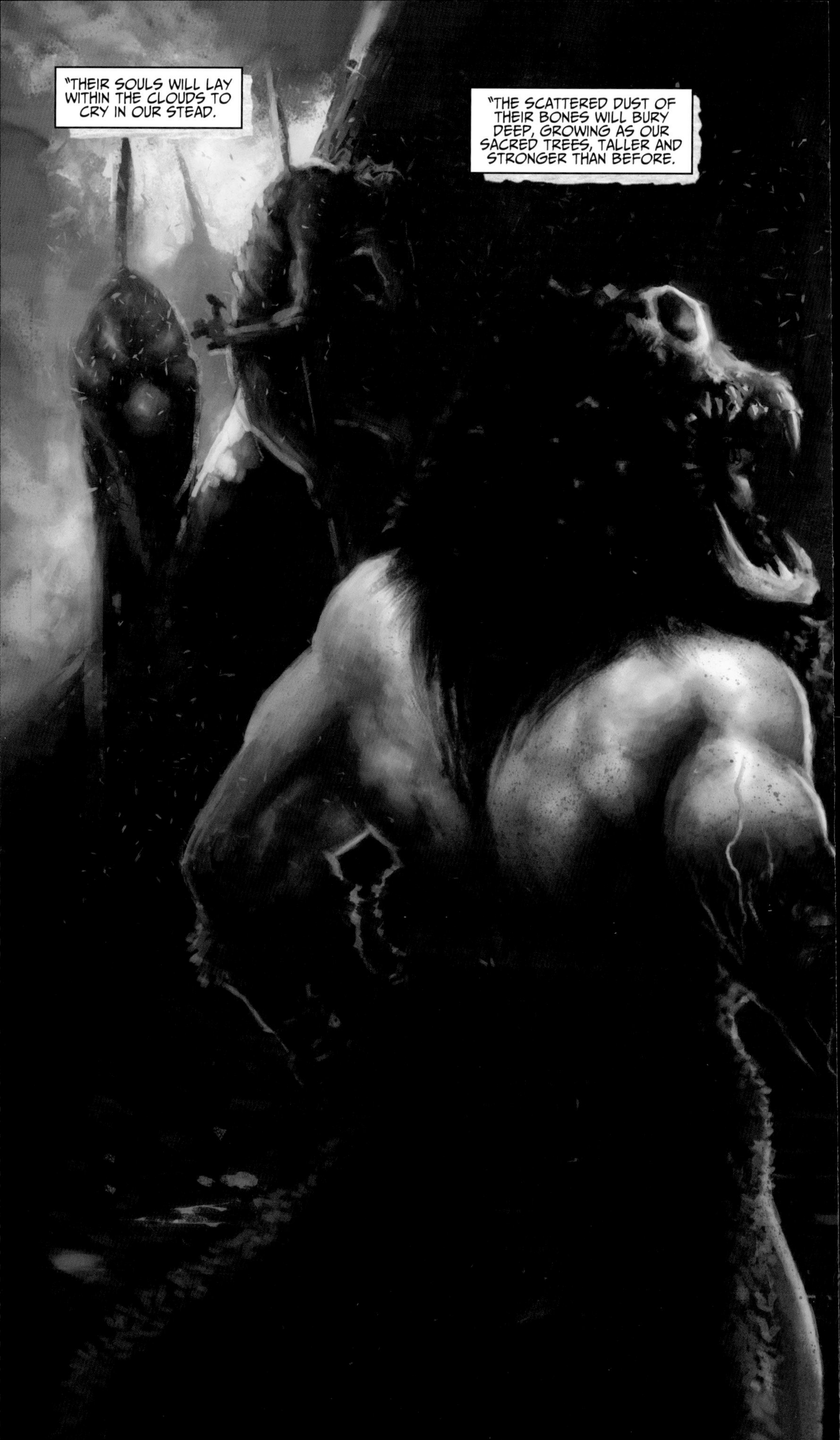
"THEIR SOULS WILL LAY WITHIN THE CLOUDS TO CRY IN OUR STEAD.
"THE SCATTERED DUST OF THEIR BONES WILL BURY DEEP, GROWING AS OUR SACRED TREES, TALLER AND STRONGER THAN BEFORE.

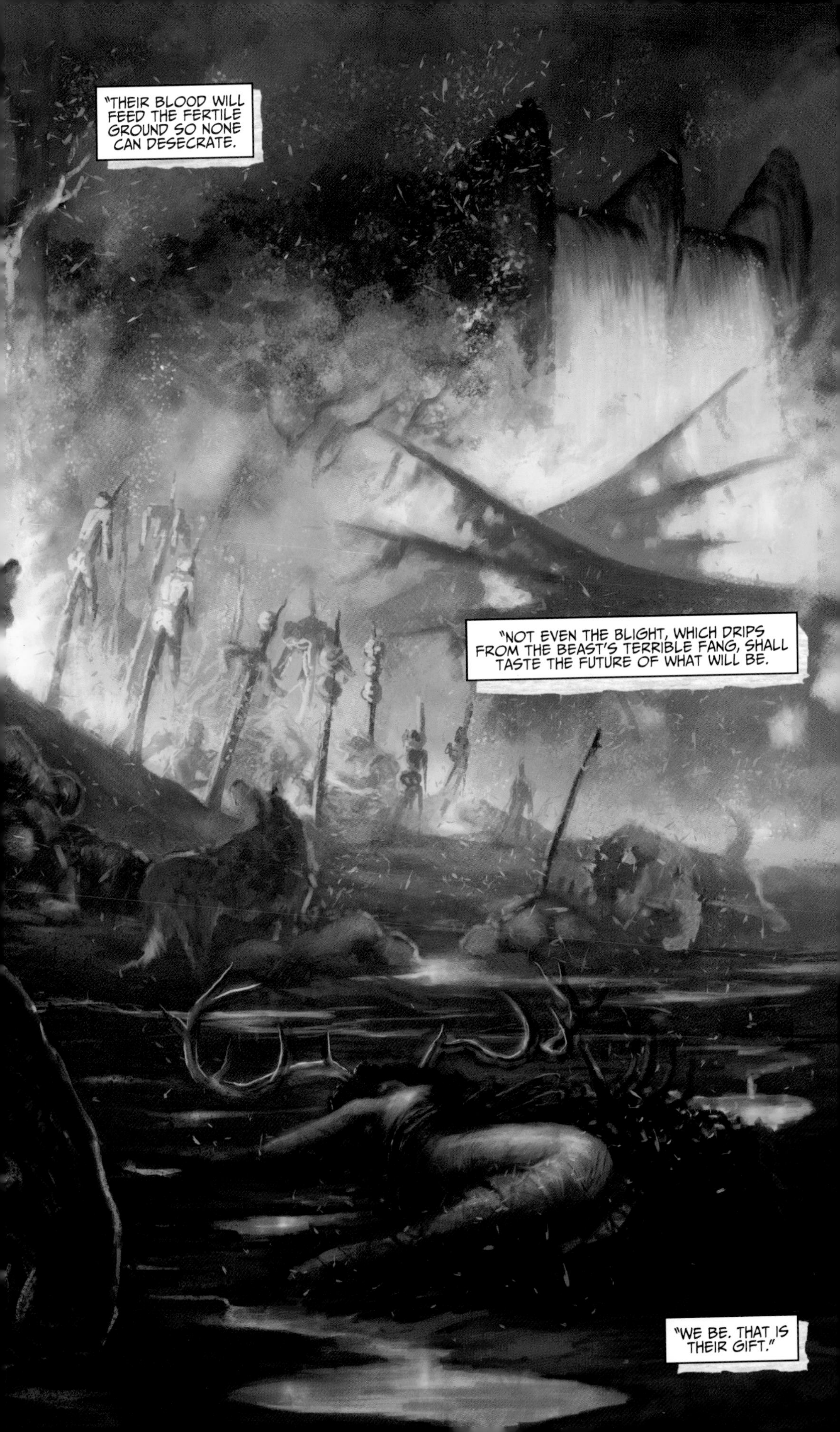
"THEIR BLOOD WILL FEED THE FERTILE GROUND SO NONE CAN DESECRATE.
"NOT EVEN THE BLIGHT, WHICH DRIPS FROM THE BEAST'S TERRIBLE FANG, SHALL TASTE THE FUTURE OF WHAT WILL BE.
"WE BE. THAT IS THEIR GIFT."

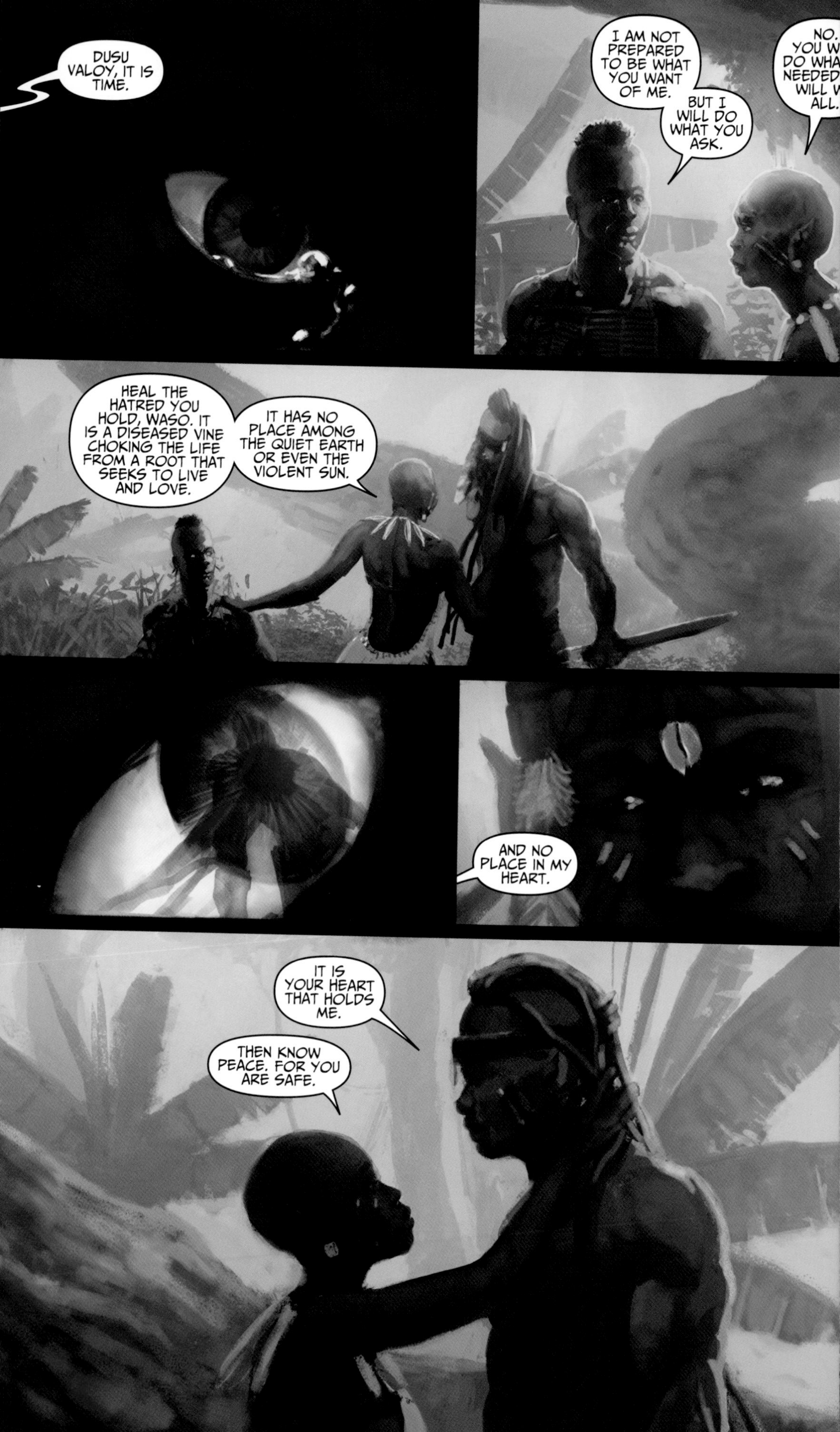
DUSU VALOY, IT IS TIME.
I AM NOT PREPARED TO BE WHAT YOU WANT OF ME.
BUT I WILL DO WHAT YOU ASK.
NO. YOU W DO WHA NEEDED WILL W ALL.
HEAL THE HATRED YOU HOLD, WASO. IT IS A DISEASED VINE CHOKING THE LIFE FROM A ROOT THAT SEEKS TO LIVE AND LOVE.
IT HAS NO PLACE AMONG THE QUIET EARTH OR EVEN THE VIOLENT SUN.
AND NO PLACE IN MY HEART.
IT IS YOUR HEART THAT HOLDS ME.
THEN KNOW PEACE. FOR YOU ARE SAFE.

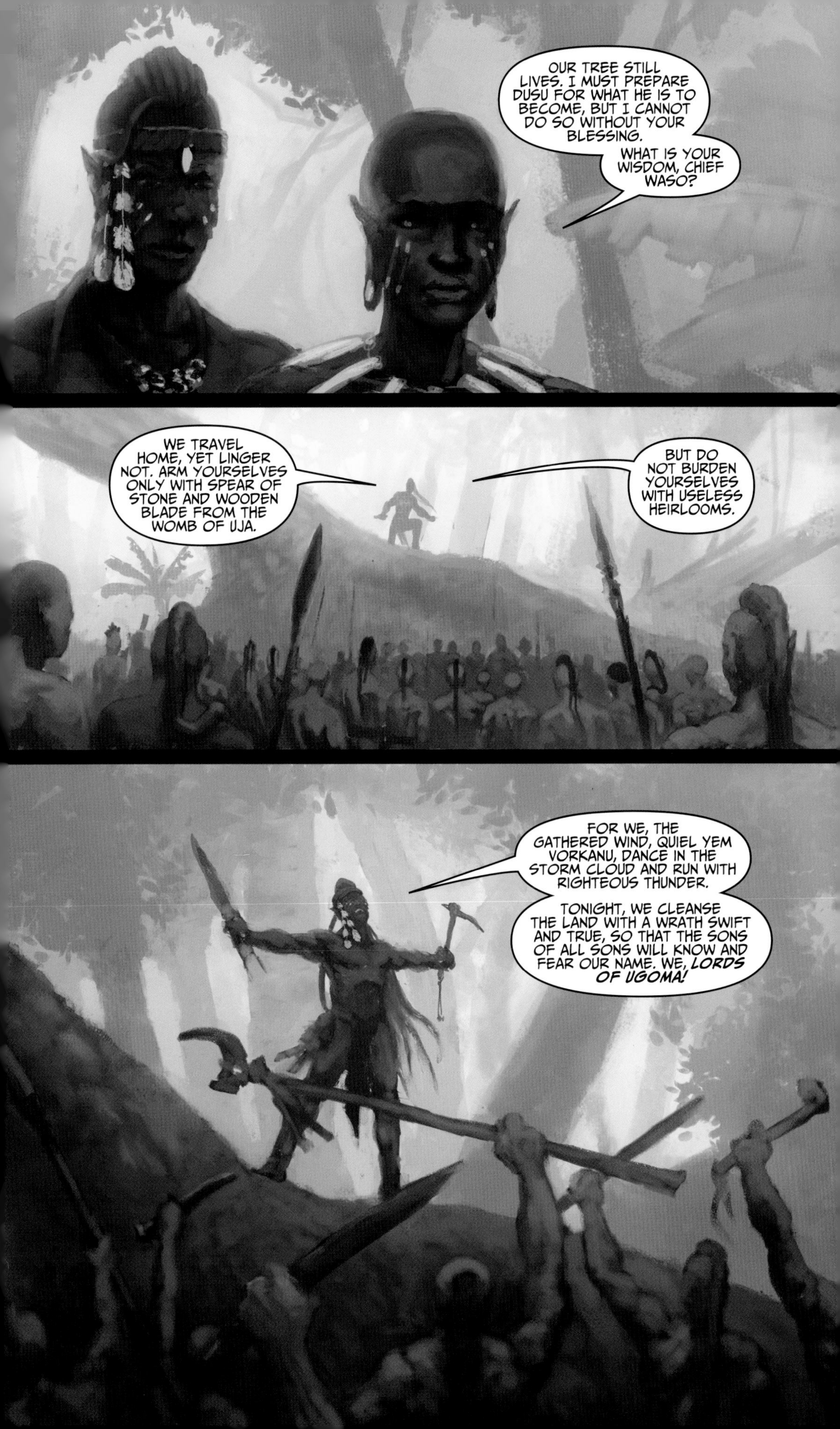
OUR TREE STILL LIVES. I MUST PREPARE DUSU FOR WHAT HE IS TO BECOME, BUT I CANNOT DO SO WITHOUT YOUR BLESSING.
WHAT IS YOUR WISDOM, CHIEF WASO?
WE TRAVEL HOME, YET LINGER NOT. ARM YOURSELVES ONLY WITH SPEAR OF STONE AND WOODEN BLADE FROM THE WOMB OF UJA.
BUT DO NOT BURDEN YOURSELVES WITH USELESS HEIRLOOMS.
FOR WE, THE GATHERED WIND, QUIEL YEM VORKANU, DANCE IN THE STORM CLOUD AND RUN WITH RIGHTEOUS THUNDER.
TONIGHT, WE CLEANSE THE LAND WITH A WRATH SWIFT AND TRUE, SO THAT THE SONS OF ALL SONS WILL KNOW AND FEAR OUR NAME. WE, *LORDS OF UGOMA!*

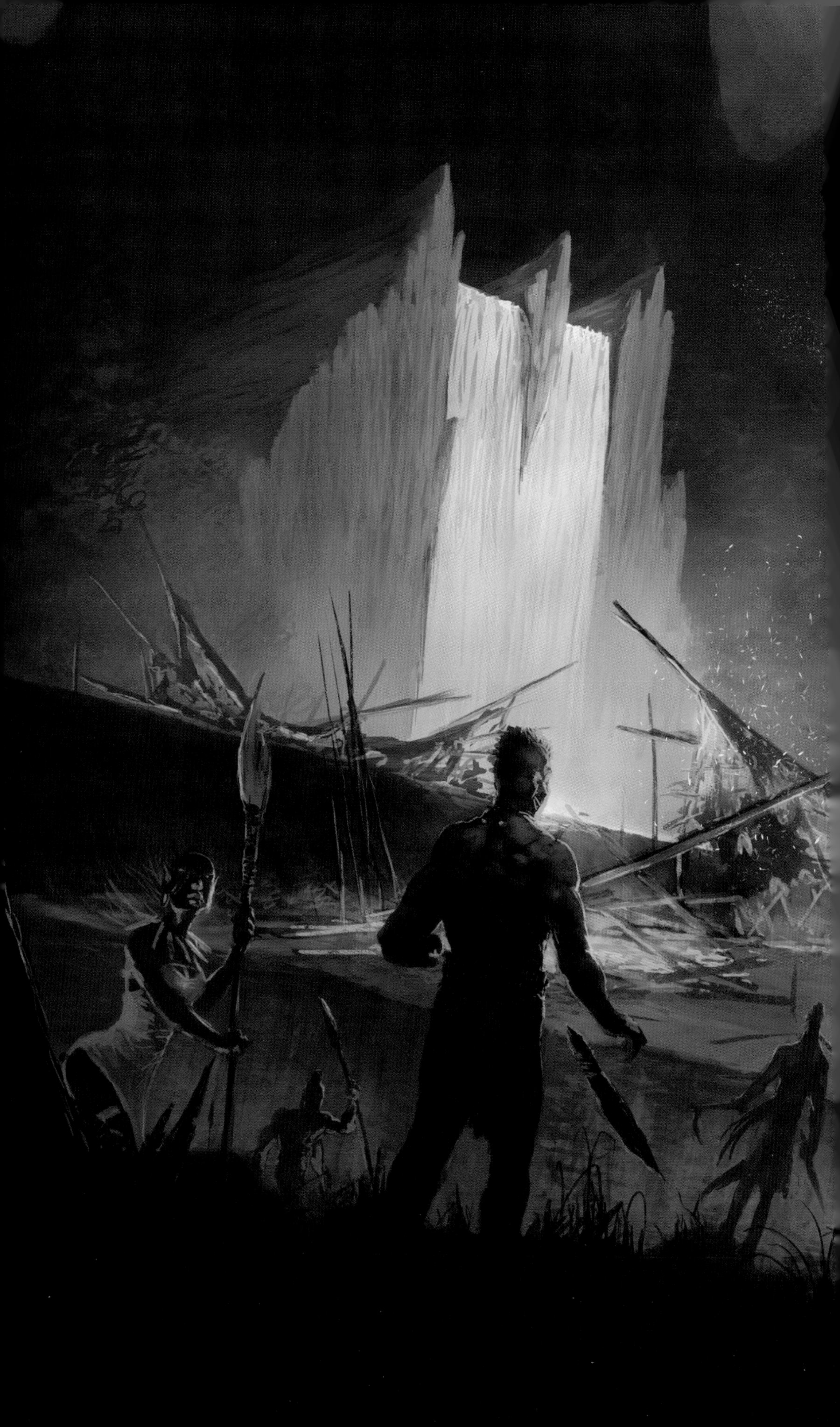

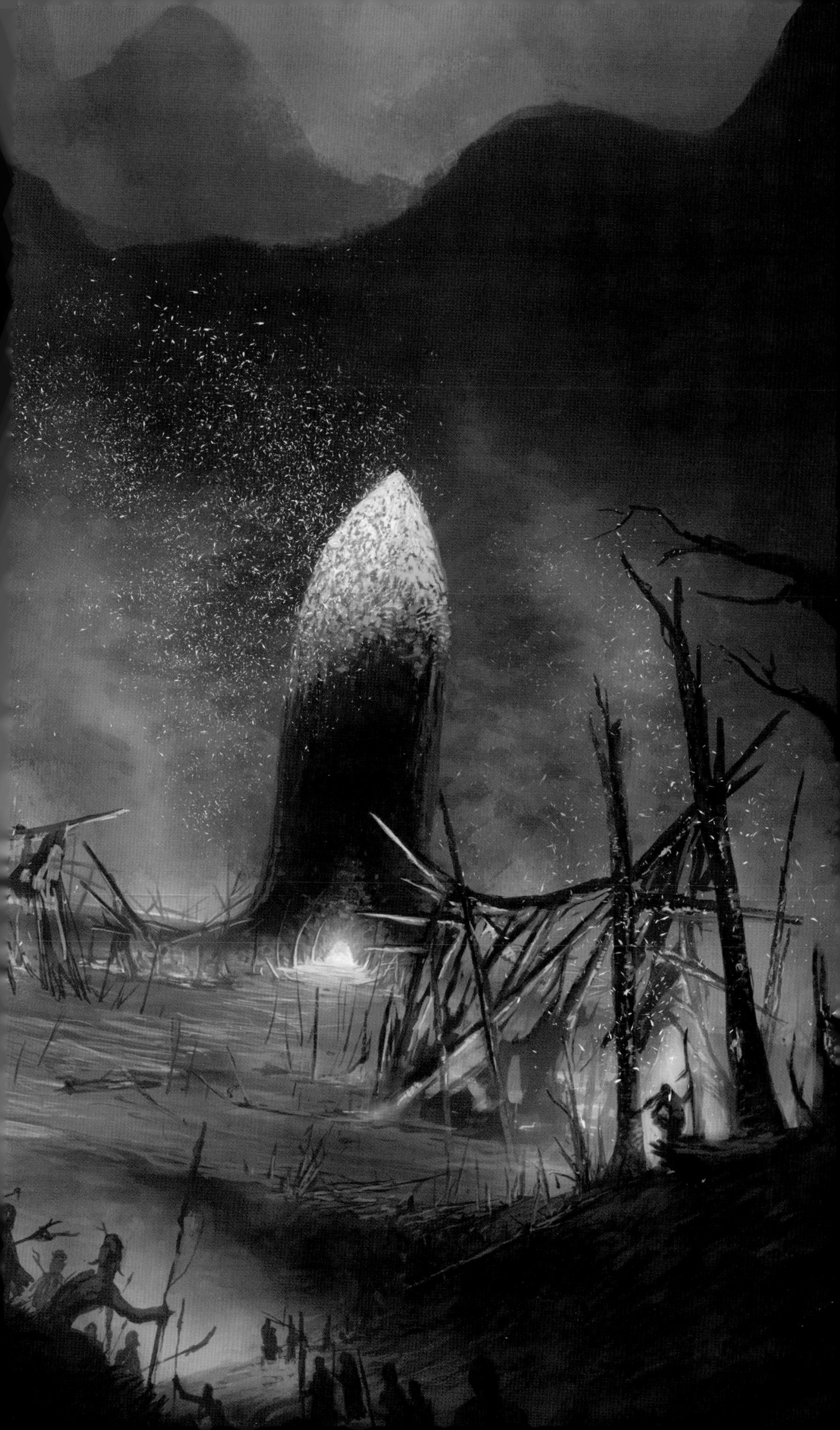

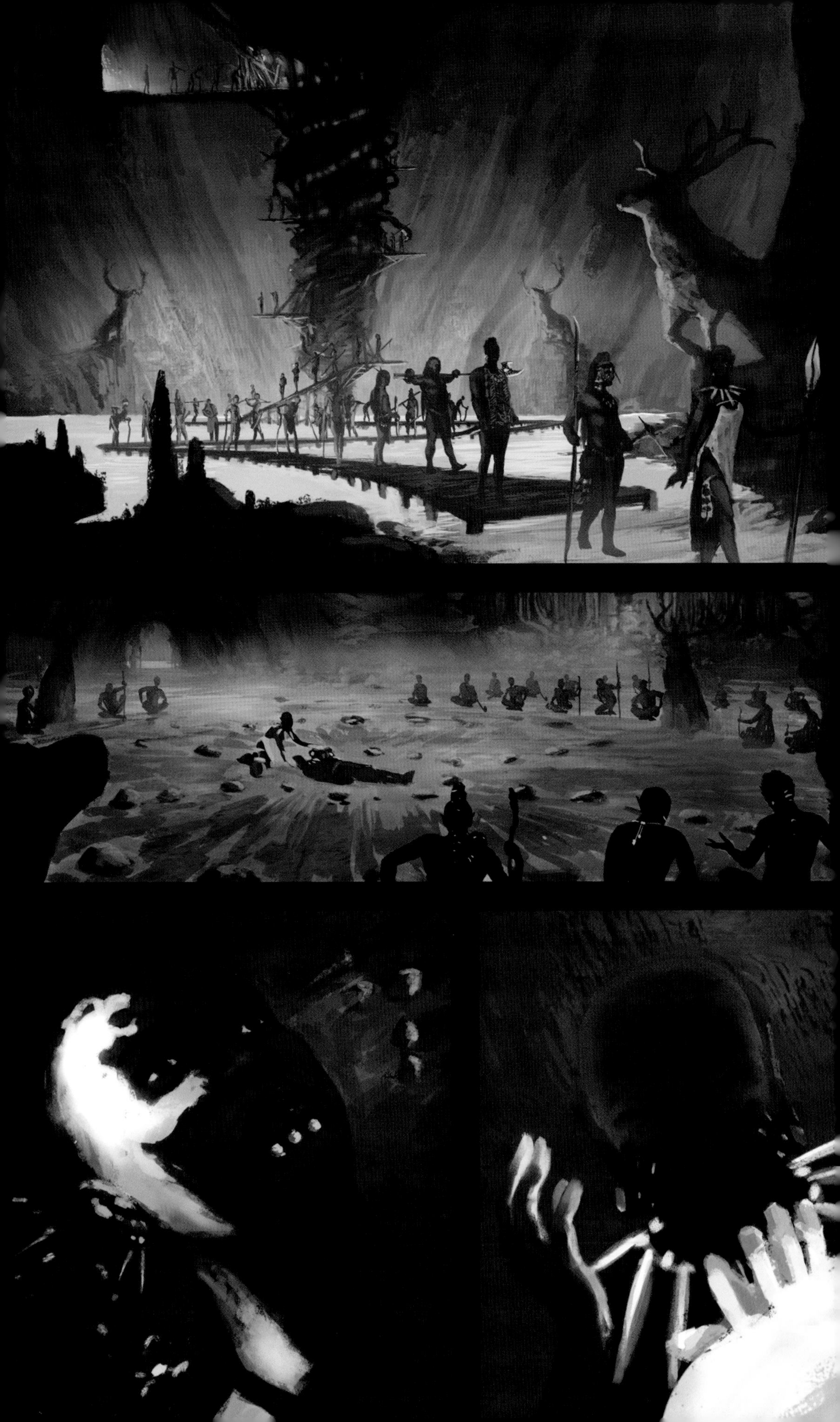

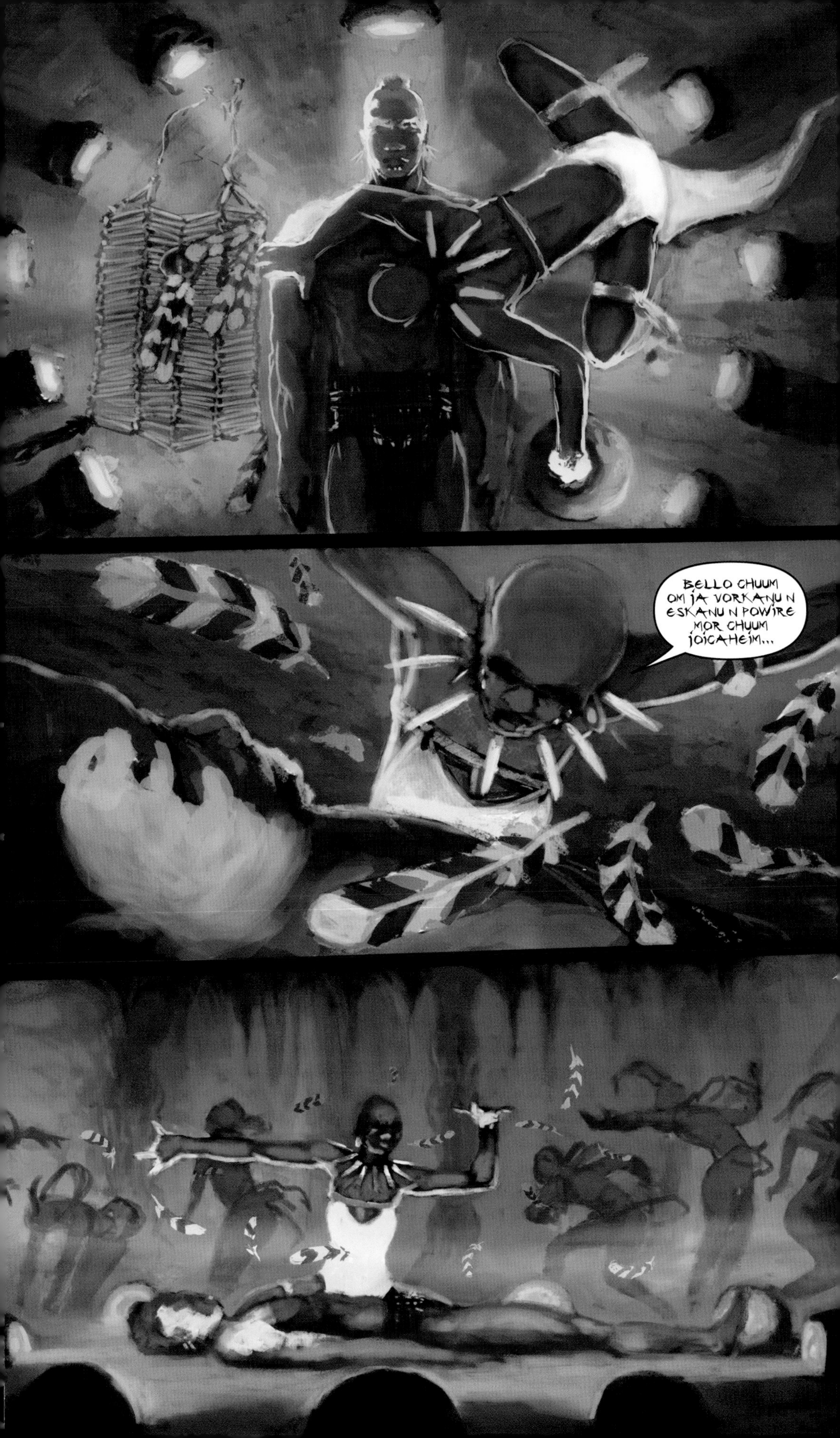
BELLO CHUUM OM JA VORKANU N ESKANU N POWIRE MOR CHUUM JOICAHEIM...

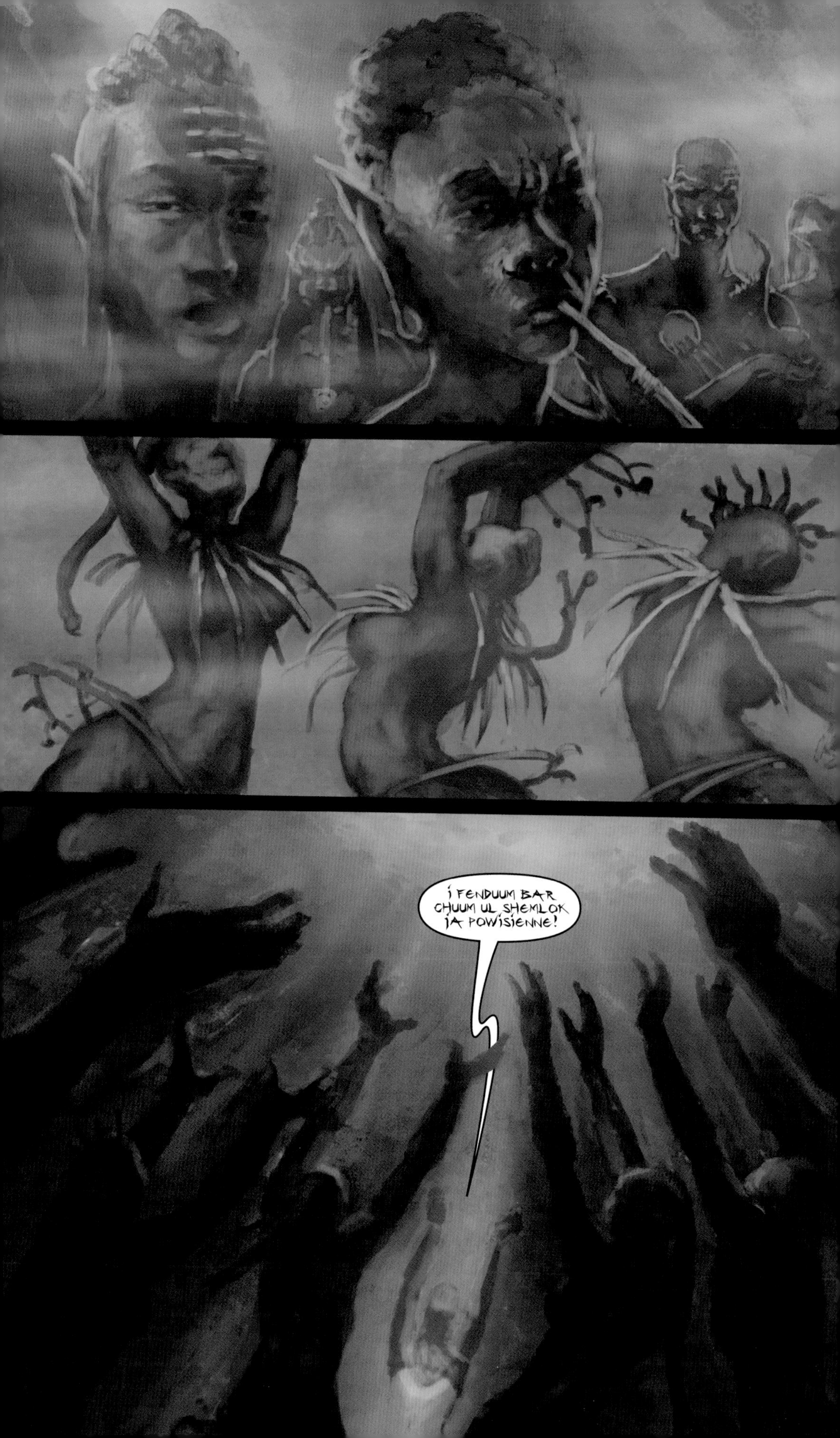
¡FENDUUM BAR CHUUM UL SHEMLOK ¡A POWISIENNE!

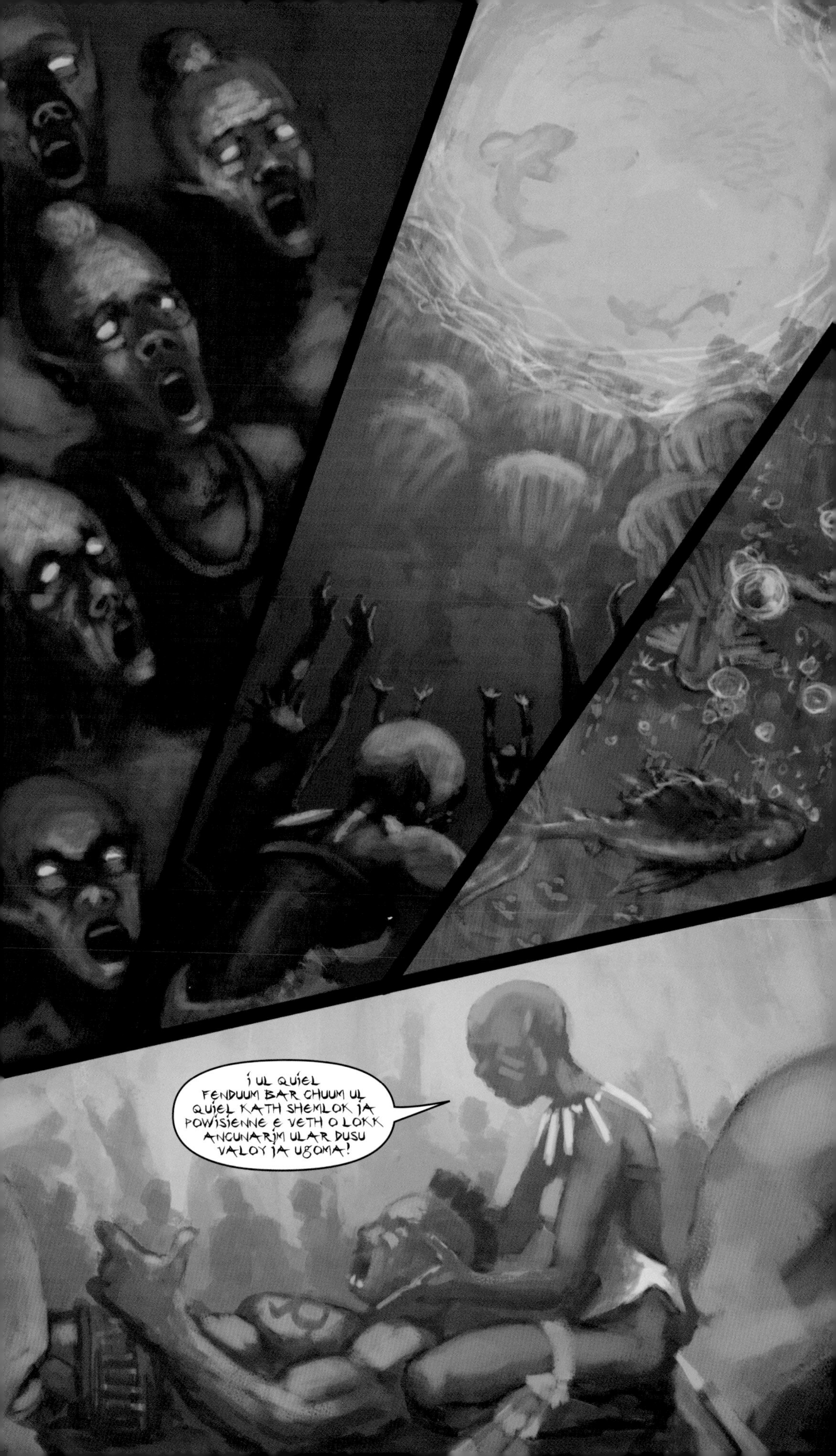
¡UL QUIEL FENDUUM BAR CHUUM UL QUIEL KATH SHEMLOK JA POWISIENNE E VETH O LOKK ANCUNARIM ULAR DUSU VALOY JA UGOMA!

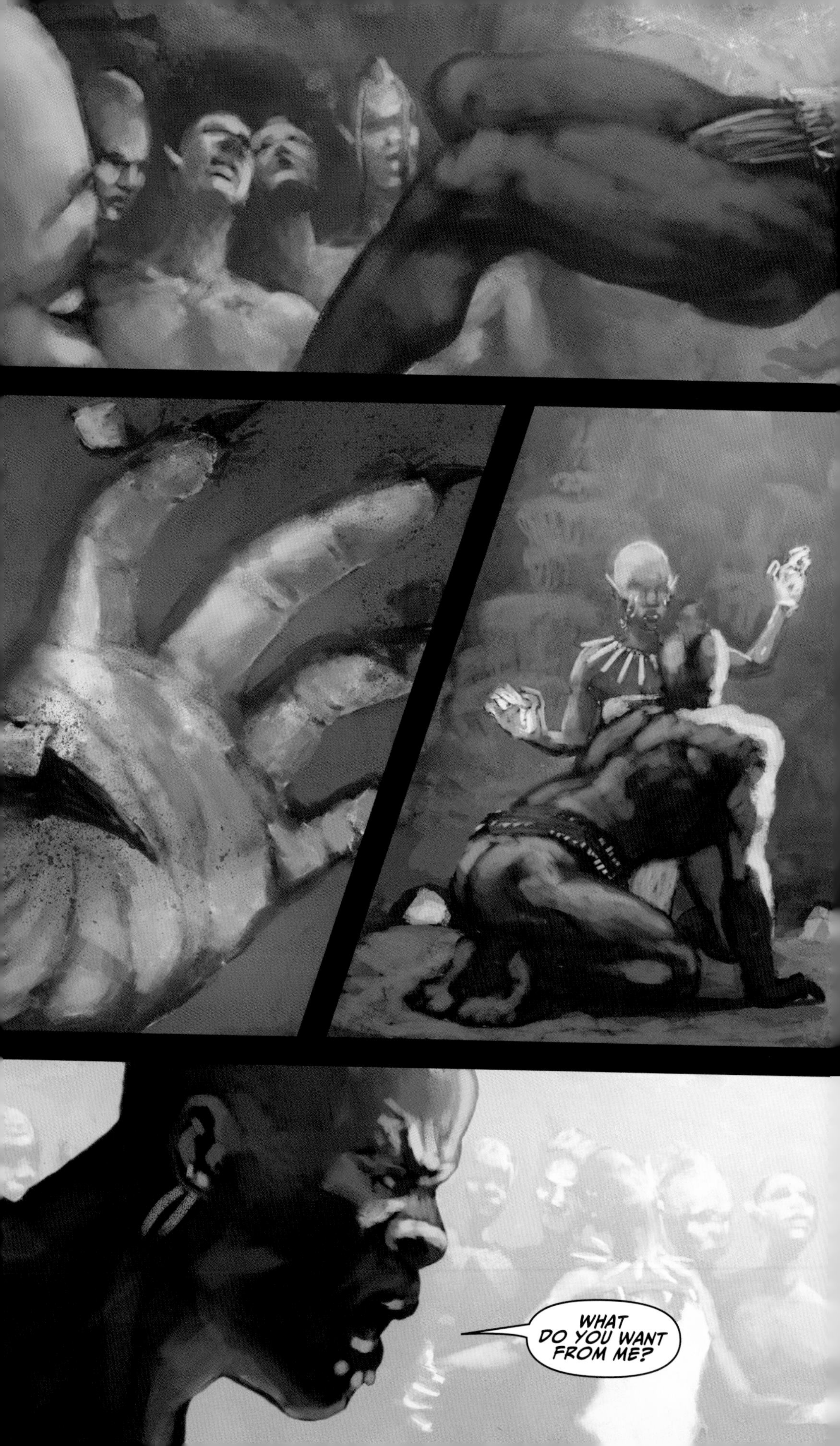
WHAT DO YOU WANT FROM ME?

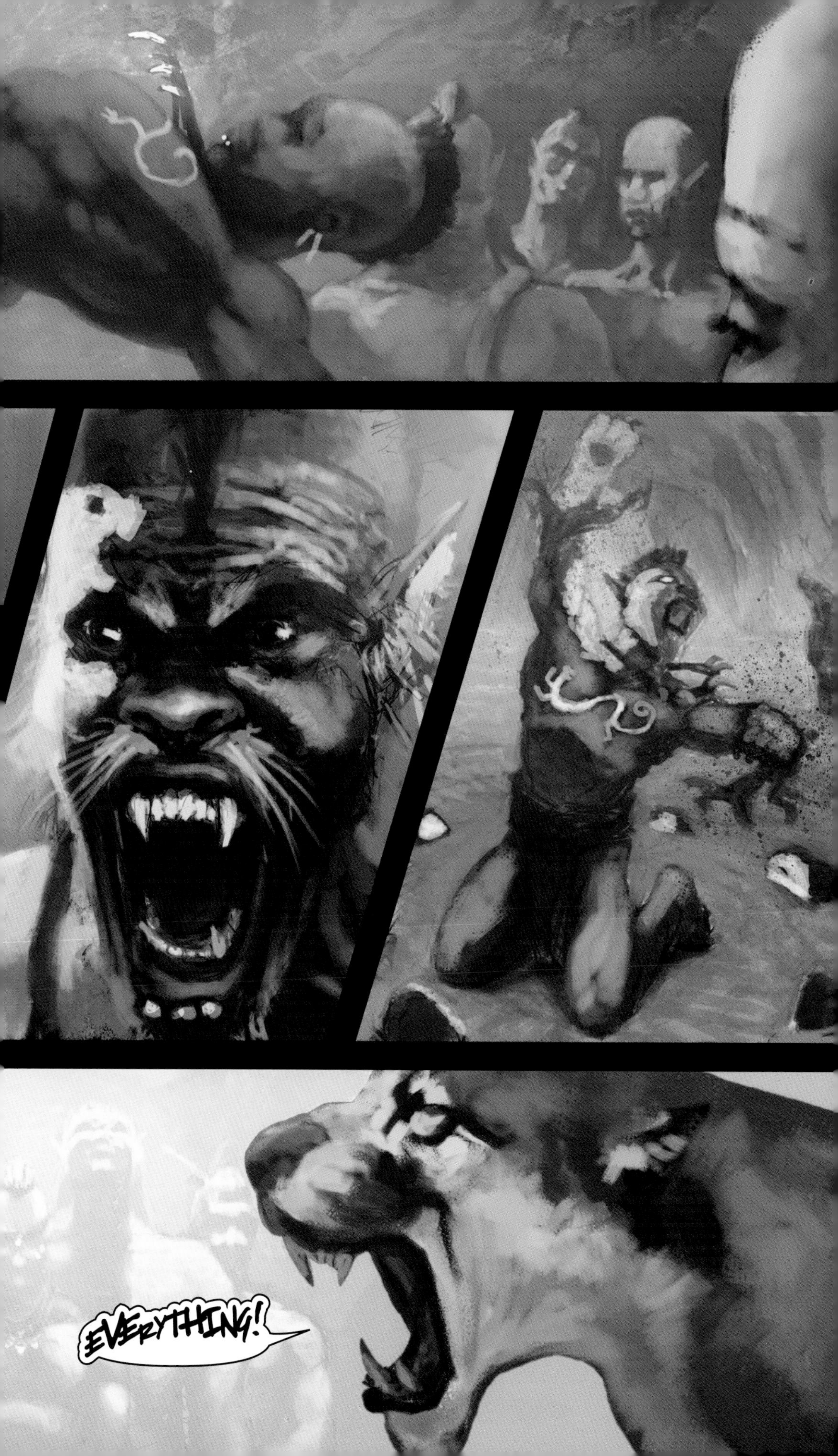
EVERYTHING!

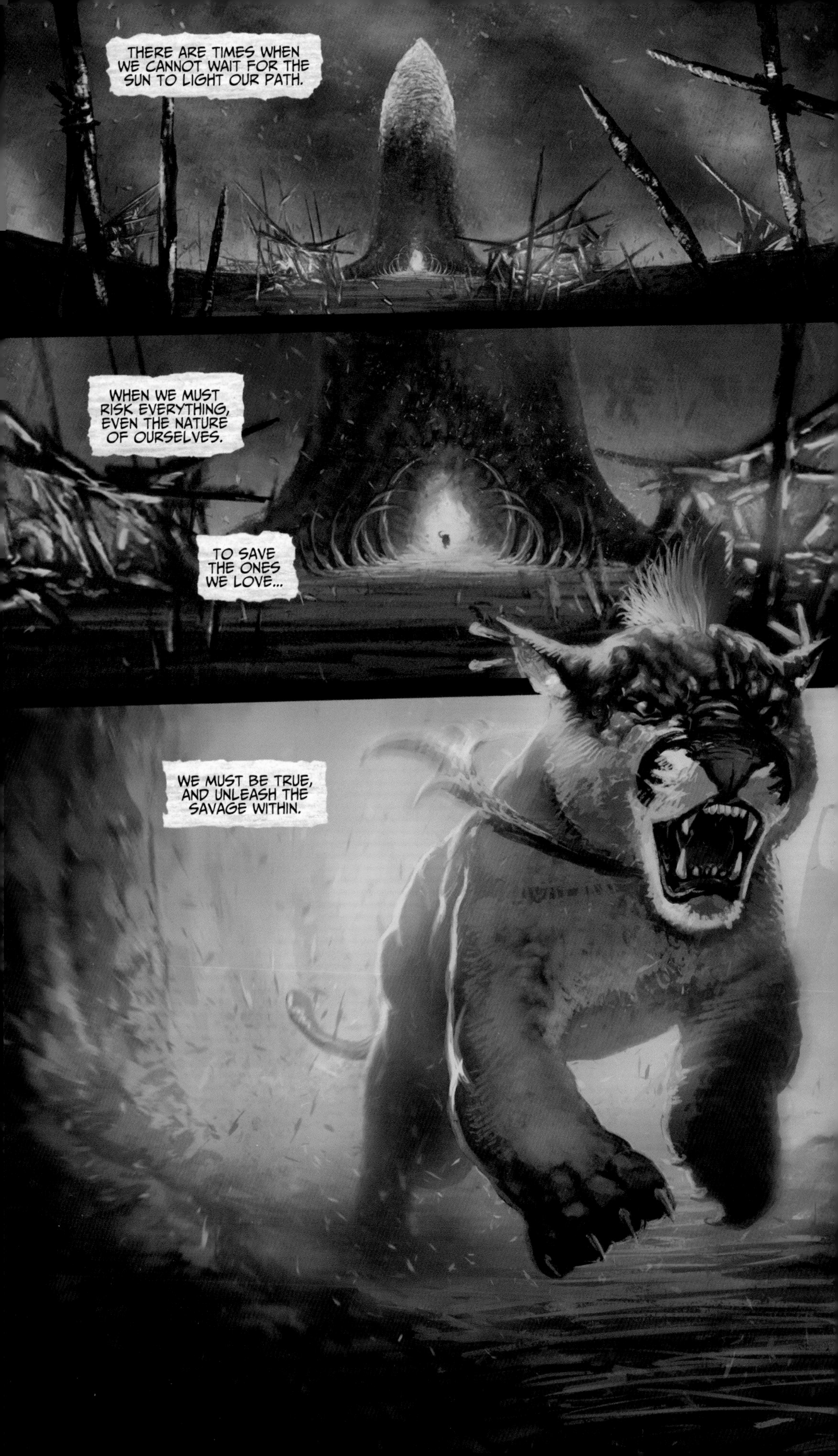
THERE ARE TIMES WHEN WE CANNOT WAIT FOR THE SUN TO LIGHT OUR PATH.
WHEN WE MUST RISK EVERYTHING, EVEN THE NATURE OF OURSELVES.
TO SAVE THE ONES WE LOVE...
WE MUST BE TRUE, AND UNLEASH THE SAVAGE WITHIN.

For some men, it is never enough. The empty void in his heart widened until the
reat and terrible nothing melded with soul and skin. Madness preyed on grief,
nd chaos, as it always does, ultimately ensued with a smile. I knew him before he
ad tasted the ruin. He was a powerful king with the strength of a giant and the
vill of a God. But his wolf crown was sharp, and fangs dug into his brow until the
ight of life dwindled, and once massive shoulders sagged low. Until finally he
ried into the nothing to be great once more, his pleas ringing through the unholy
orners of the earth and beyond."

– Salem Ravensong

It was The Untamed who ended Eternity and created Chaos. And so shall it be all of
our undoing... as well as his.

Arukas, the Devil, first child of Andarcil and Madraq, took his white and unholy
sword and plunged it deep into the soul of Celebrius (God of Life and Eternity), and
now we are doomed to an end. When it shall happen, few of us know, but the day
shall come when sons slay fathers and mothers abandon their young in their darkest
need, for all hope shall be lost.

The Universe, Esu, the Mother Dragon, mourned the loss of her spirit mate,
Celebrius. Yet grief soon turned to rage at his murder, and the Mother soon became
consumed with this new feeling, this hatred. A great shadow of nothing festered
within her until it could be contained no longer and tore itself away.

It became Requethax, the Dragon of Blight and the Devourer of All Things. His
tainted essence spreads like a disease, and so his symbol is that of a dark, cancerous
Blight spreading across the face of the globe. For born of hatred for all, Requethax
feeds upon the very fabric of existence, and his hunger will only be sated when he
has consumed everything that lives, whether mortal, God, or Dragon, upon the vast
and volatile world of…

ASUNDA

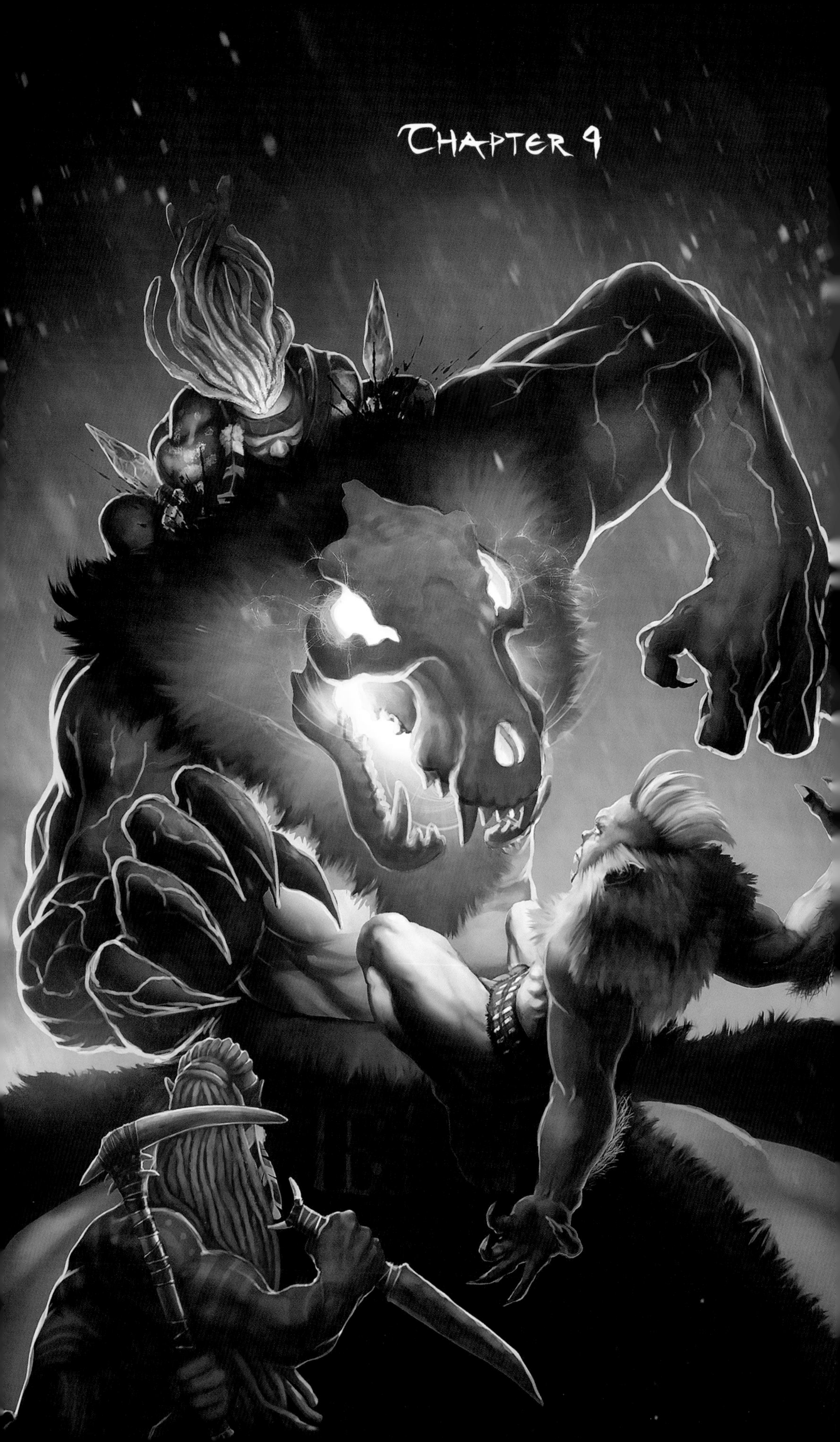
CHAPTER 9

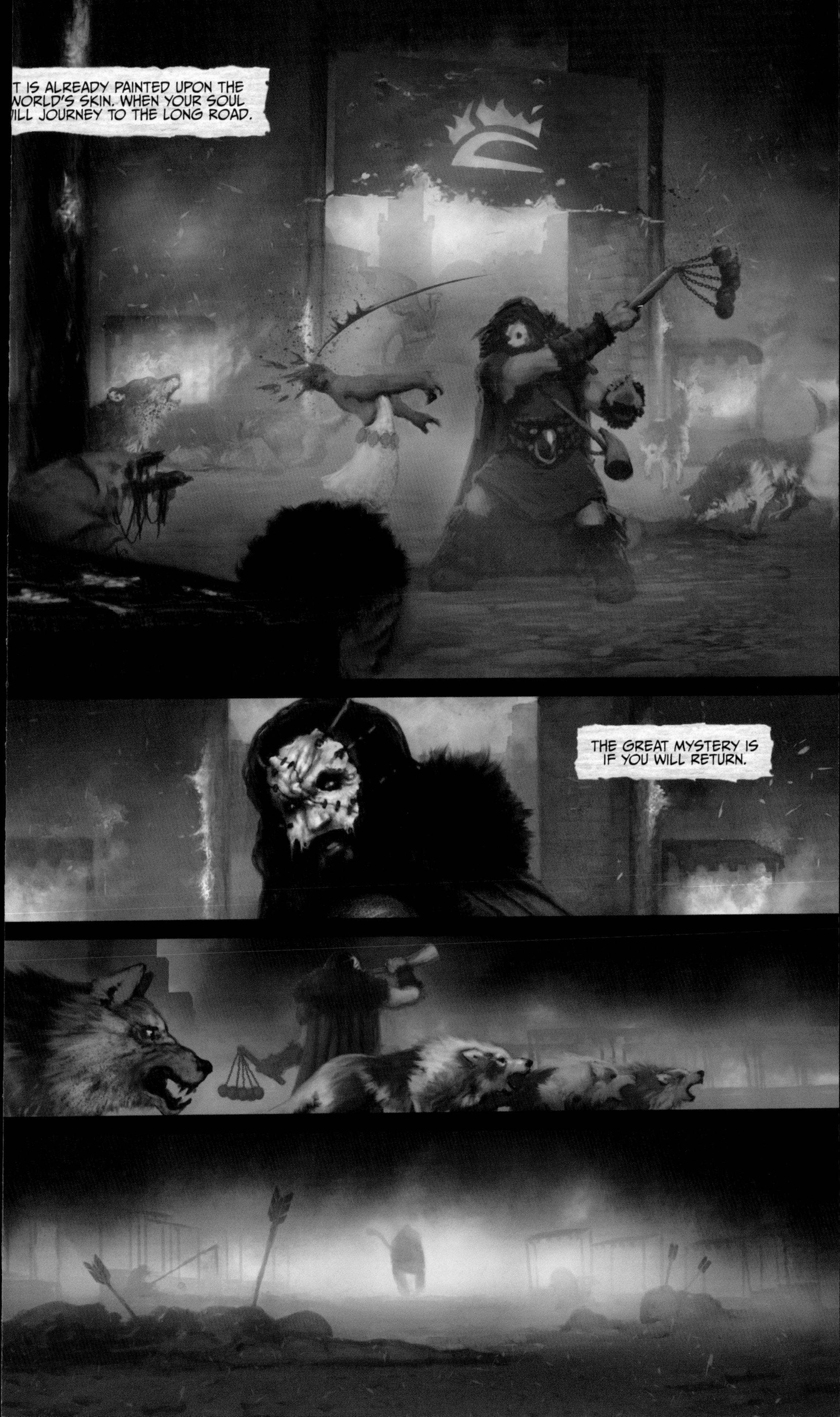
T IS ALREADY PAINTED UPON THE WORLD'S SKIN. WHEN YOUR SOUL WILL JOURNEY TO THE LONG ROAD.
THE GREAT MYSTERY IS IF YOU WILL RETURN.

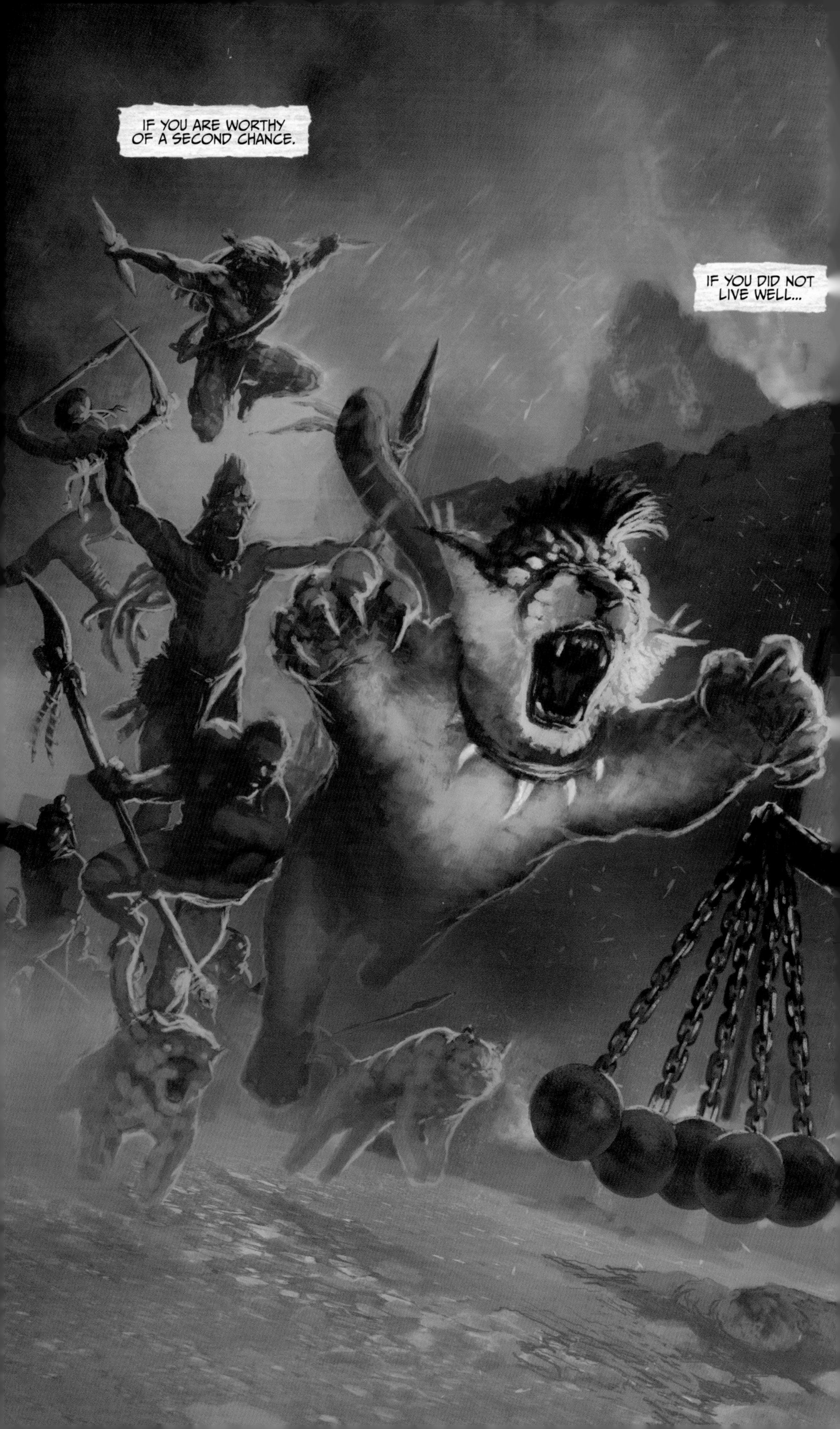
IF YOU ARE WORTHY OF A SECOND CHANCE.
IF YOU DID NOT LIVE WELL...

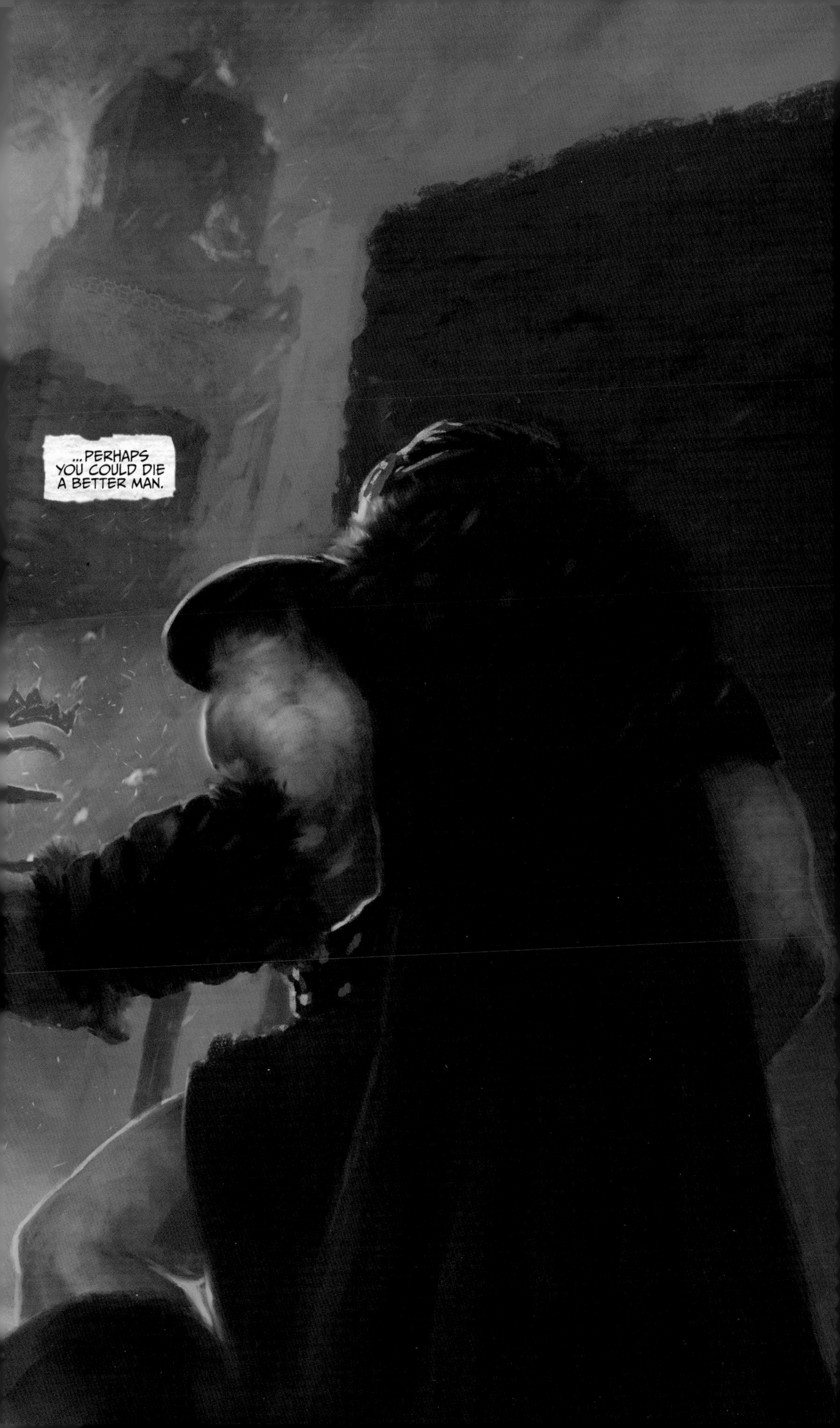
...PERHAPS YOU COULD DIE A BETTER MAN.

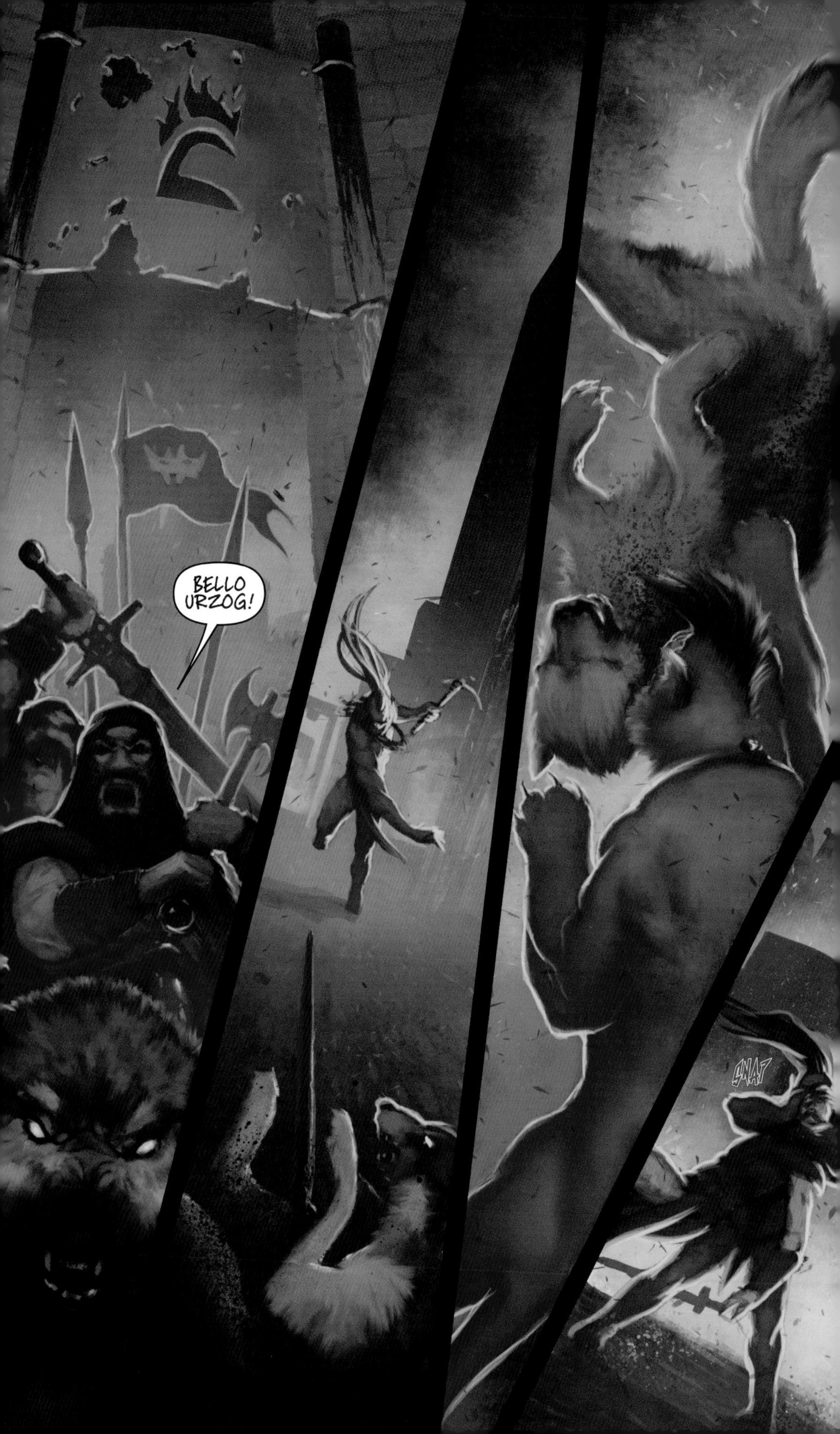
BELLO URZOG!
SNAT

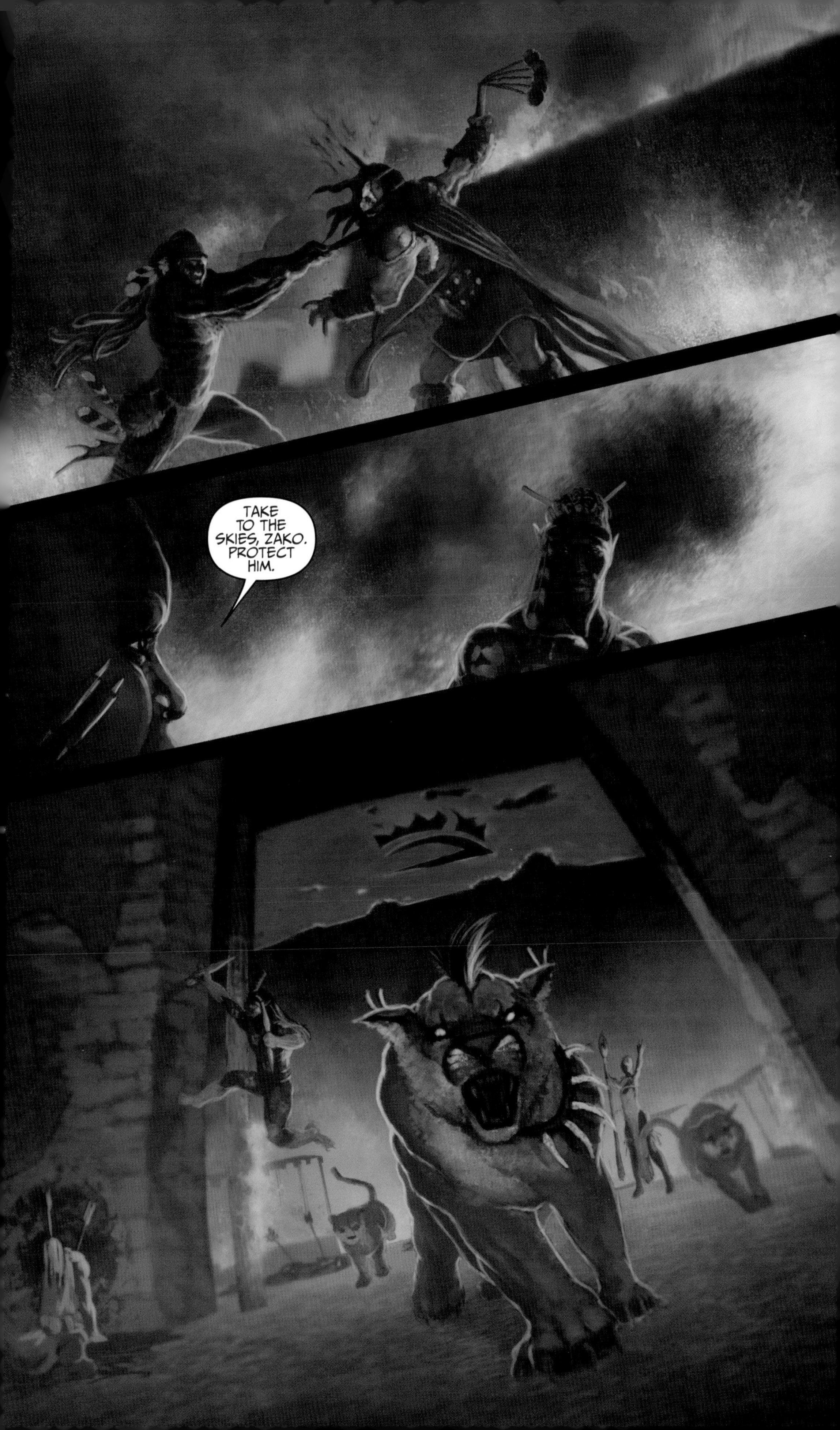
TAKE TO THE SKIES, ZAKO. PROTECT HIM.

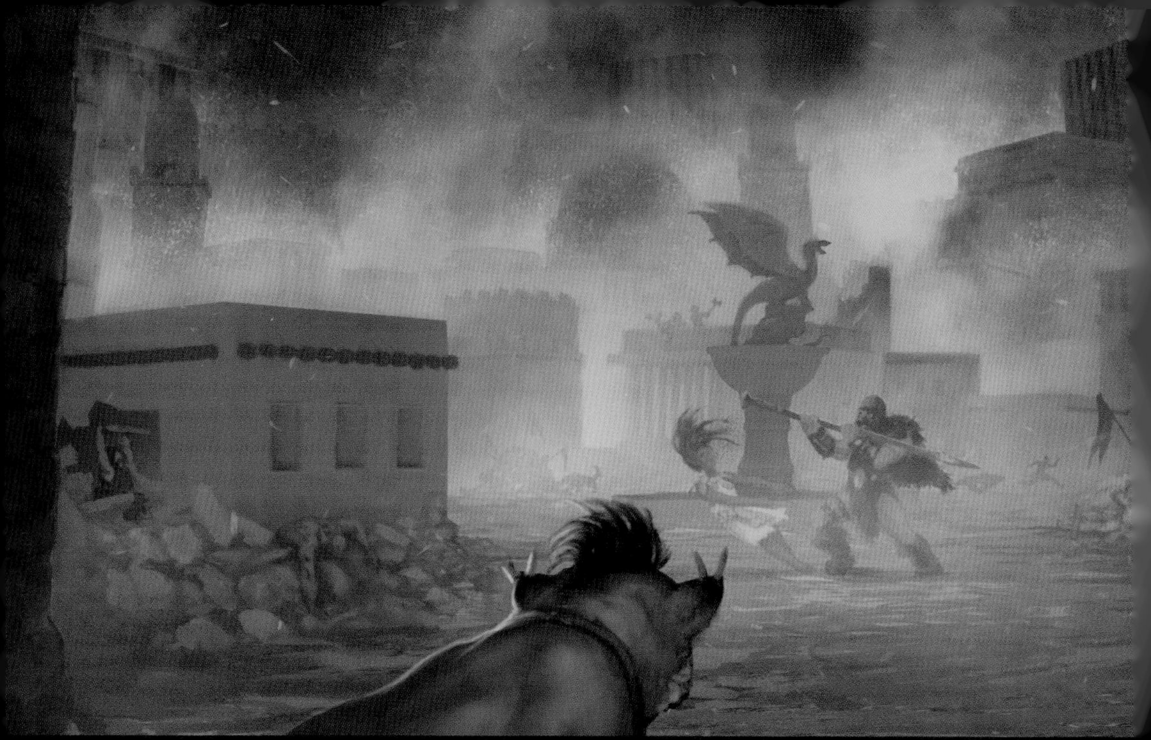

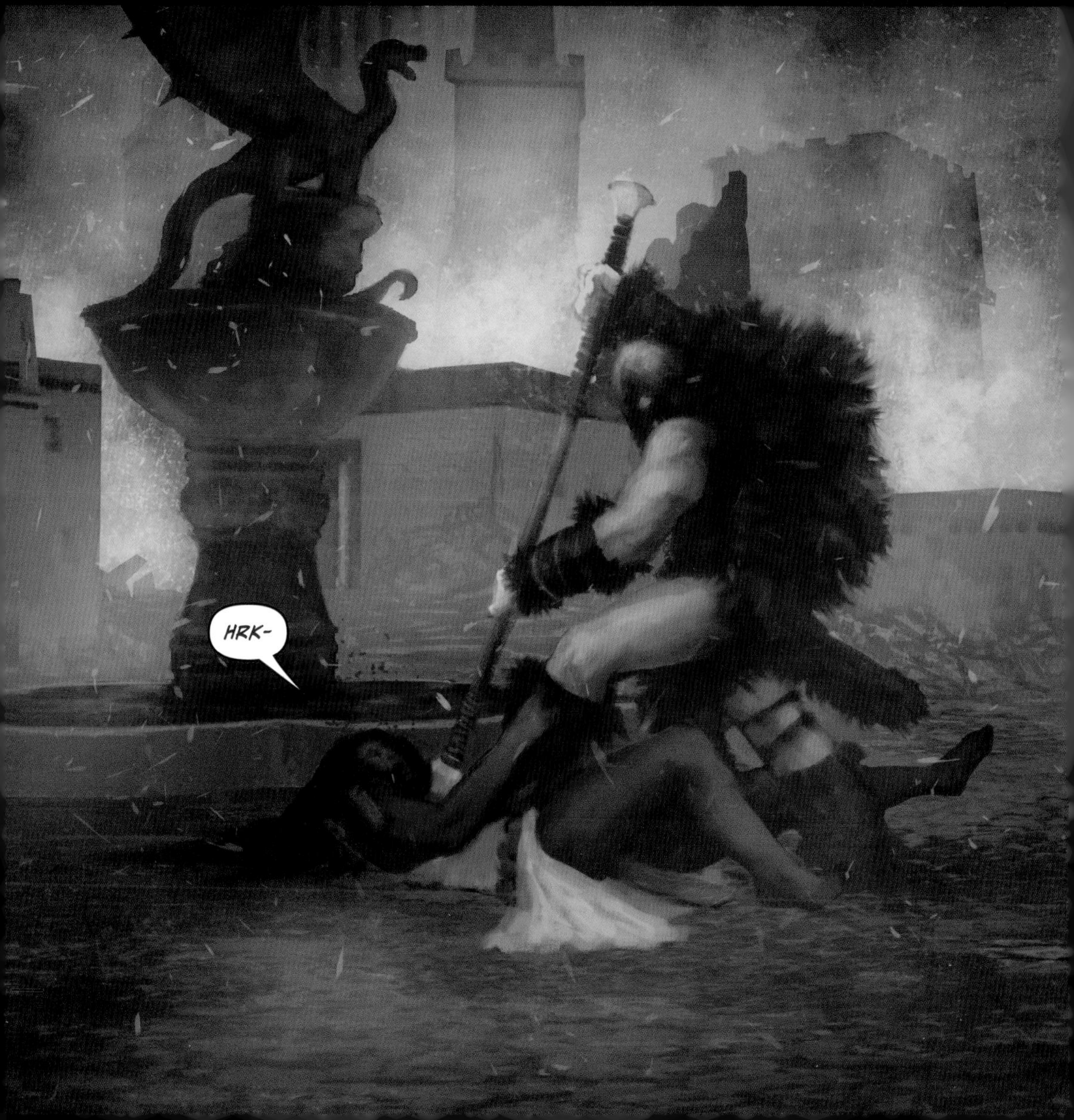
HRK-

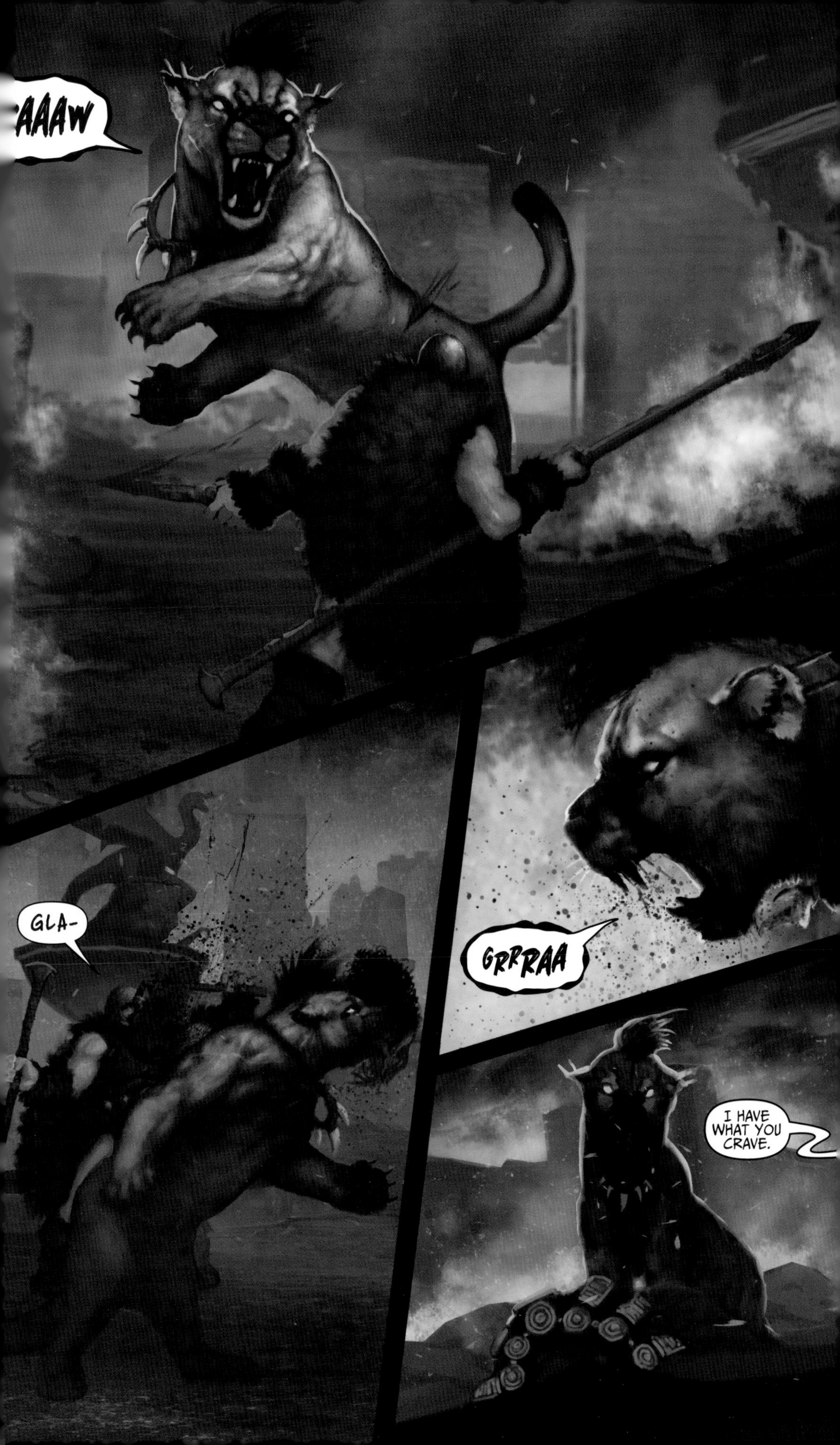

AAAW
GLA-
GRRRAA
I HAVE WHAT YOU CRAVE.

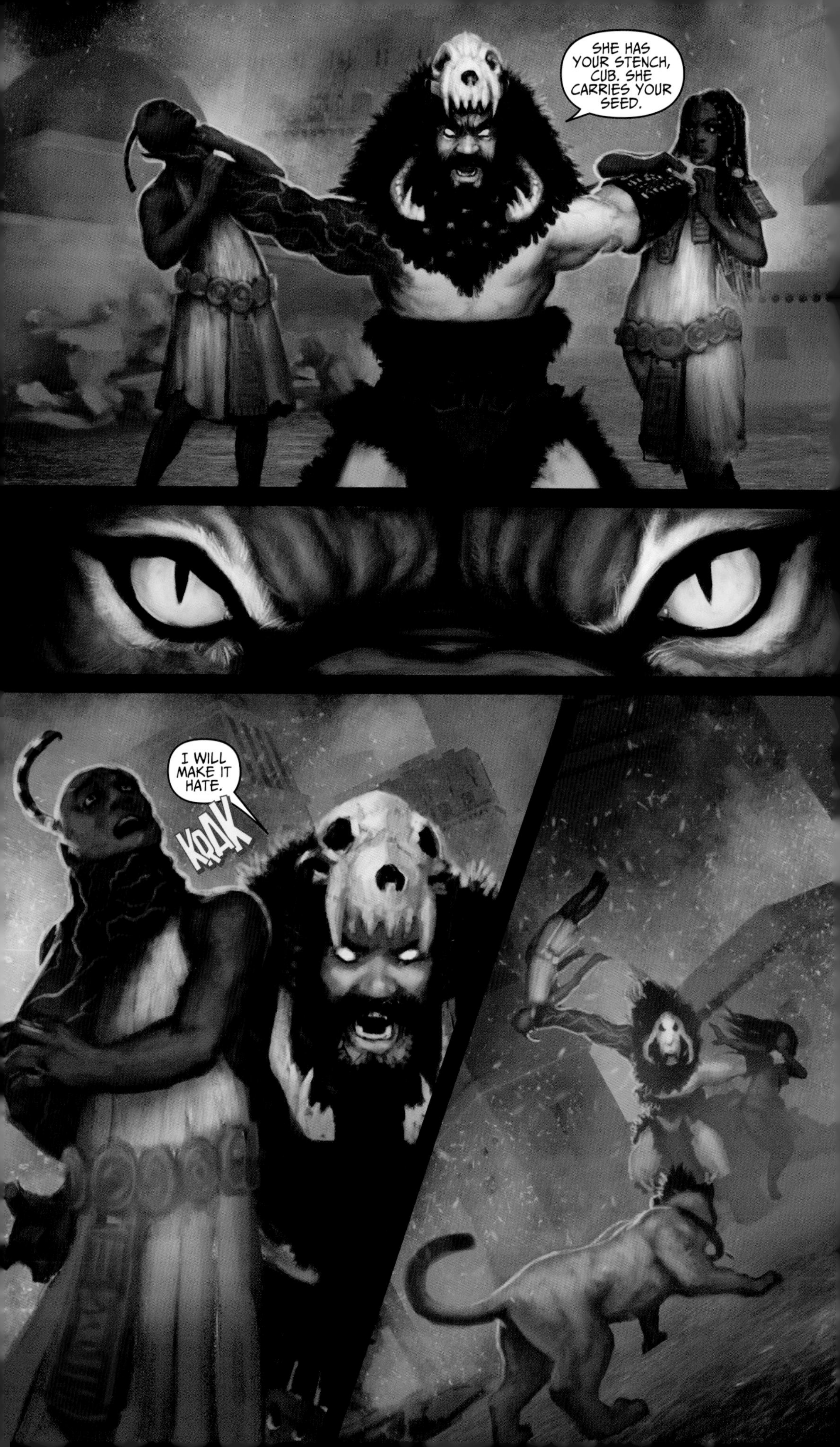
SHE HAS YOUR STENCH, CUB. SHE CARRIES YOUR SEED.
I WILL MAKE IT HATE.
KRAK

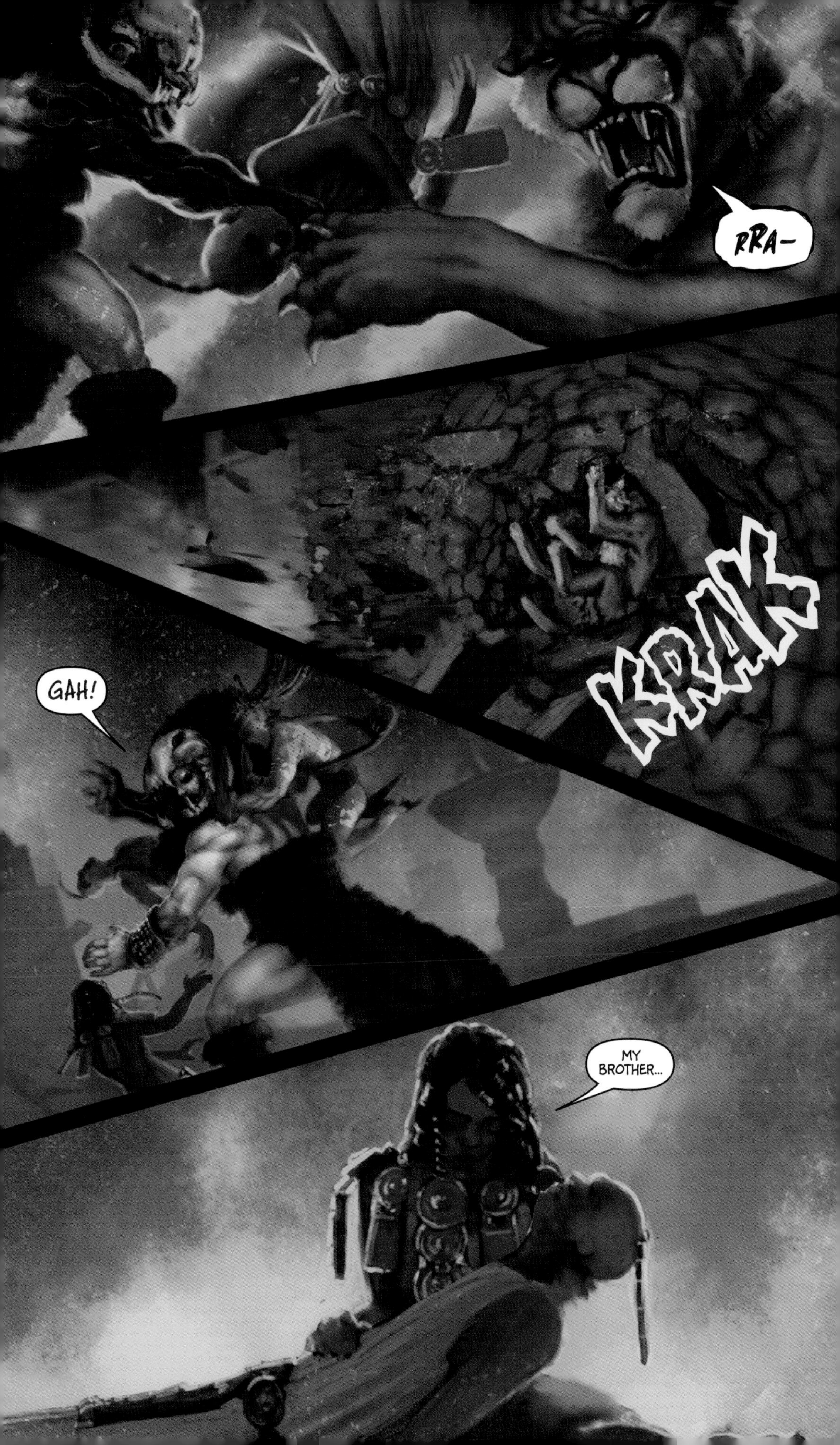
RRA-
KRAK
GAH!
MY BROTHER...

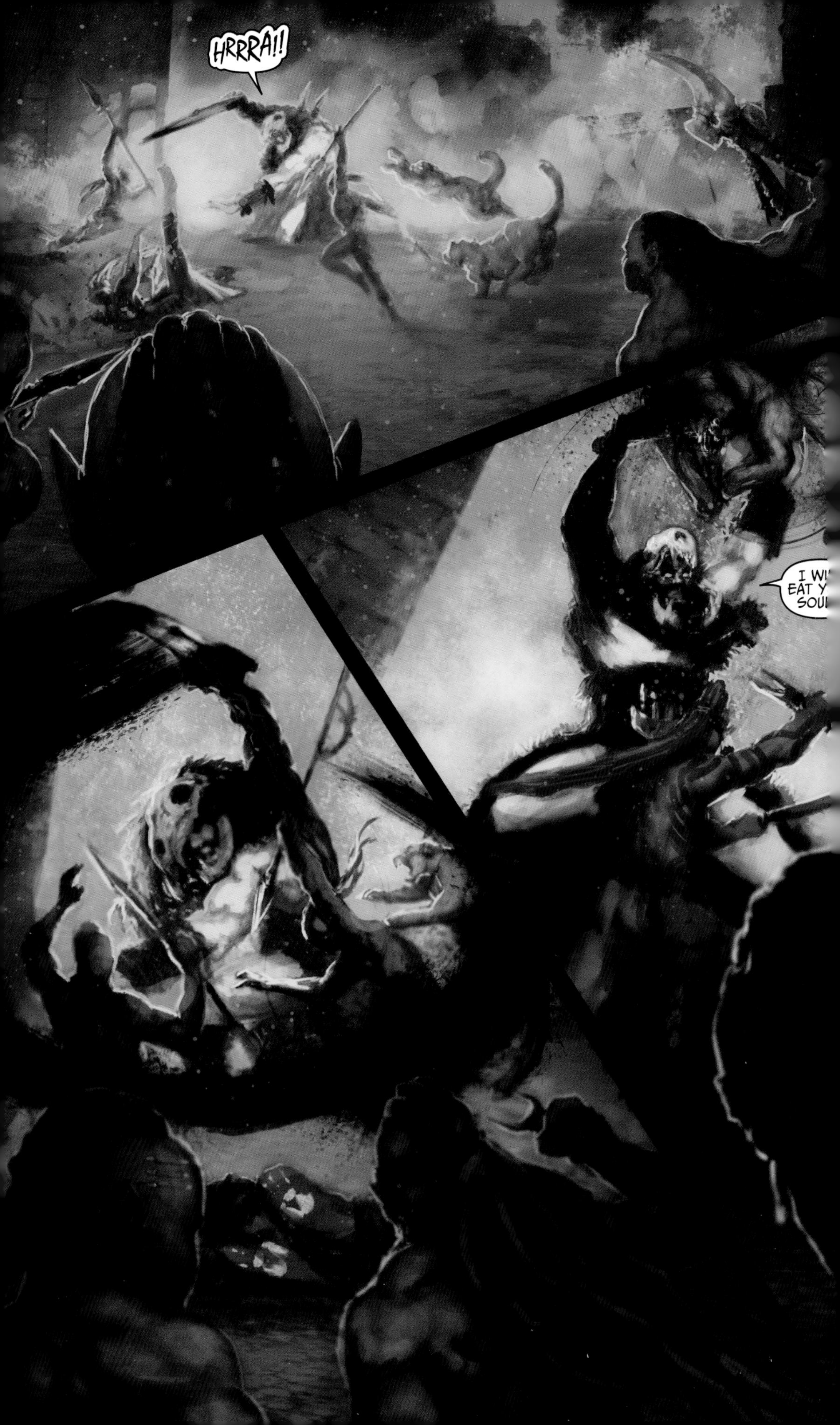
HRRRA!!
I WI
EAT Y
SOU

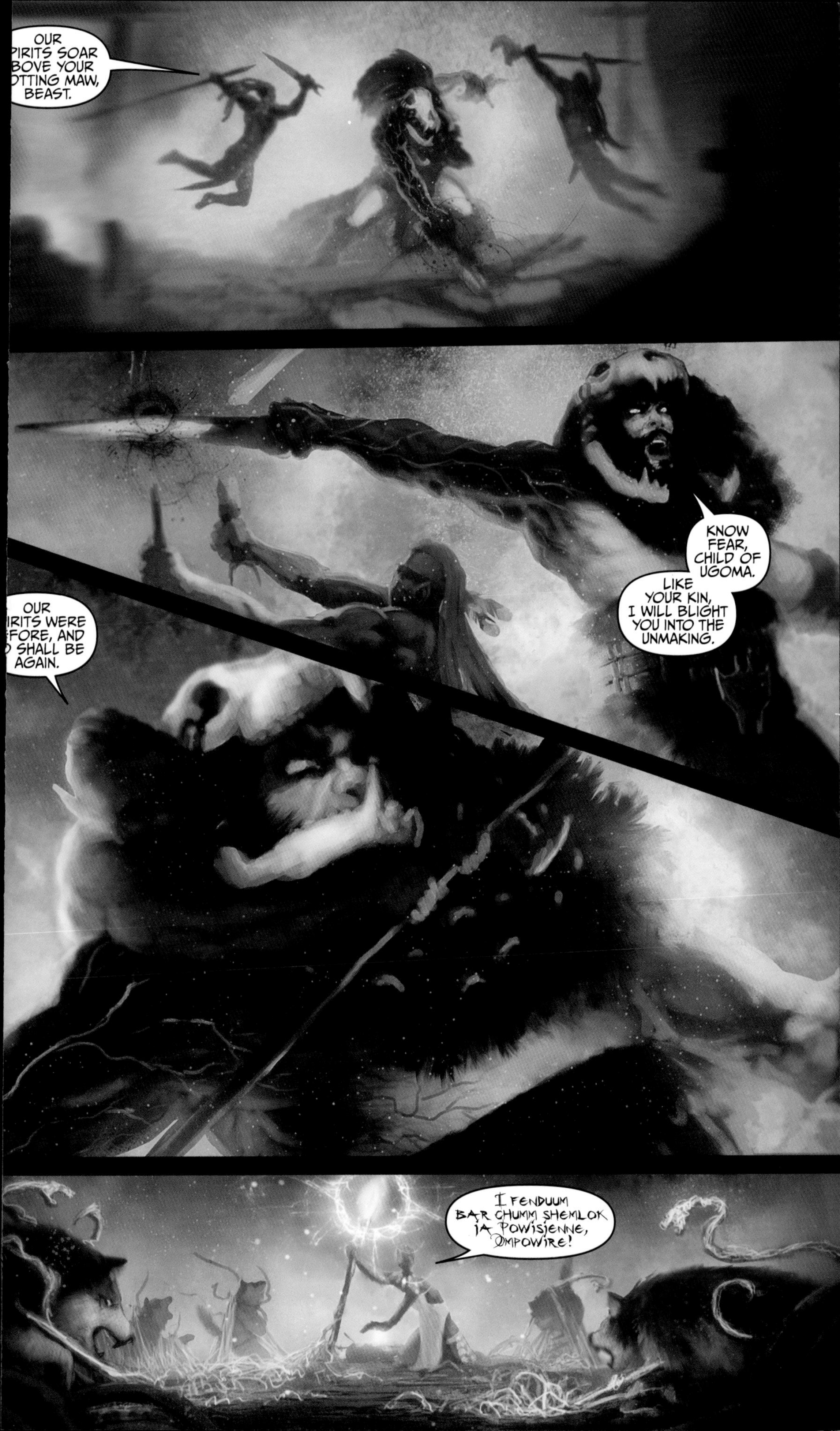
OUR PIRITS SOAR BOVE YOUR OTTING MAW, BEAST.
KNOW FEAR, CHILD OF UGOMA.
LIKE YOUR KIN, I WILL BLIGHT YOU INTO THE UNMAKING.
OUR IRITS WERE FORE, AND SHALL BE AGAIN.
I FENDUUM BAR CHUMM SHEMLOK JA POWISJENNE, OMPOWIRE!

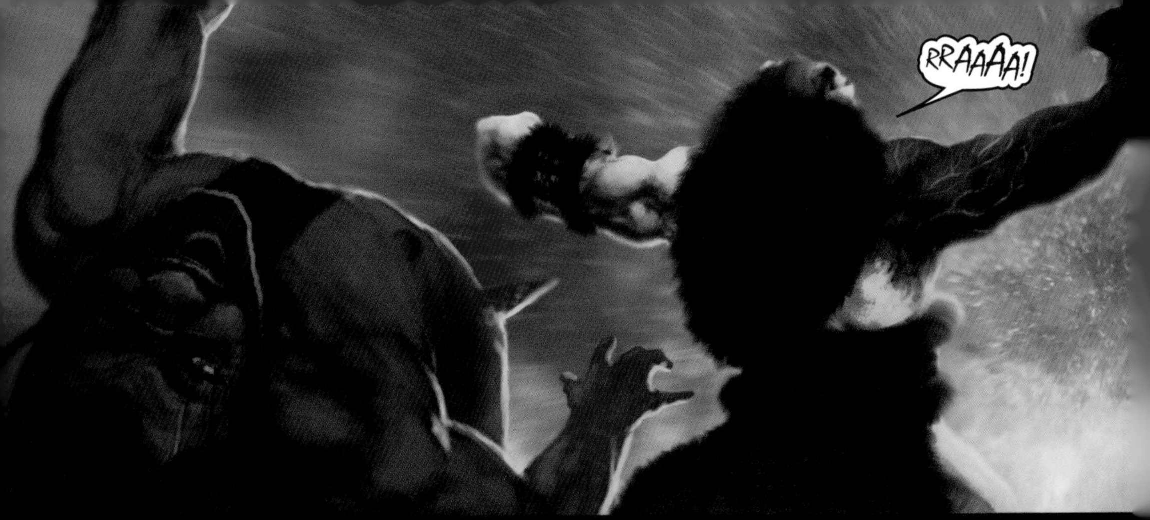
RRAAAA!

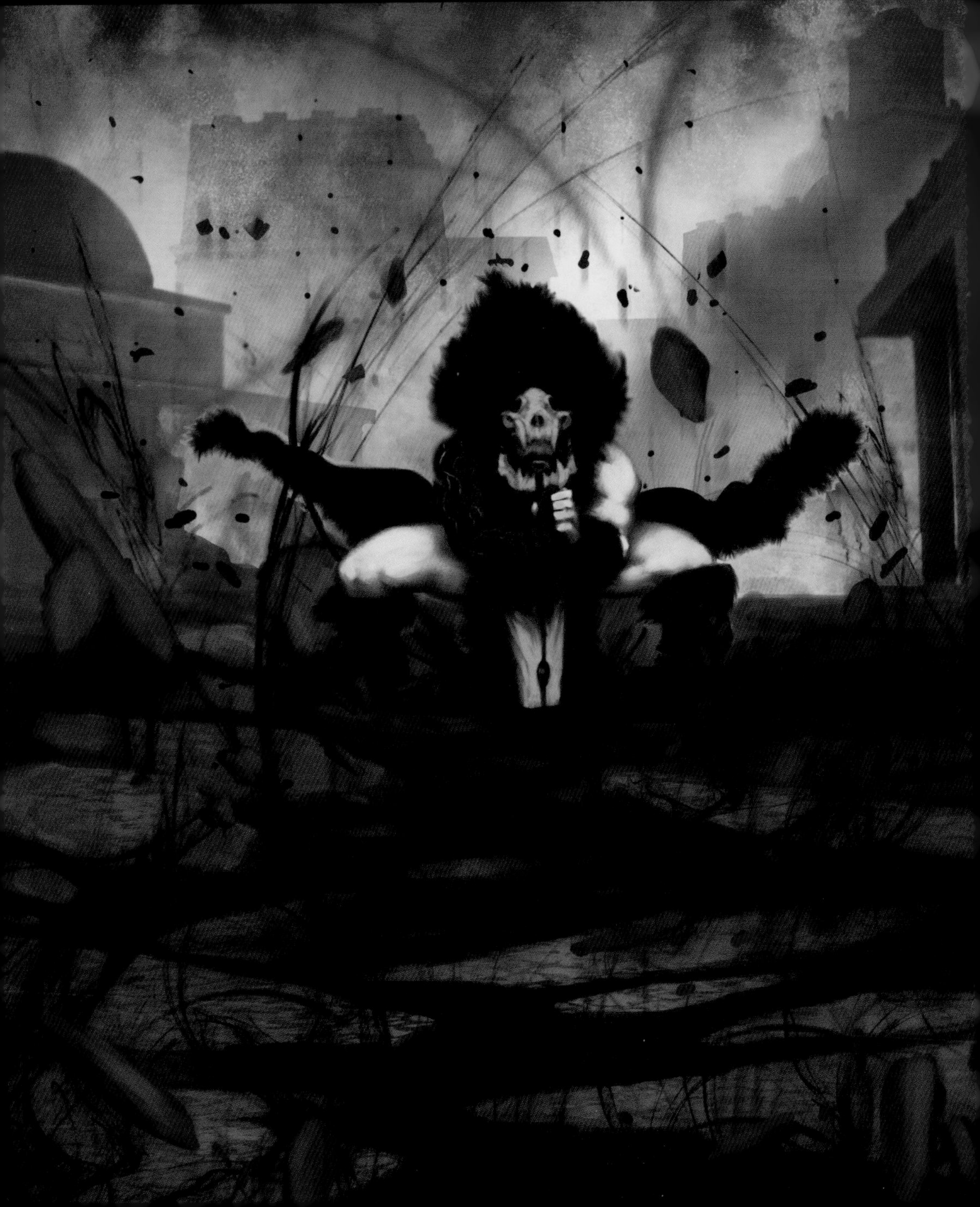

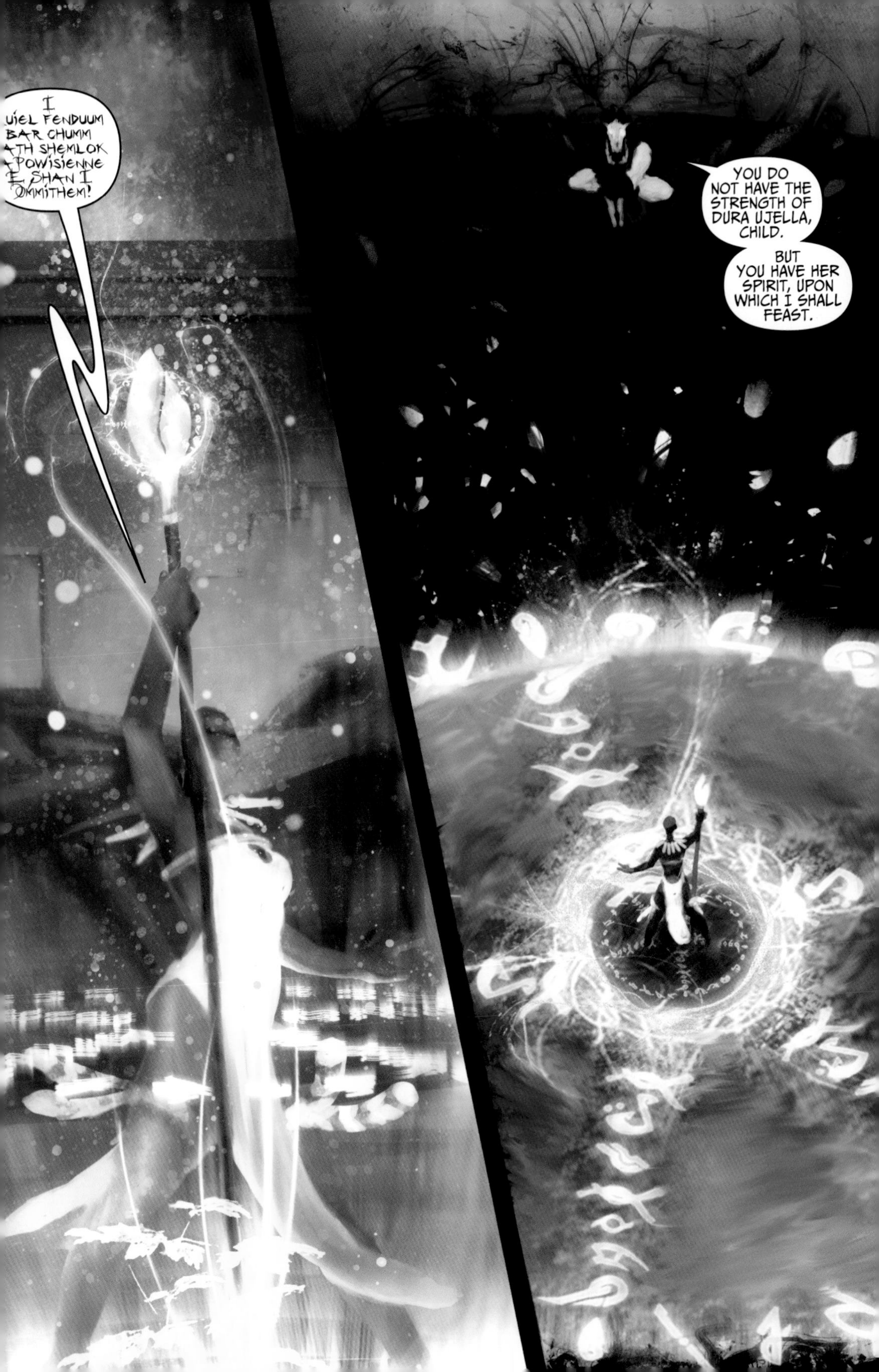
I UIEL FENDUUM BAR CHUMM ATH SHEMLOK POWISIENNE E SHAN I OMMITHEM!
YOU DO NOT HAVE THE STRENGTH OF DURA UJELLA, CHILD.
BUT YOU HAVE HER SPIRIT, UPON WHICH I SHALL FEAST.

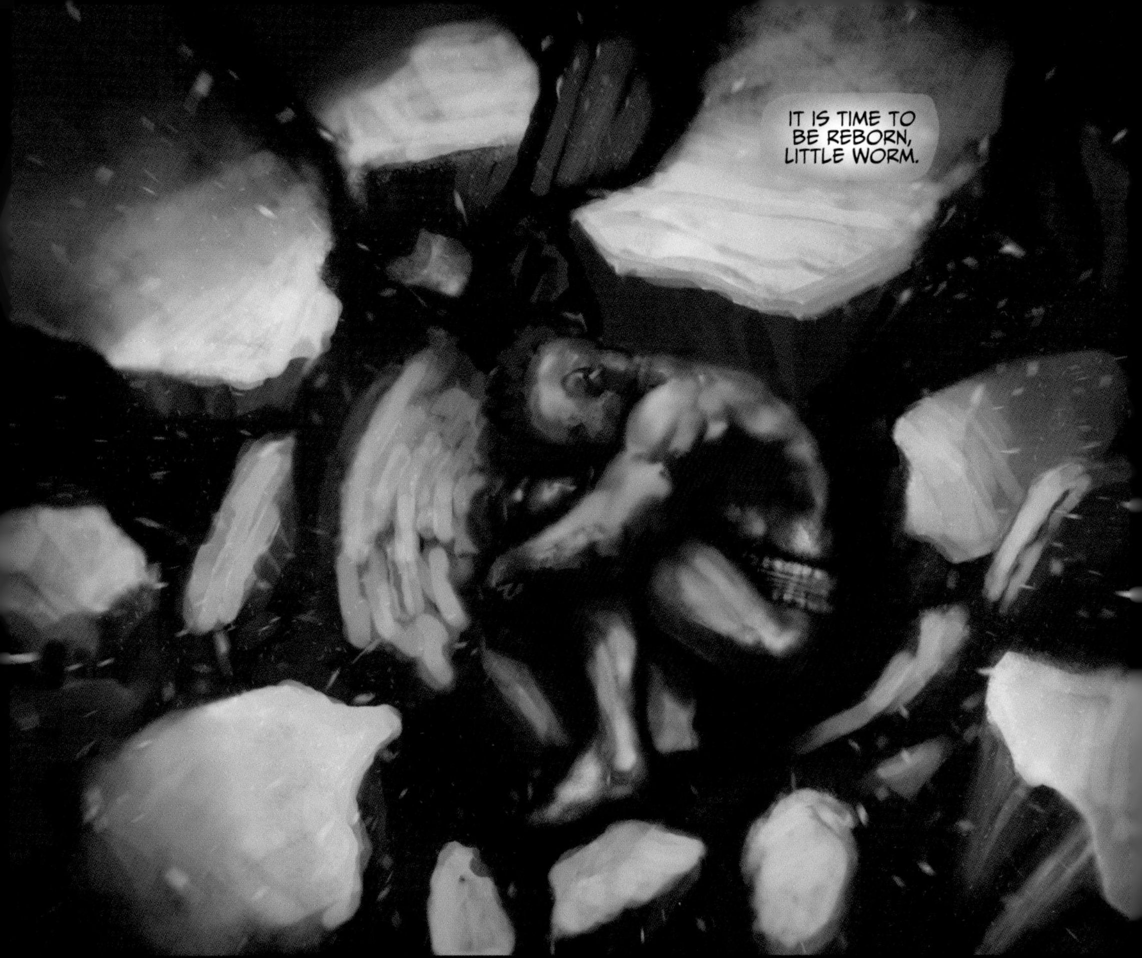
IT IS TIME TO
BE REBORN,
LITTLE WORM.

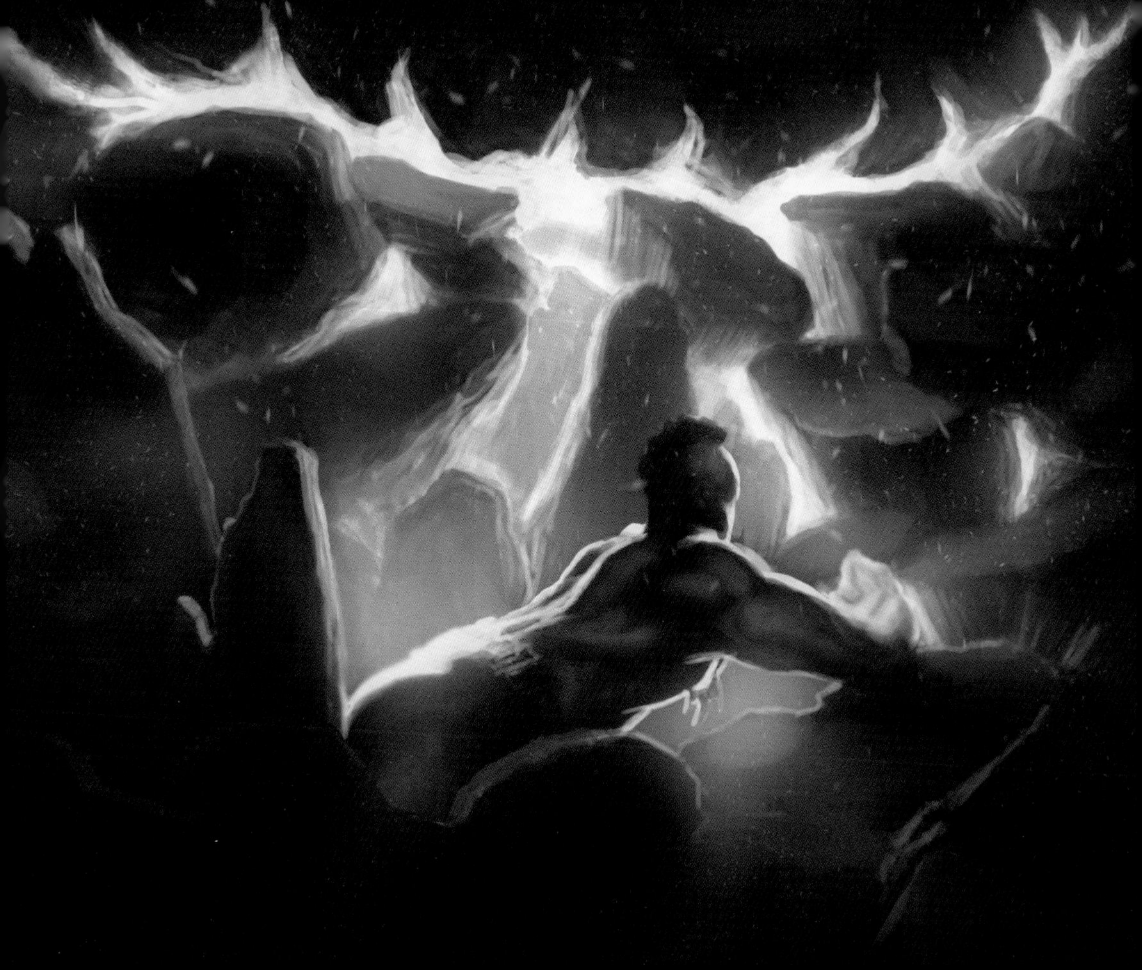

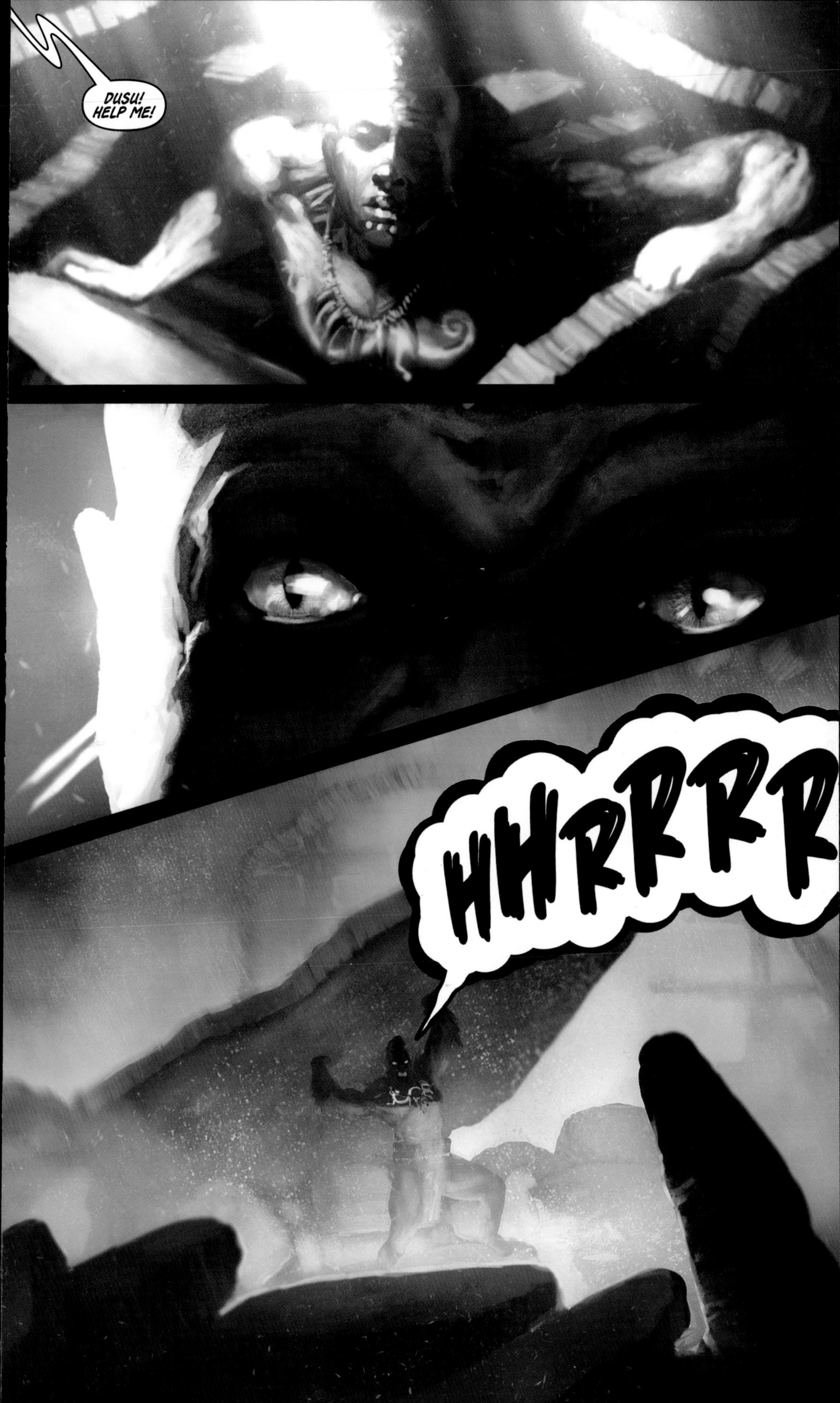
DUSU! HELP ME!
HHRRRR

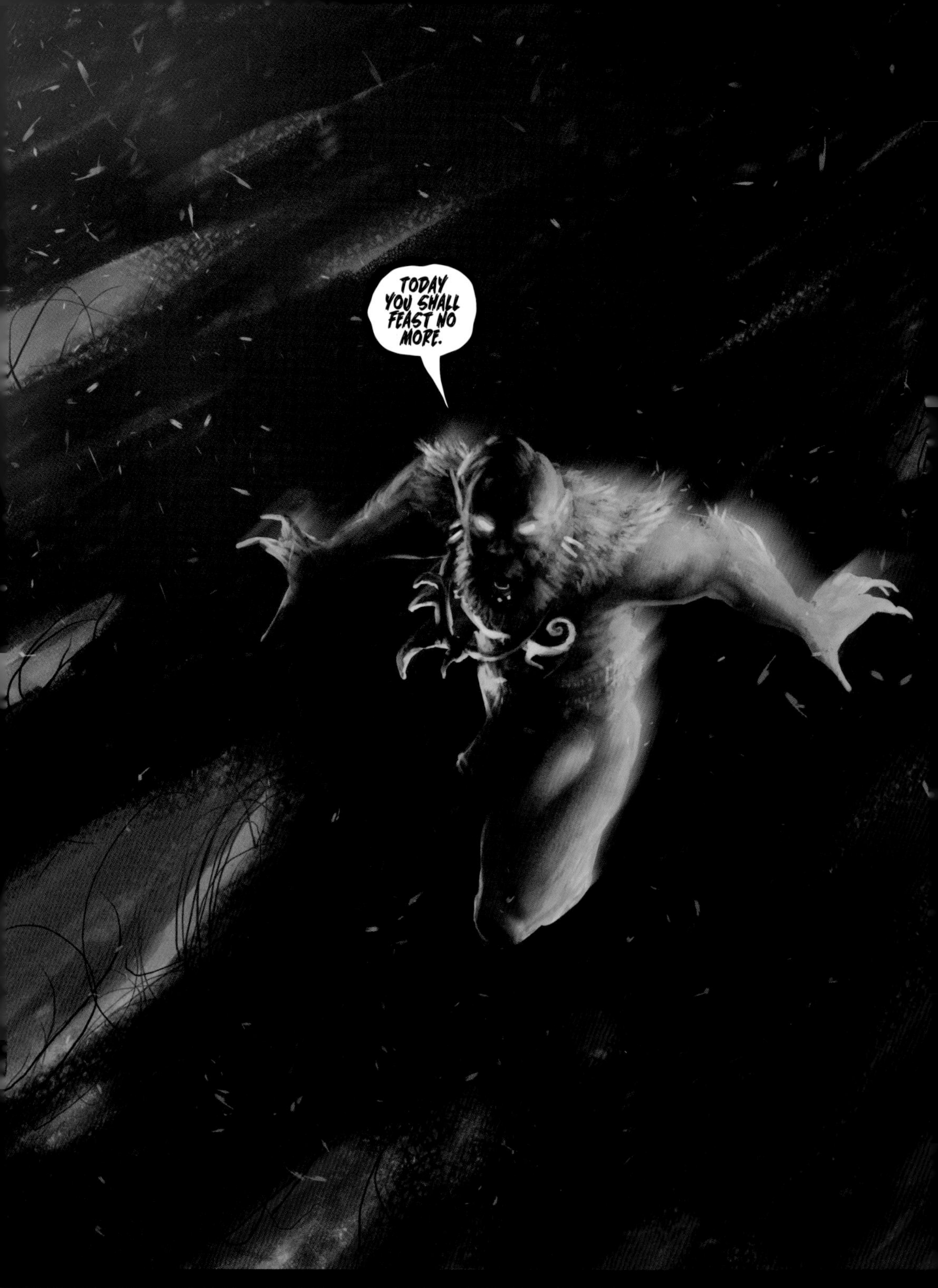
TODAY YOU SHALL FEAST NO MORE.

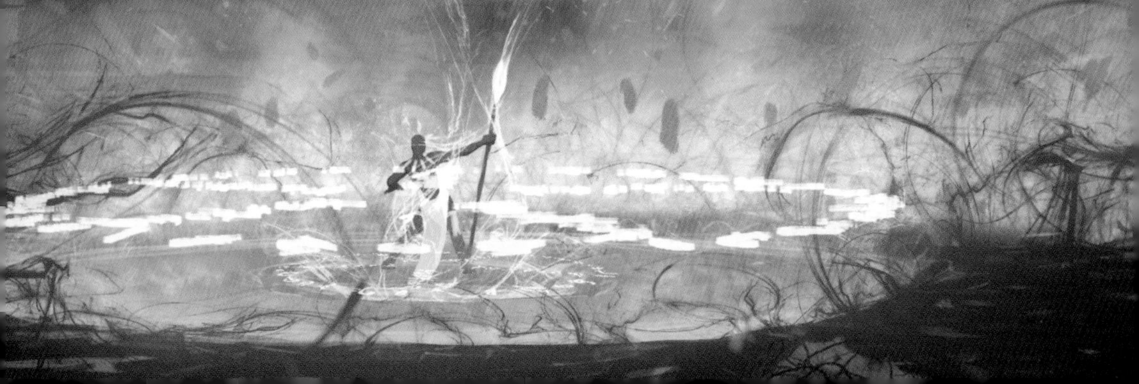

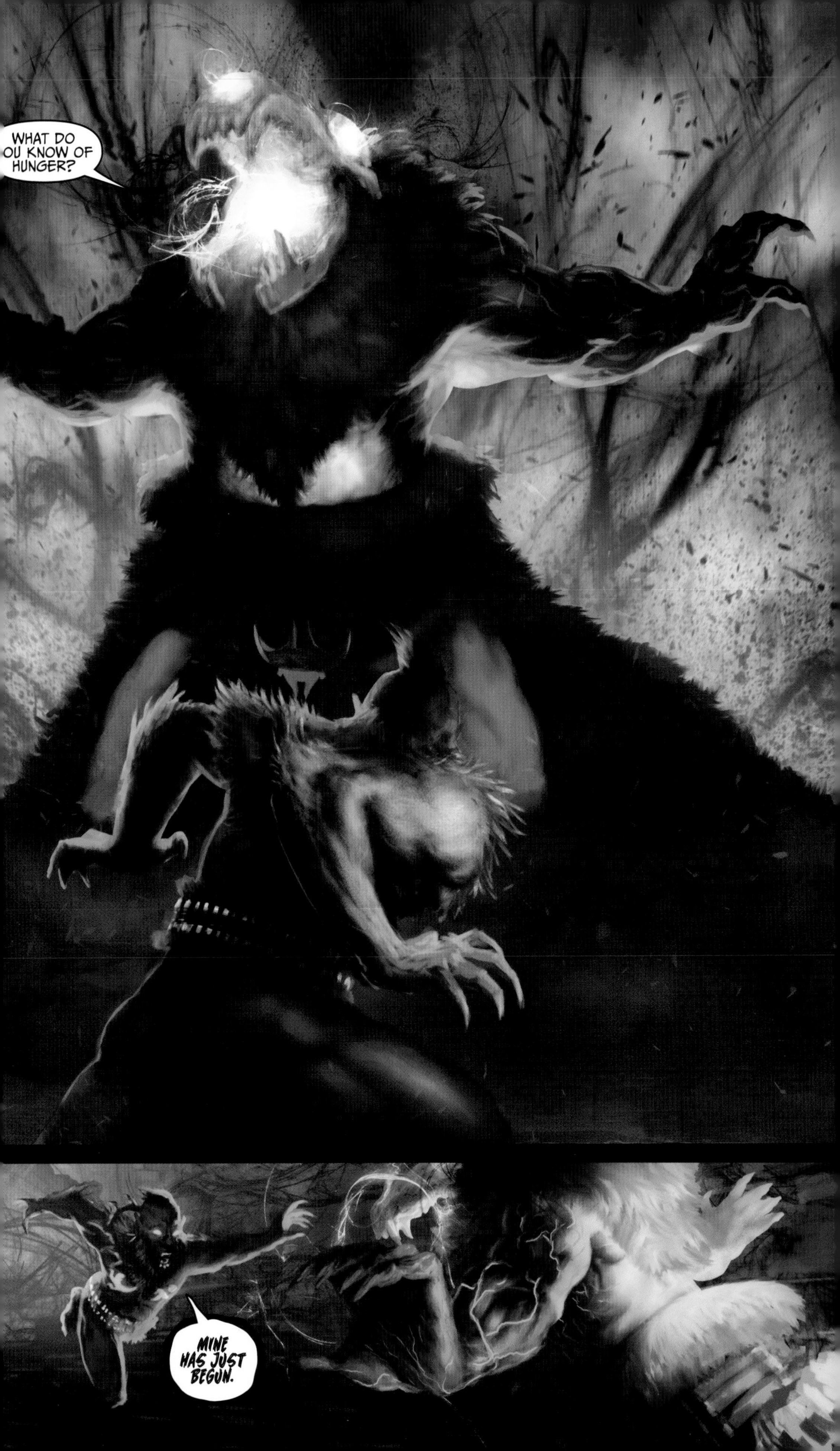
WHAT DO OU KNOW OF HUNGER?
MINE HAS JUST BEGUN.

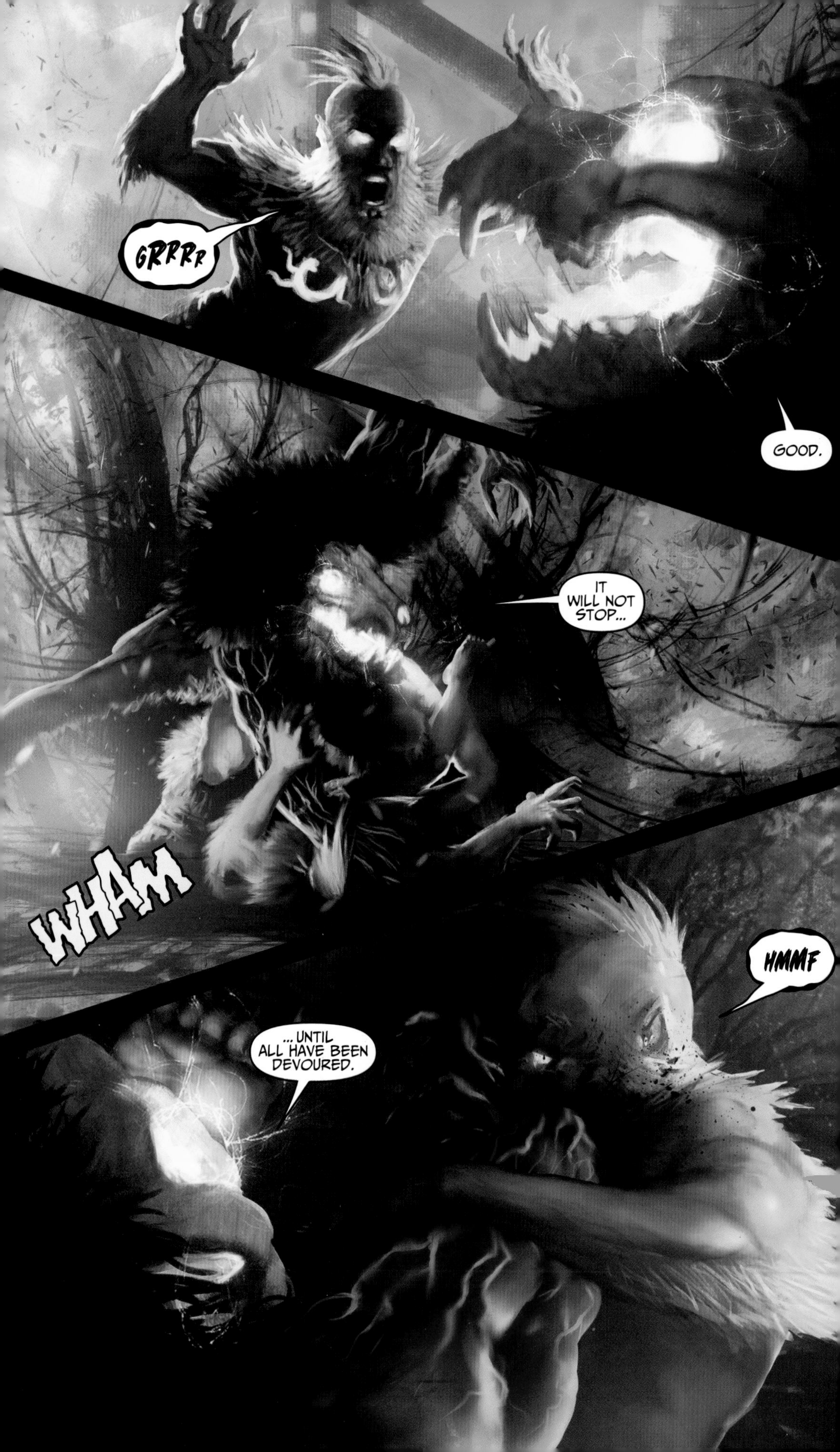
GRRRR
GOOD.
IT WILL NOT STOP...
WHAM
HMMF
...UNTIL ALL HAVE BEEN DEVOURED.

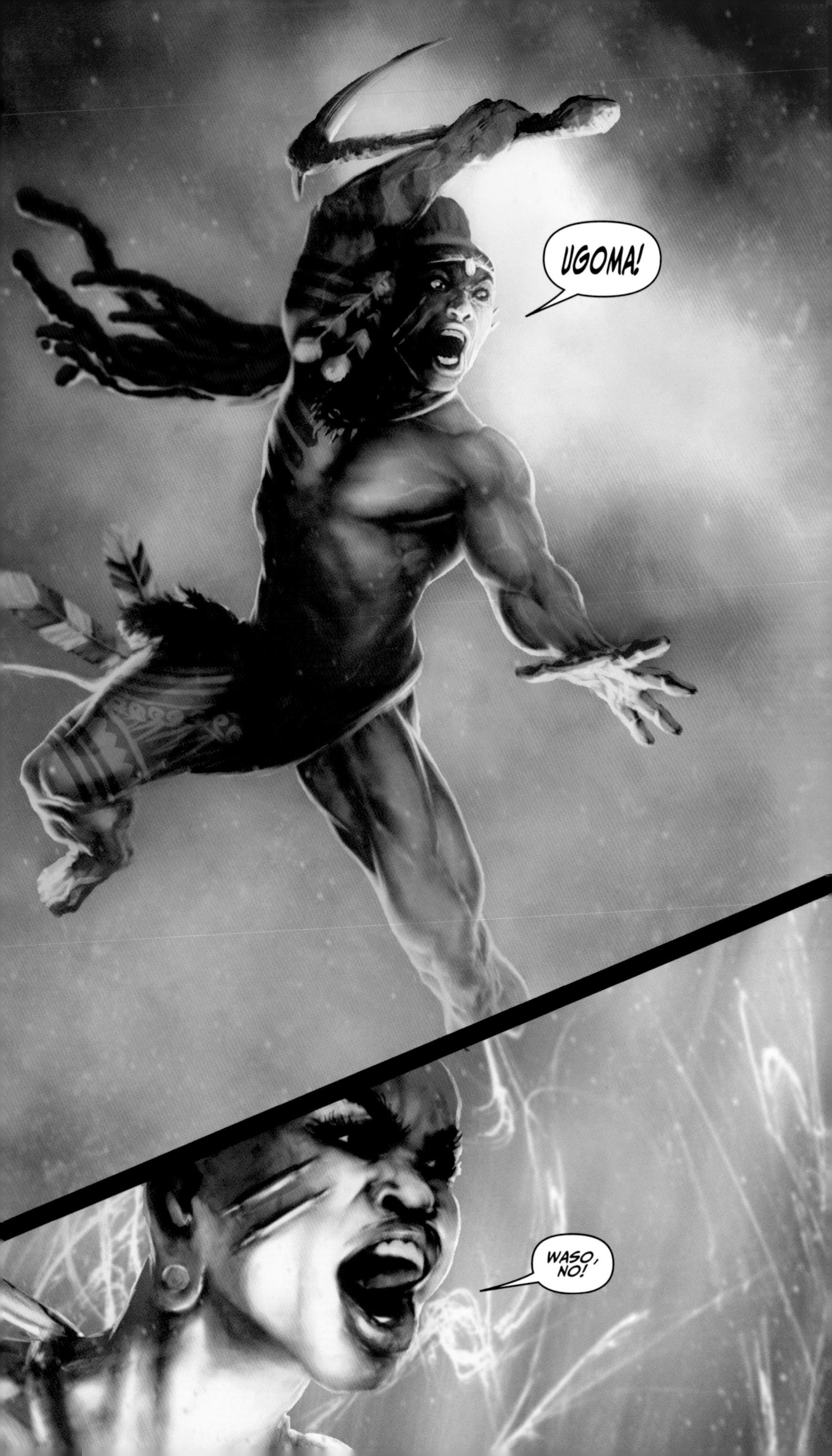
UGOMA!
WASO, NO!

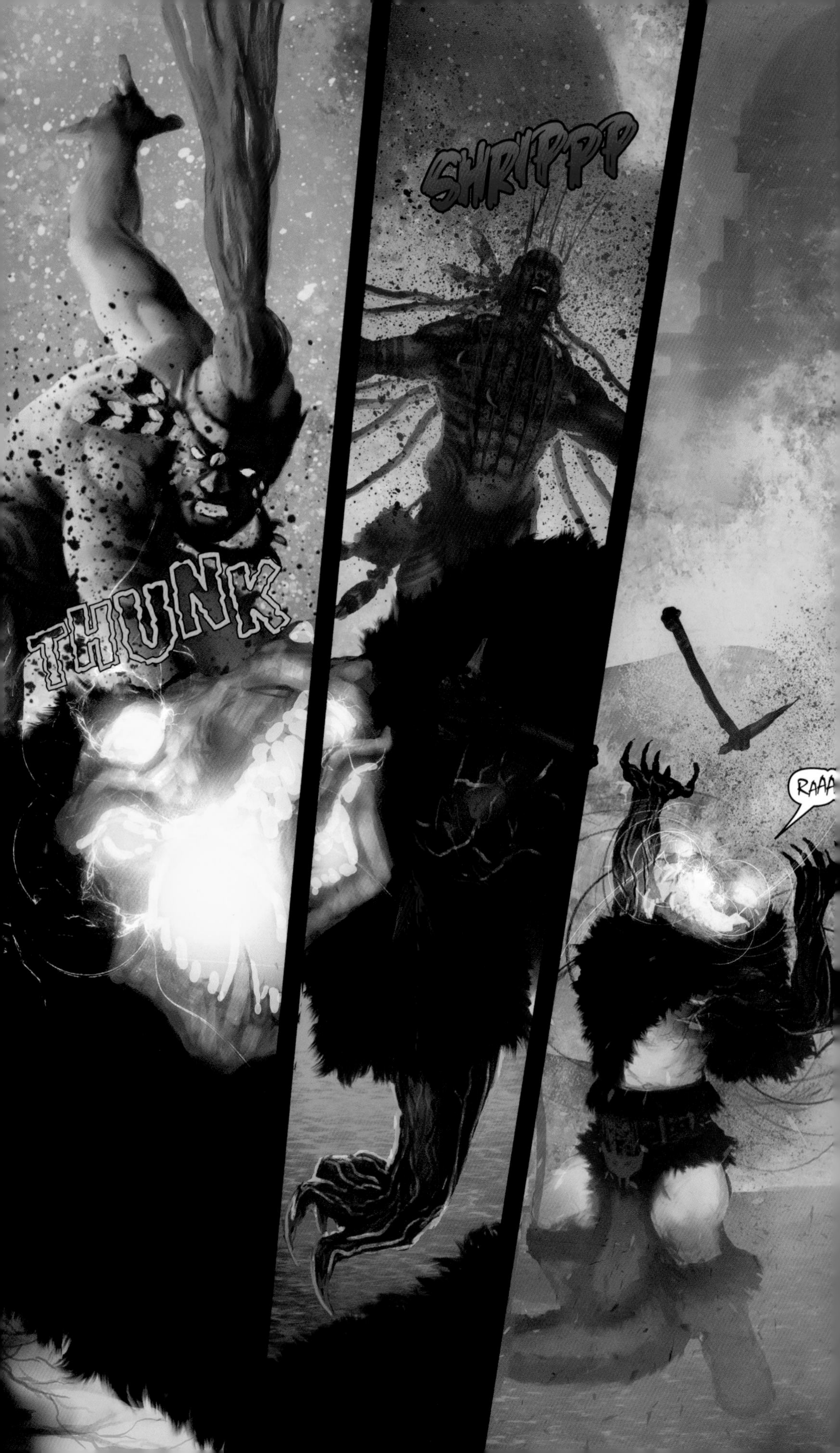
THUNK
SHRIPPP
RAAA

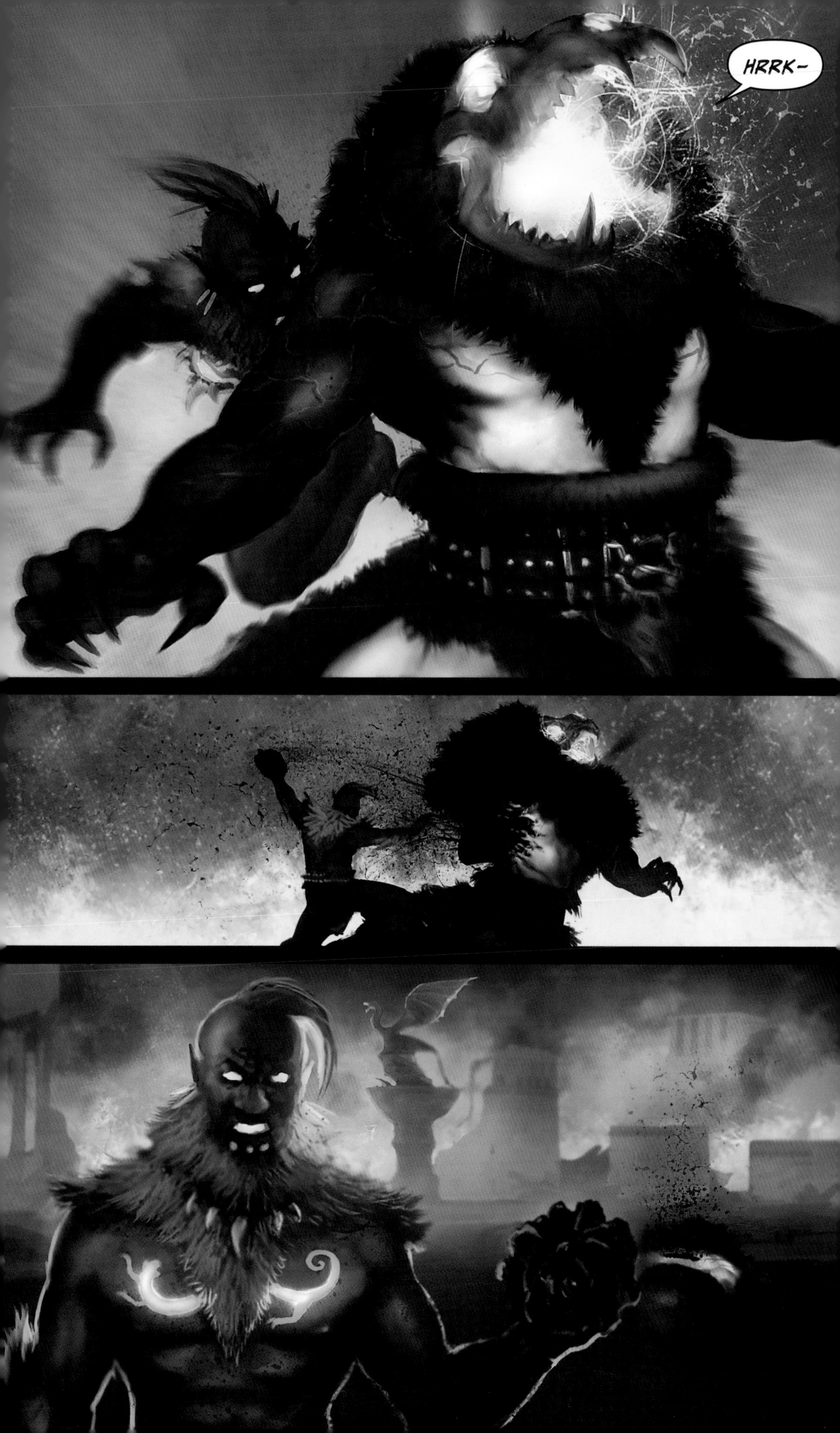
HRRK-

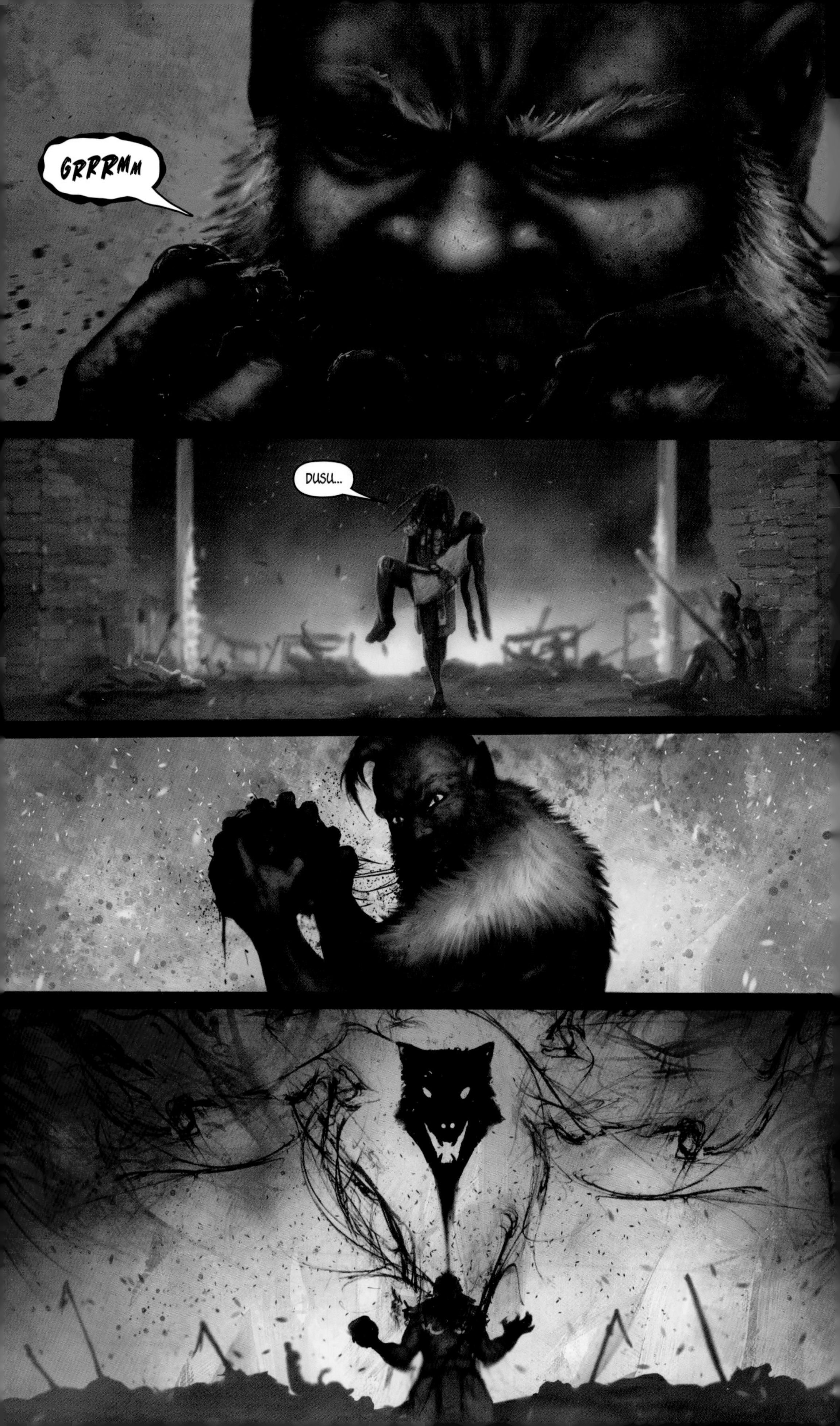
GRRRMM
DUSU...

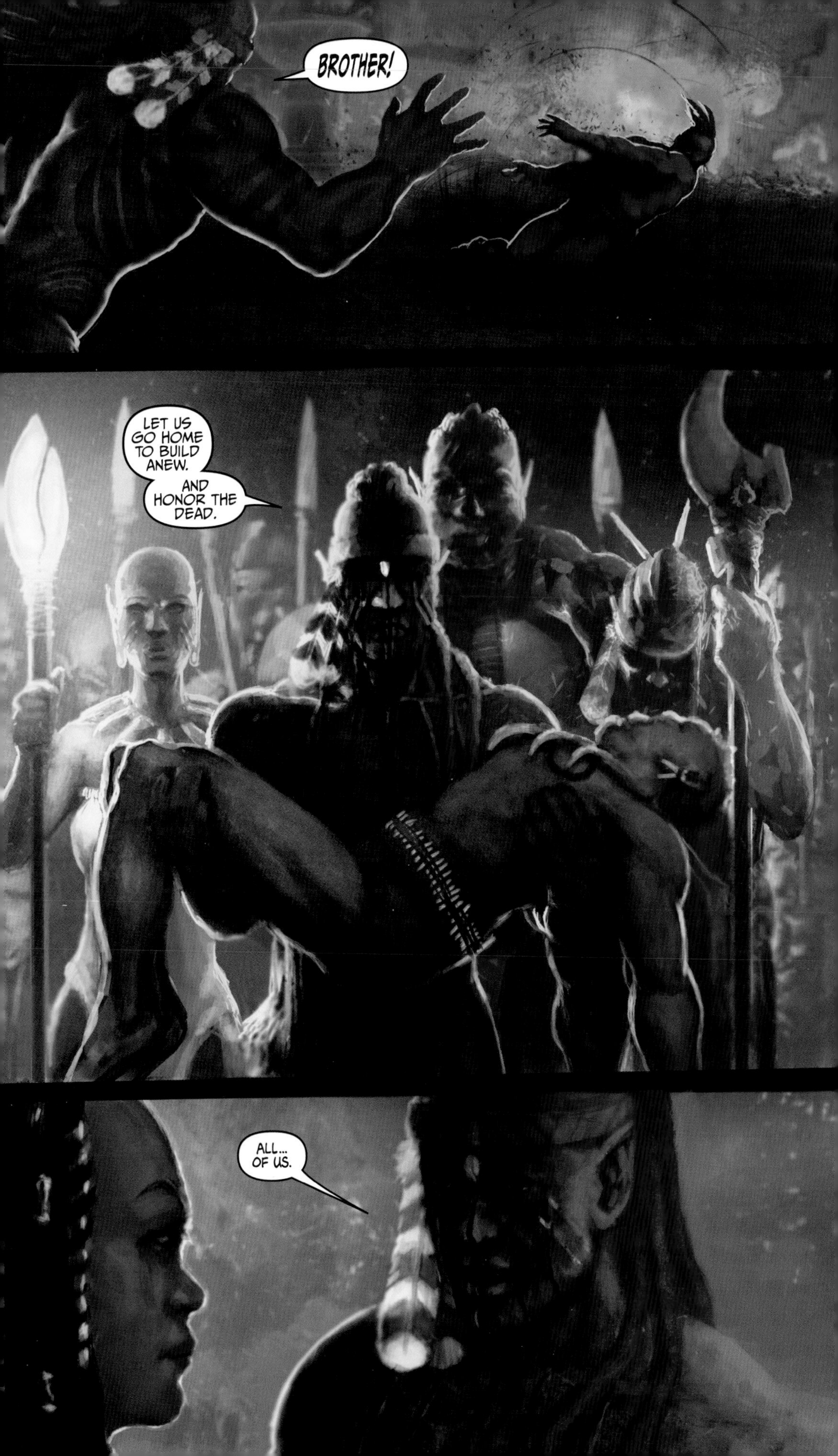
BROTHER!
LET US GO HOME TO BUILD ANEW.
AND HONOR THE DEAD.
ALL... OF US.

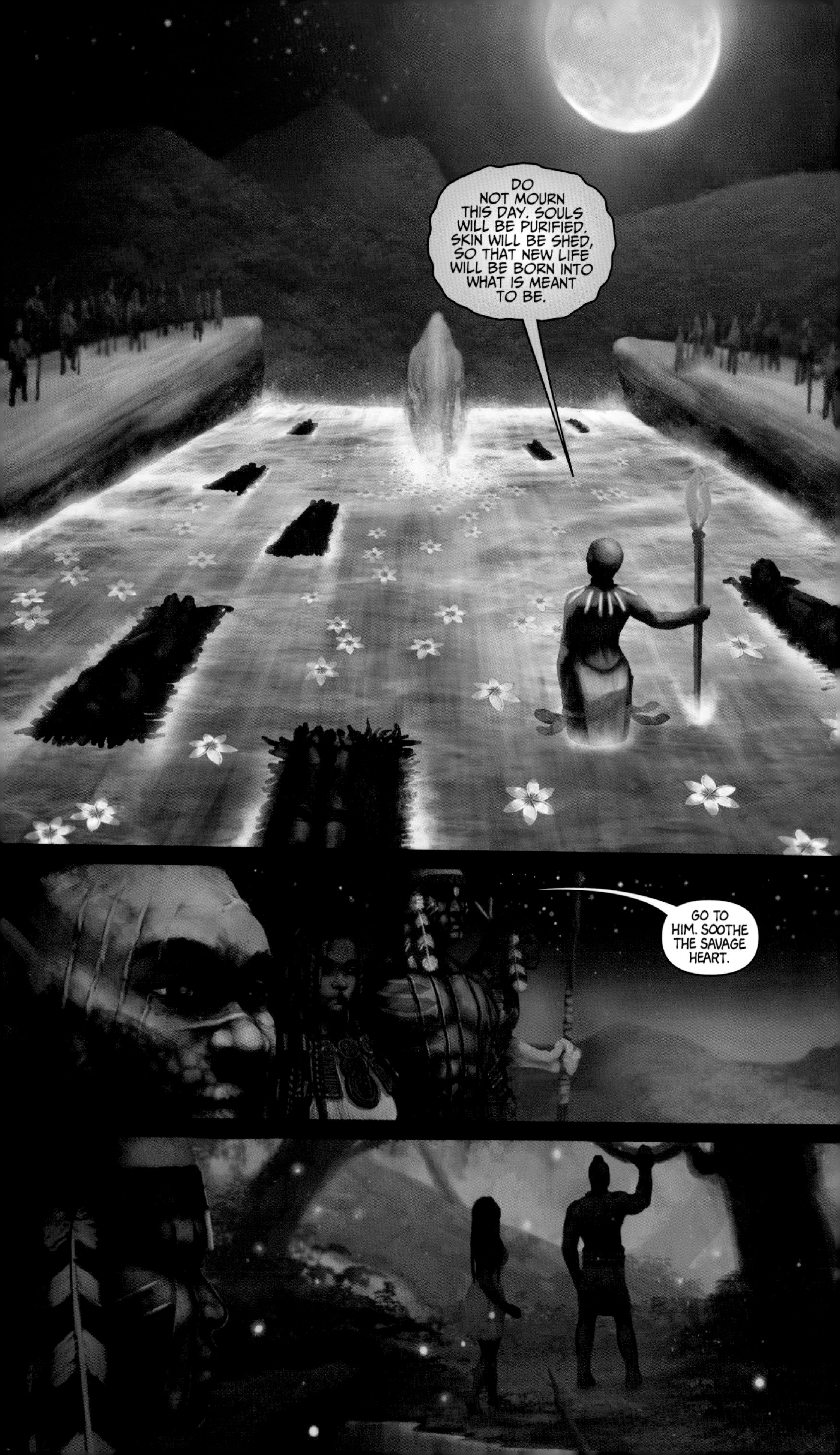
DO NOT MOURN THIS DAY. SOULS WILL BE PURIFIED. SKIN WILL BE SHED, SO THAT NEW LIFE WILL BE BORN INTO WHAT IS MEANT TO BE.
GO TO HIM. SOOTHE THE SAVAGE HEART.

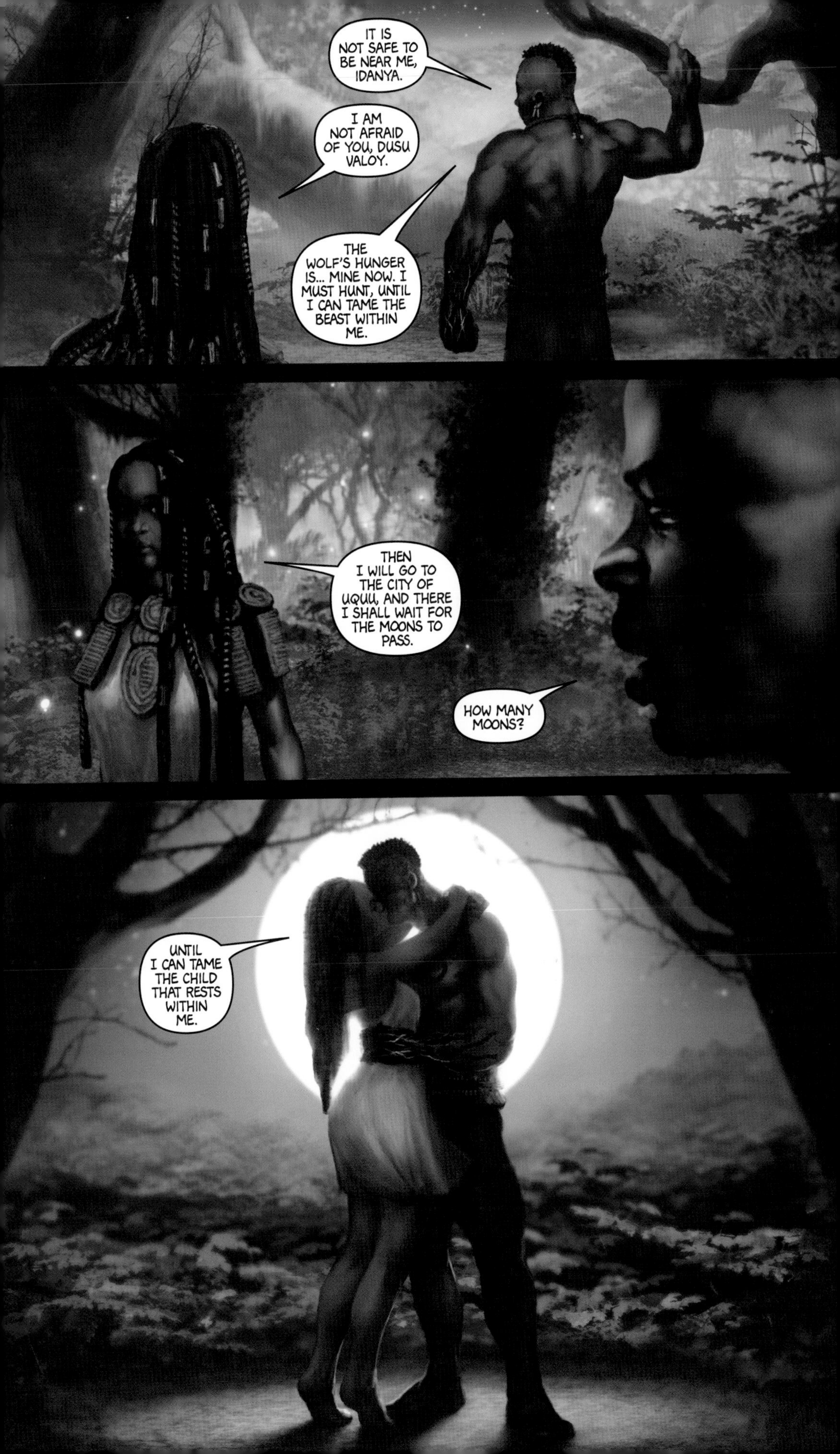
IT IS NOT SAFE TO BE NEAR ME, IDANYA.
I AM NOT AFRAID OF YOU, DUSU VALOY.
THE WOLF'S HUNGER IS... MINE NOW. I MUST HUNT, UNTIL I CAN TAME THE BEAST WITHIN ME.
THEN I WILL GO TO THE CITY OF UQUU, AND THERE I SHALL WAIT FOR THE MOONS TO PASS.
HOW MANY MOONS?
UNTIL I CAN TAME THE CHILD THAT RESTS WITHIN ME.

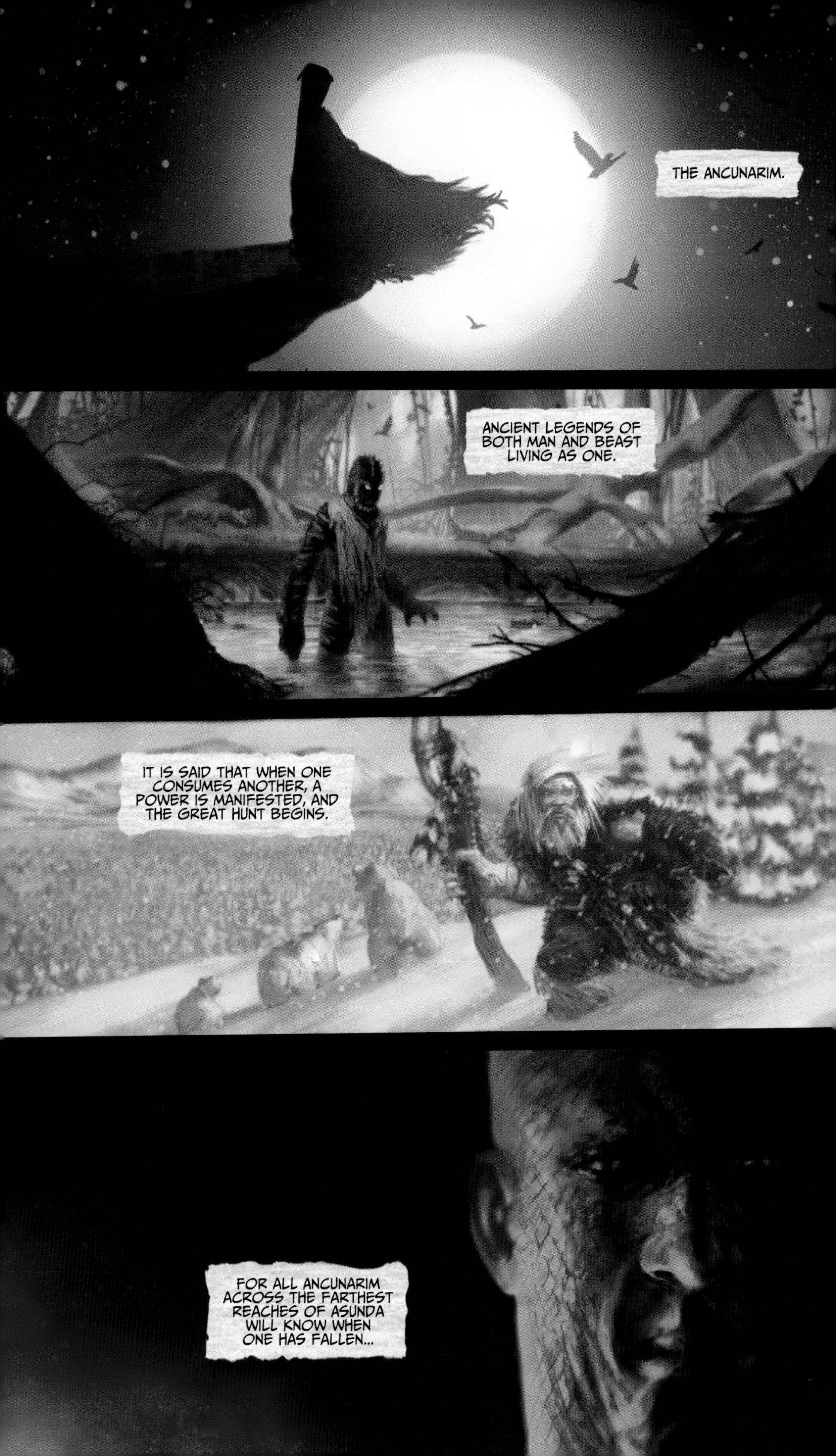
THE ANCUNARIM.
ANCIENT LEGENDS OF BOTH MAN AND BEAST LIVING AS ONE.
IT IS SAID THAT WHEN ONE CONSUMES ANOTHER, A POWER IS MANIFESTED, AND THE GREAT HUNT BEGINS.
FOR ALL ANCUNARIM ACROSS THE FARTHEST REACHES OF ASUNDA WILL KNOW WHEN ONE HAS FALLEN...

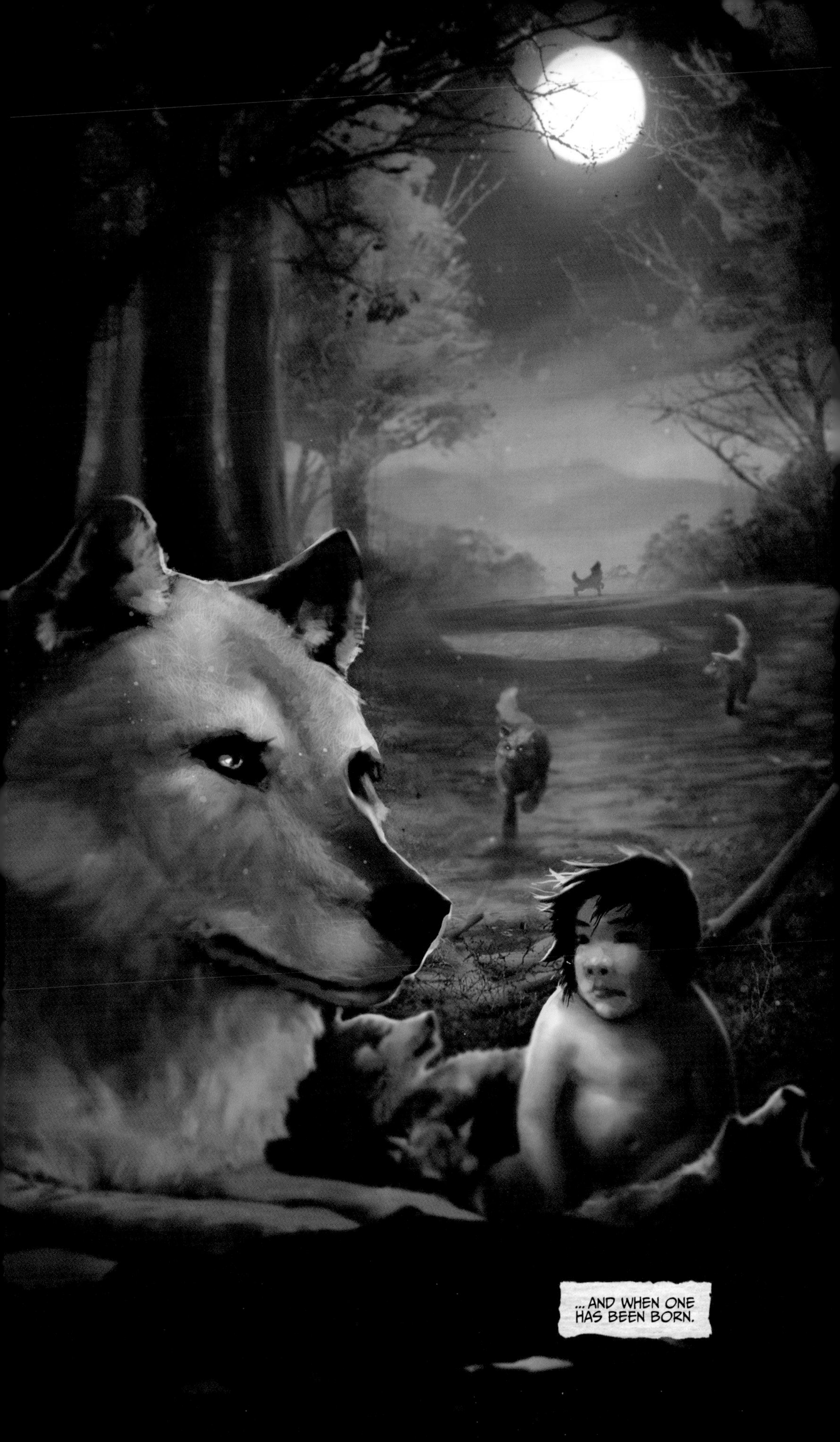
...AND WHEN ONE HAS BEEN BORN.

Hello Stranger

As the mother's arms grew cold around him, a sadness enveloped me. It was not the first time I had caused a mother's screams to ring in a child's ears upon a coal black night, but this death occurred not due to malice or greed, but to foresight. This life needed to be taken.

The cougars howled as they surrounded him, for they knew a champion had awoken. I watched the boy child squirm in the muck and considered whether to pluck his tiny heart for my own ravenous greed, thus stealing from fate and defying the Ancient pact Kilandrum and I had bound upon our kind in an epoch past.

The moon was now full, glittering silver and beautiful, the night akin to a still black sea. My power was full, and I was aroused with the knowing that only she, my mistress, my lover queen Magga, would witness. It was as if she was teasing me, tempting with a greater power than loyalty to my own Ancient kind. I am Ancunarim! I am predator and prey; although none would dare name me the latter, and here was a worm to satisfy the urges of the former. Too easy. Or perhaps I did not want even Magga the Moon Dragon knowing, a card she would play later when the game unfolds. But the choice would not be mine to make, for before I could swoop down from the limber branch upon which I was perched, Powisienne settled my debate.

Omdar Shem Powirre, the chief of the Gathering Wind Tribe, had come with spear of stone. It had been many years since a human had set foot in these sacred glades and lived, not since a Galemren queen had danced for a human king and he bade me steal her away against her will. I fulfilled his wish not to be of service but because it led to the birth of a savior. Now another child of prophecy sat before the man I had wronged. I wondered, would Omdar kill this boy or would he show mercy?

We both watched the cougar lick the boy as a mother does her cubs, cleaning him as his own mother no longer could. We both knew this to be a sign from Powisienne, and so the Galemren chief took the boy to raise as his own, and I took to the skies…

Only when I heard the cry of a wolf would I return.

~ Salem Ravensong

Ancients, or Ancunarim in the old tongue, are totem beings of great power, blessed by Powisienne, the Shepherd God and World Sculptor. There is one Ancunarim for each species, and although it is understood they are not to kill one another, some cannot resist the primal urge to seek and slay as a snake would a rat. And so the hunt is on, where none are safe, as predator becomes prey across the vast and volatile world of...

Gallery

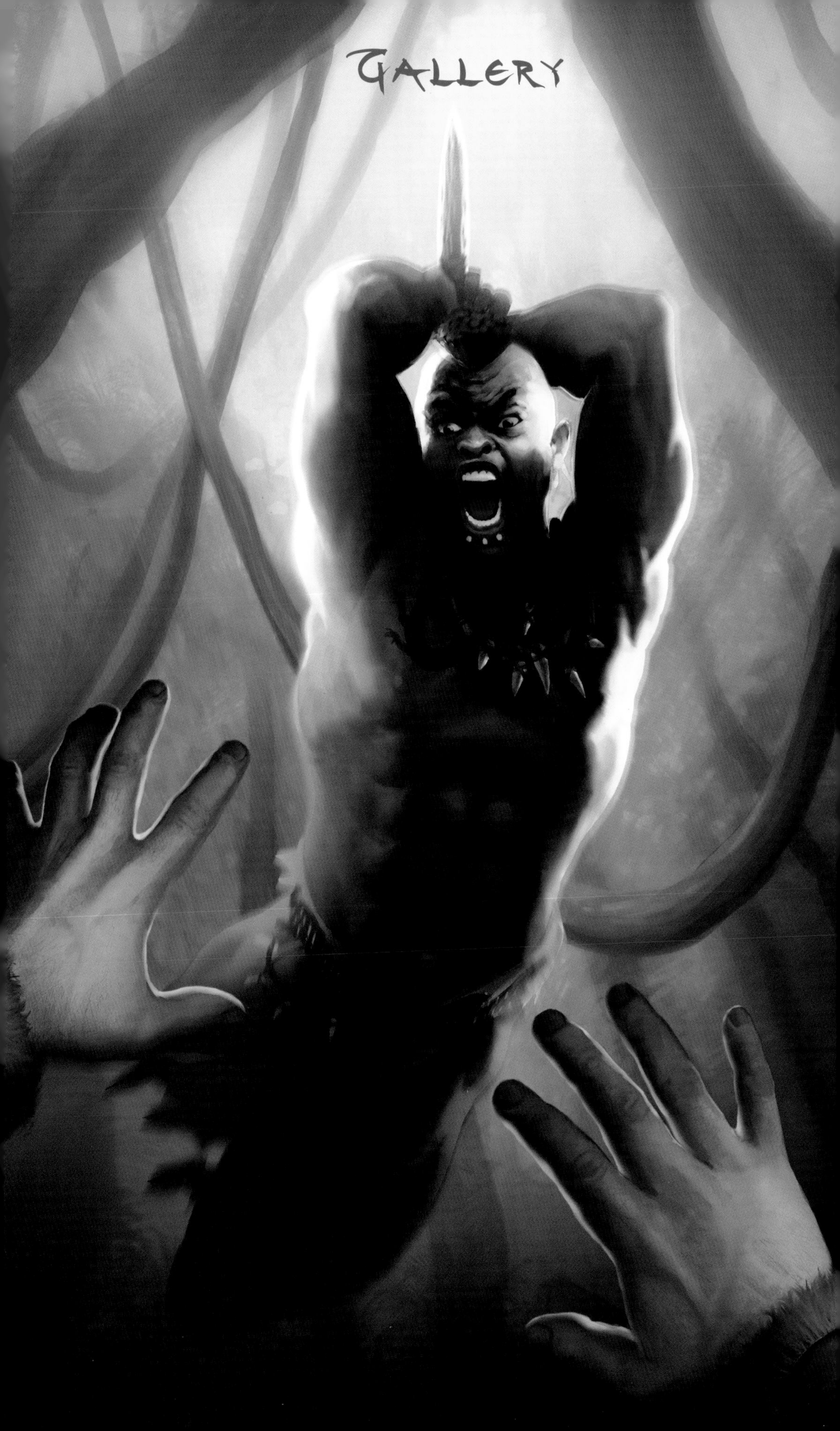

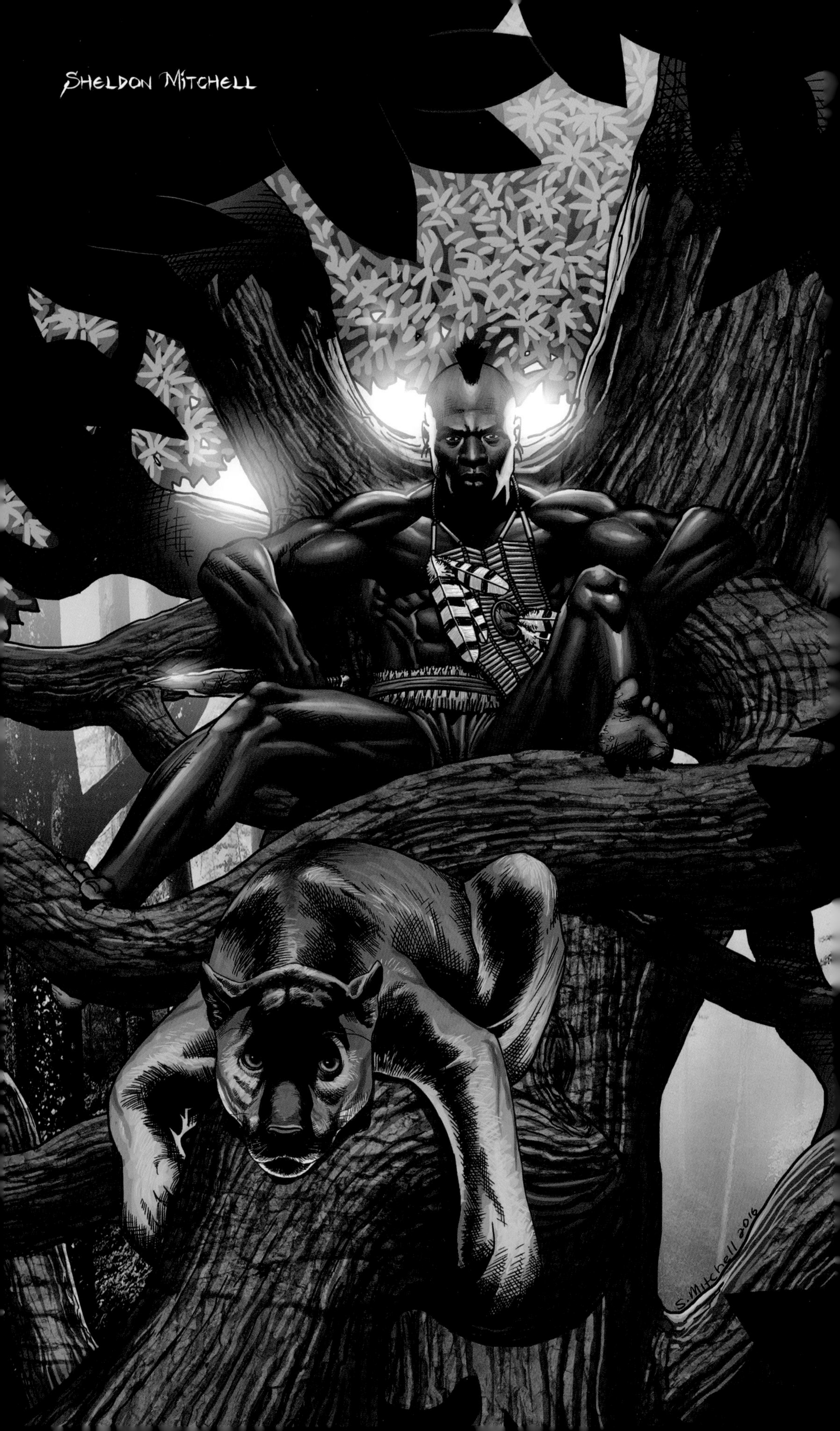
SHELDON MITCHELL
S.Mitchell 2016

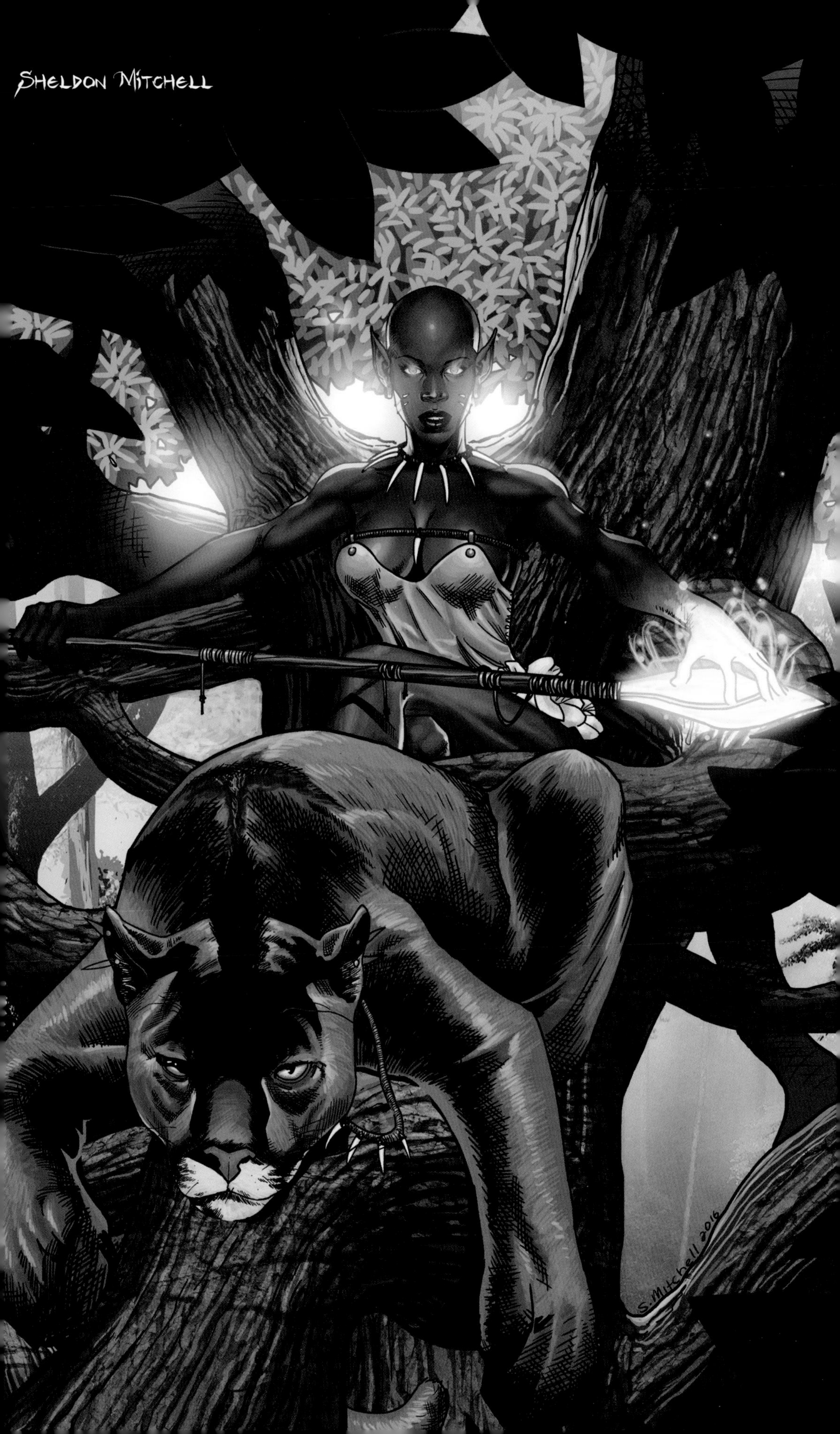
SHELDON MITCHELL
S. Mitchell 2016

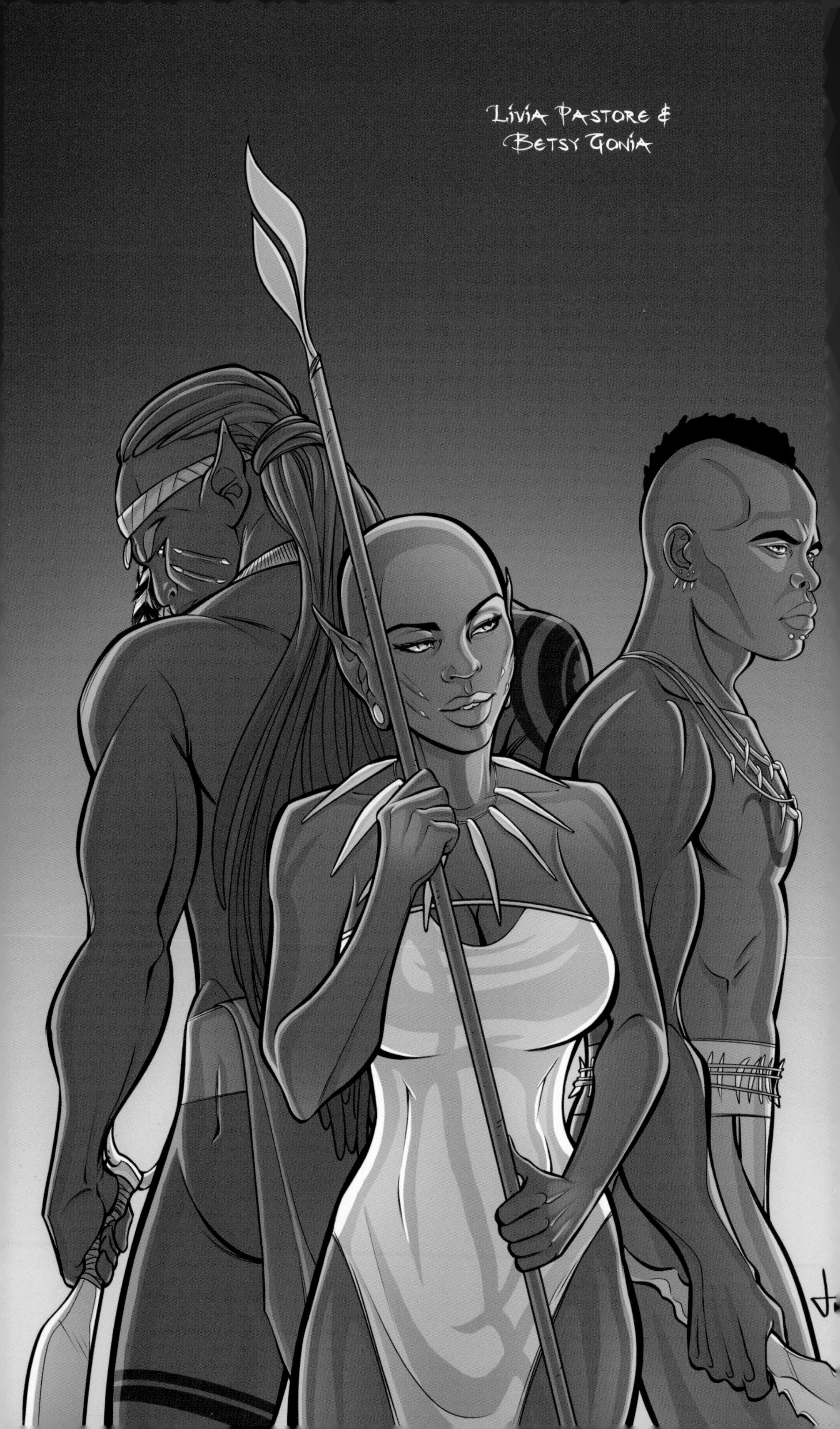
Livia Pastore &
Betsy Gonia

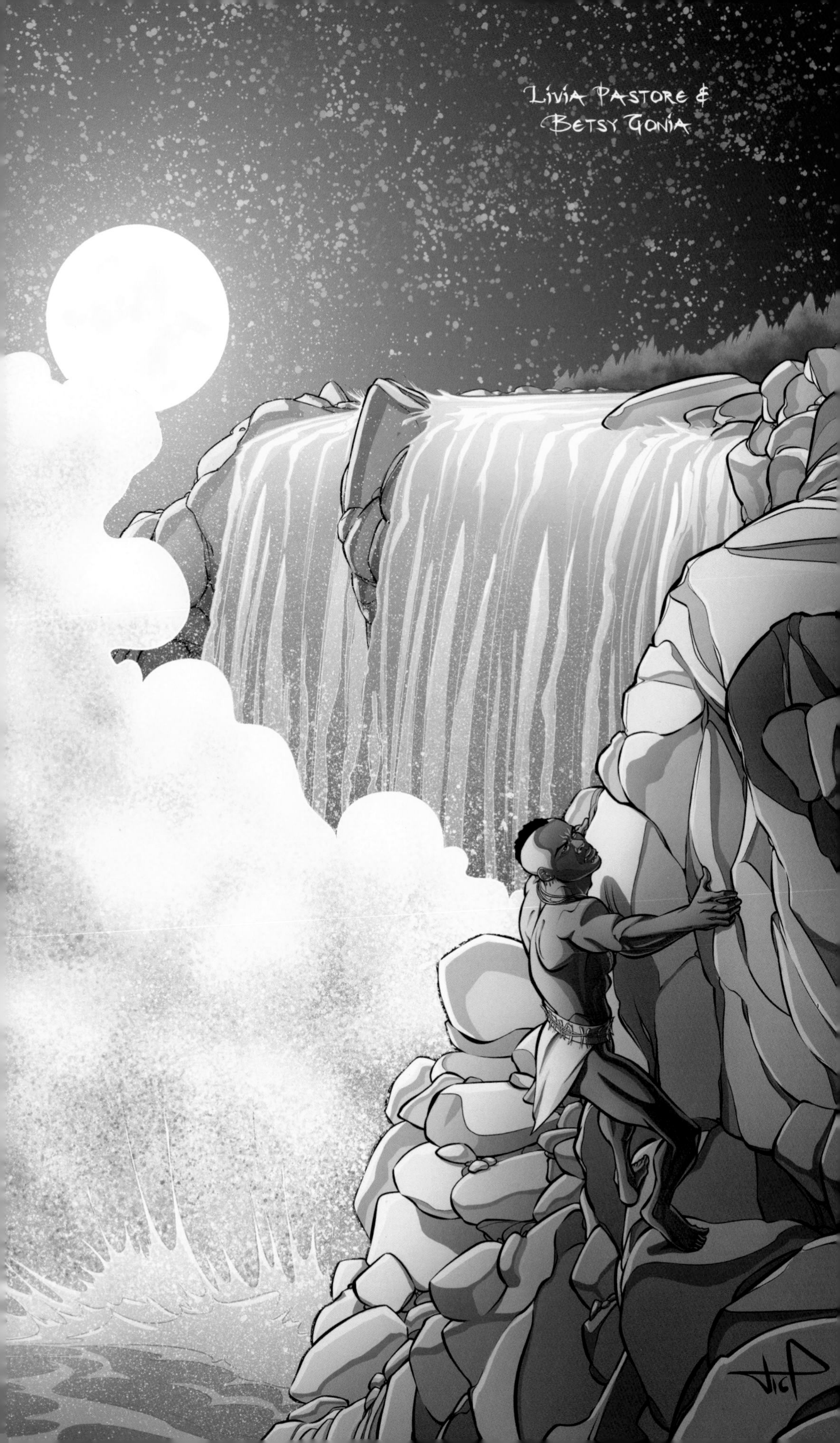

Livia Pastore &
Betsy Gonia

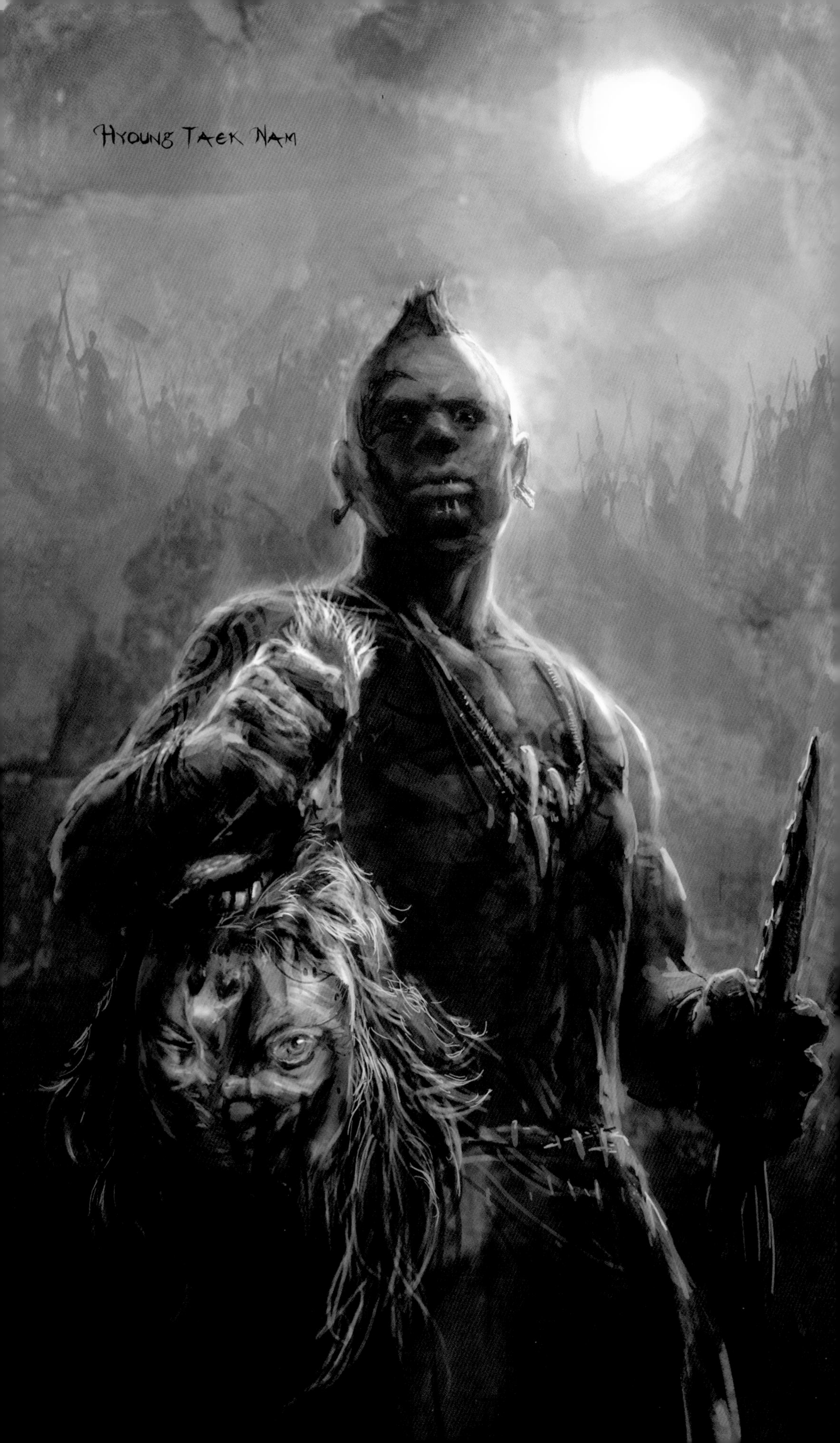
Hyoung Taek Nam

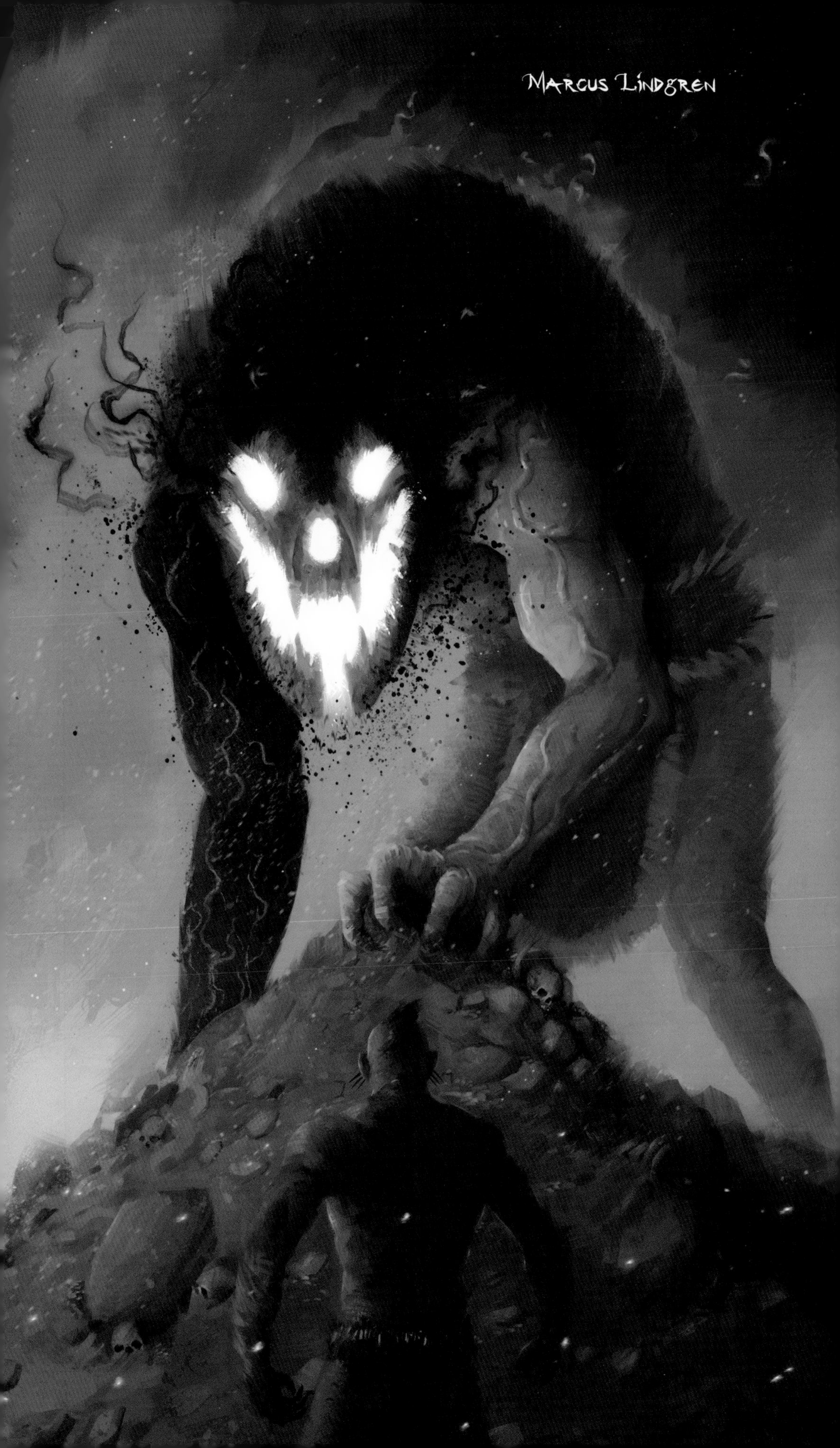
Marcus Lindgren

JOHN JENNINGS

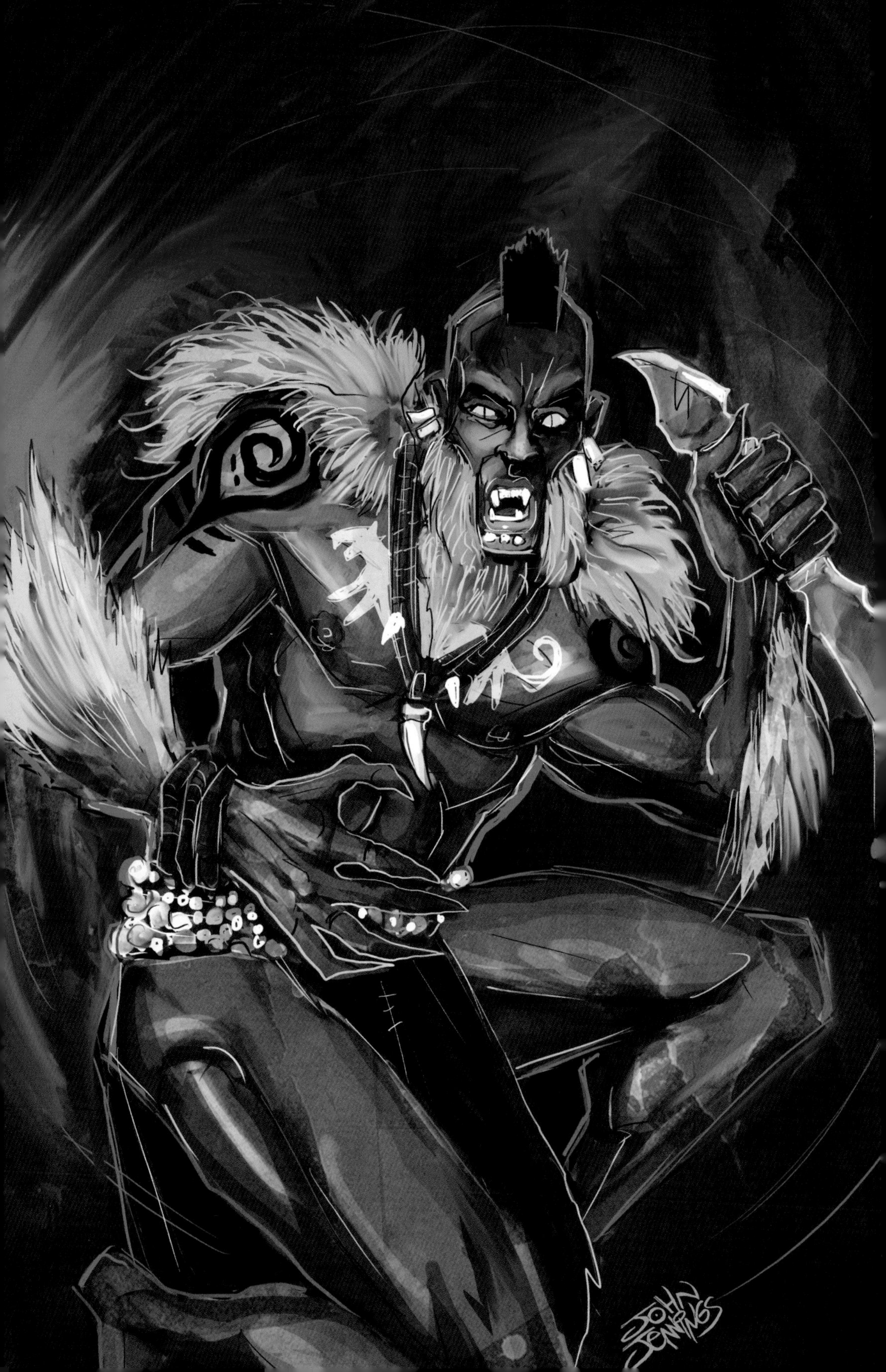
JOHN JENNINGS

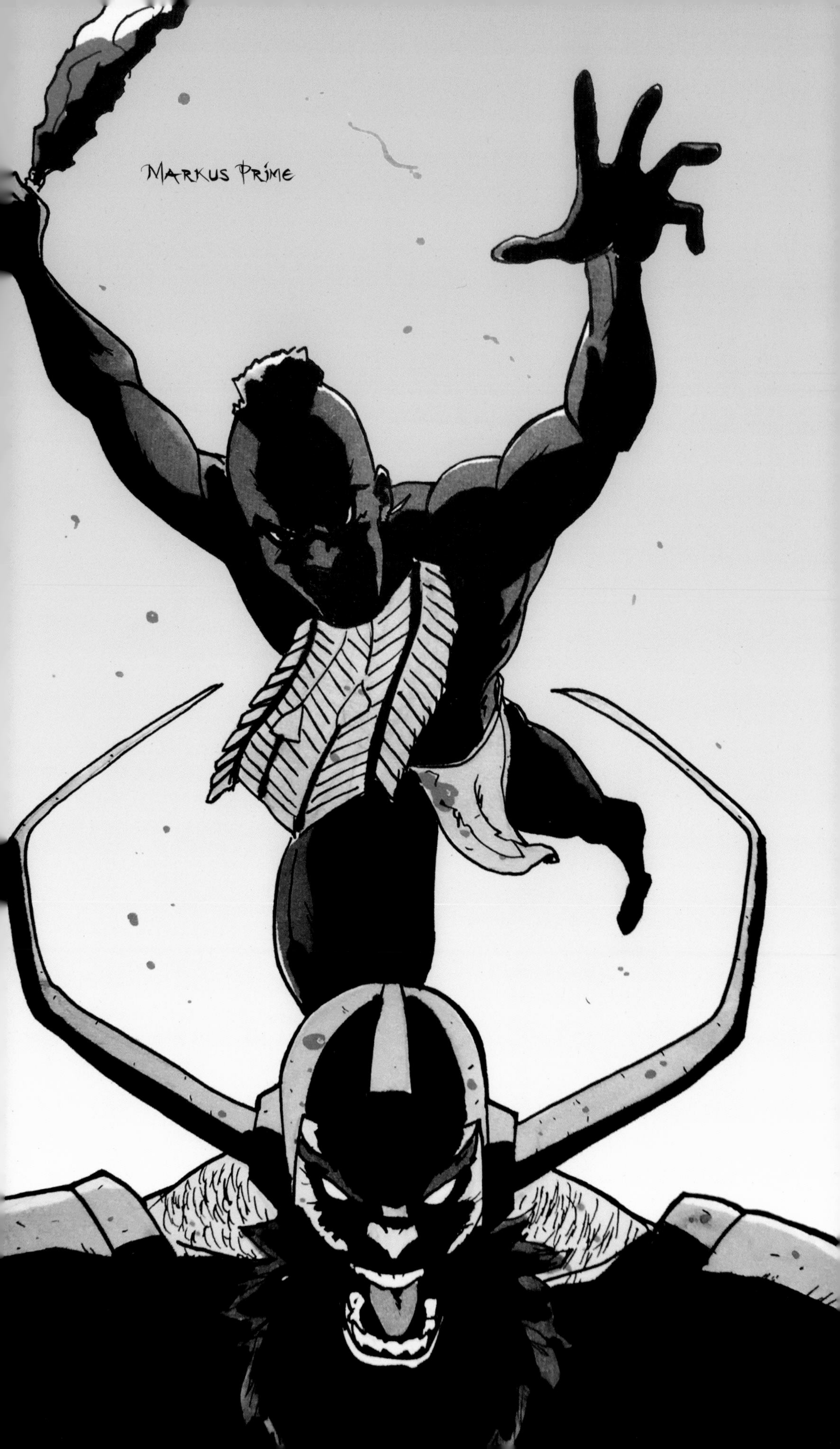
MARKUS PRIME

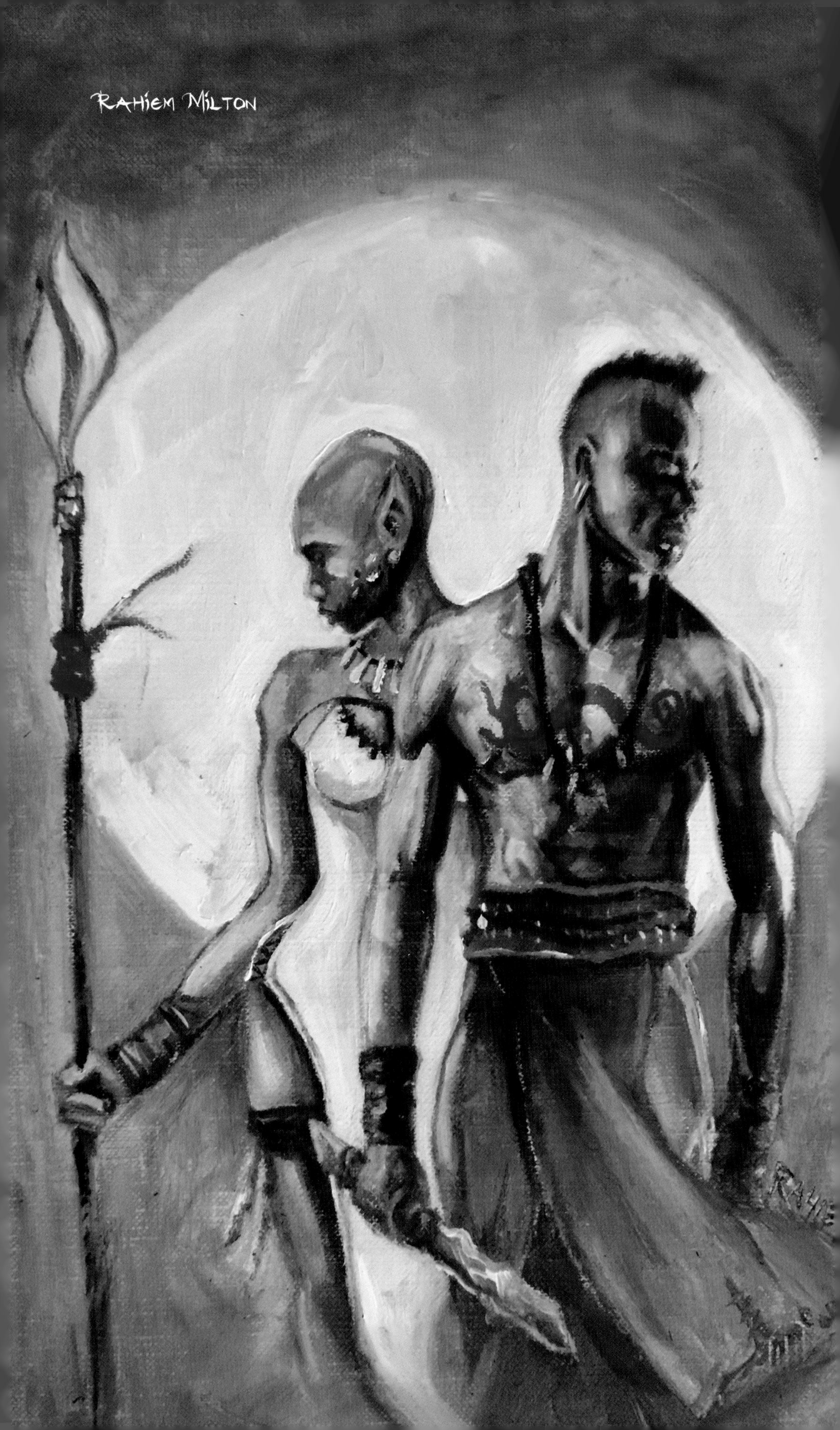
RAHIEM MILTON

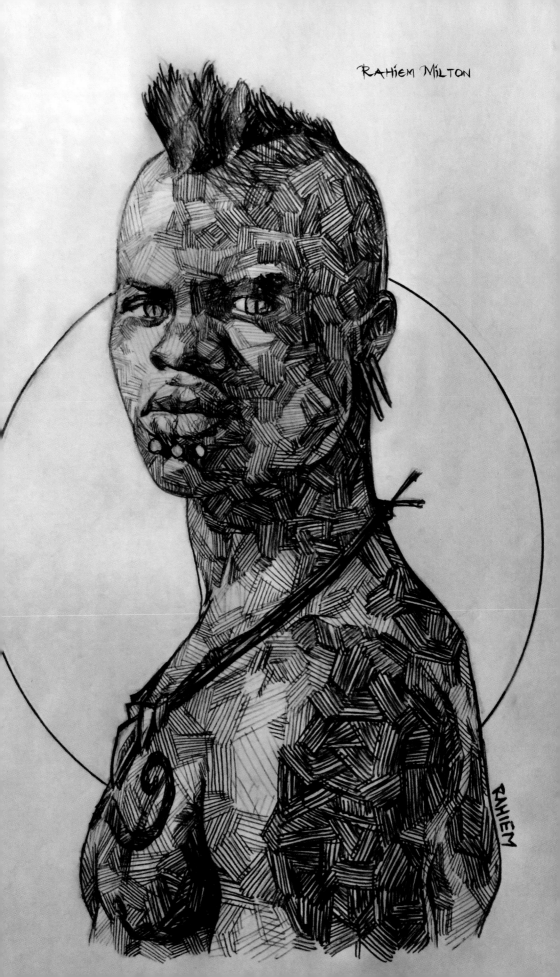

RAHIEM MILTON

RAHIEM

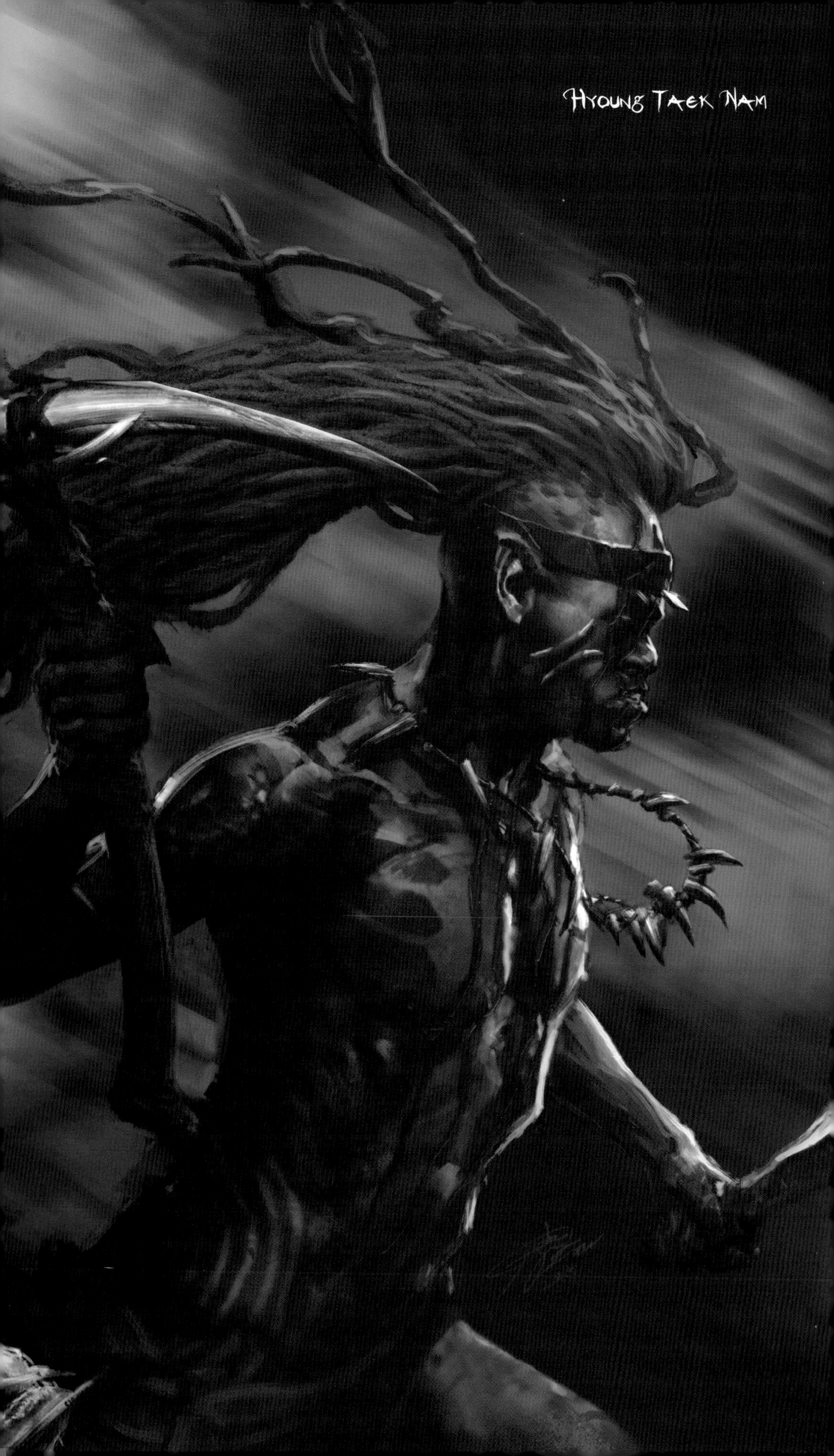

Hyoung Taek Nam

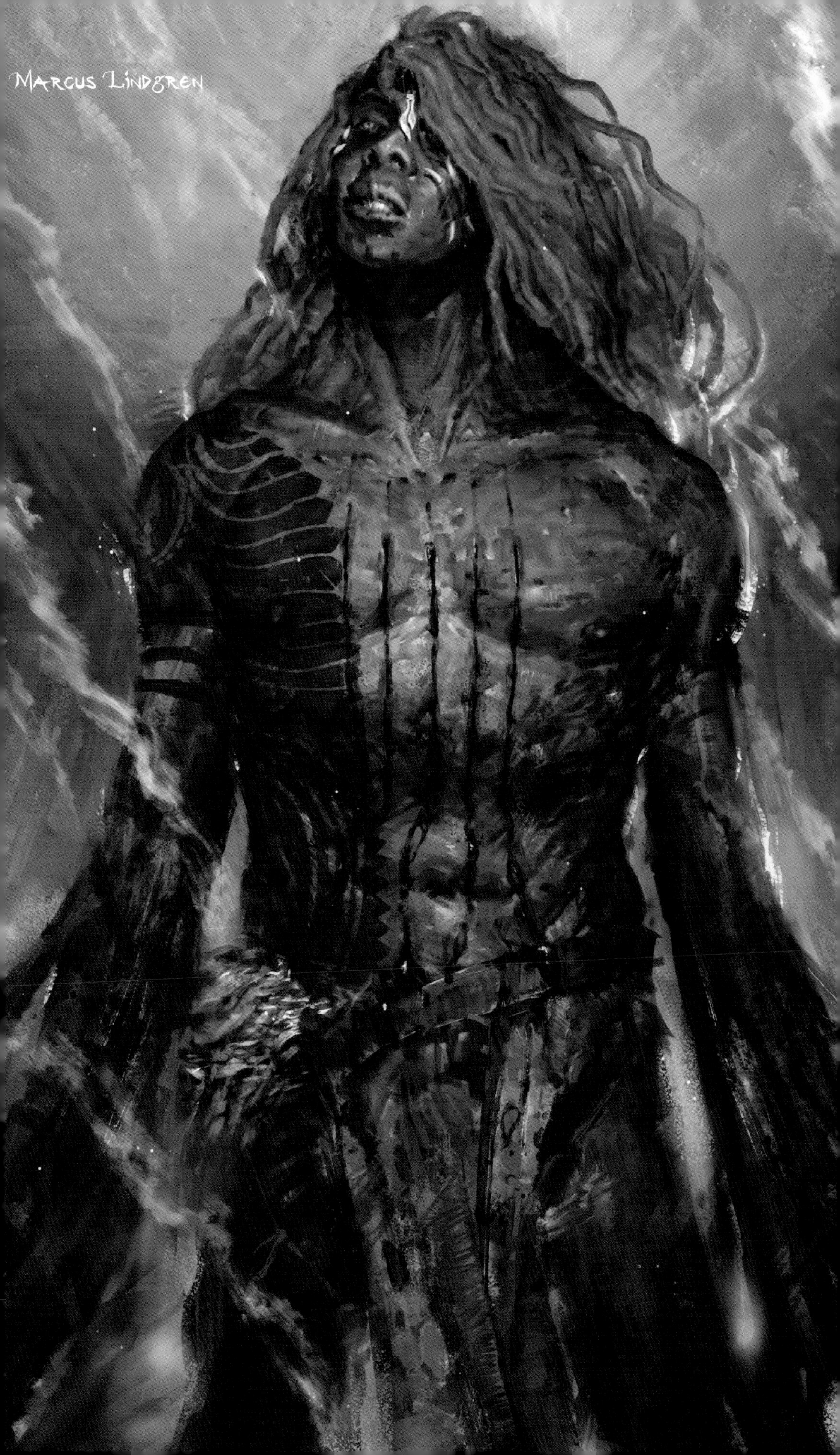
Marcus Lindgren

Matt Waite

DUSU

Path of the Ancient

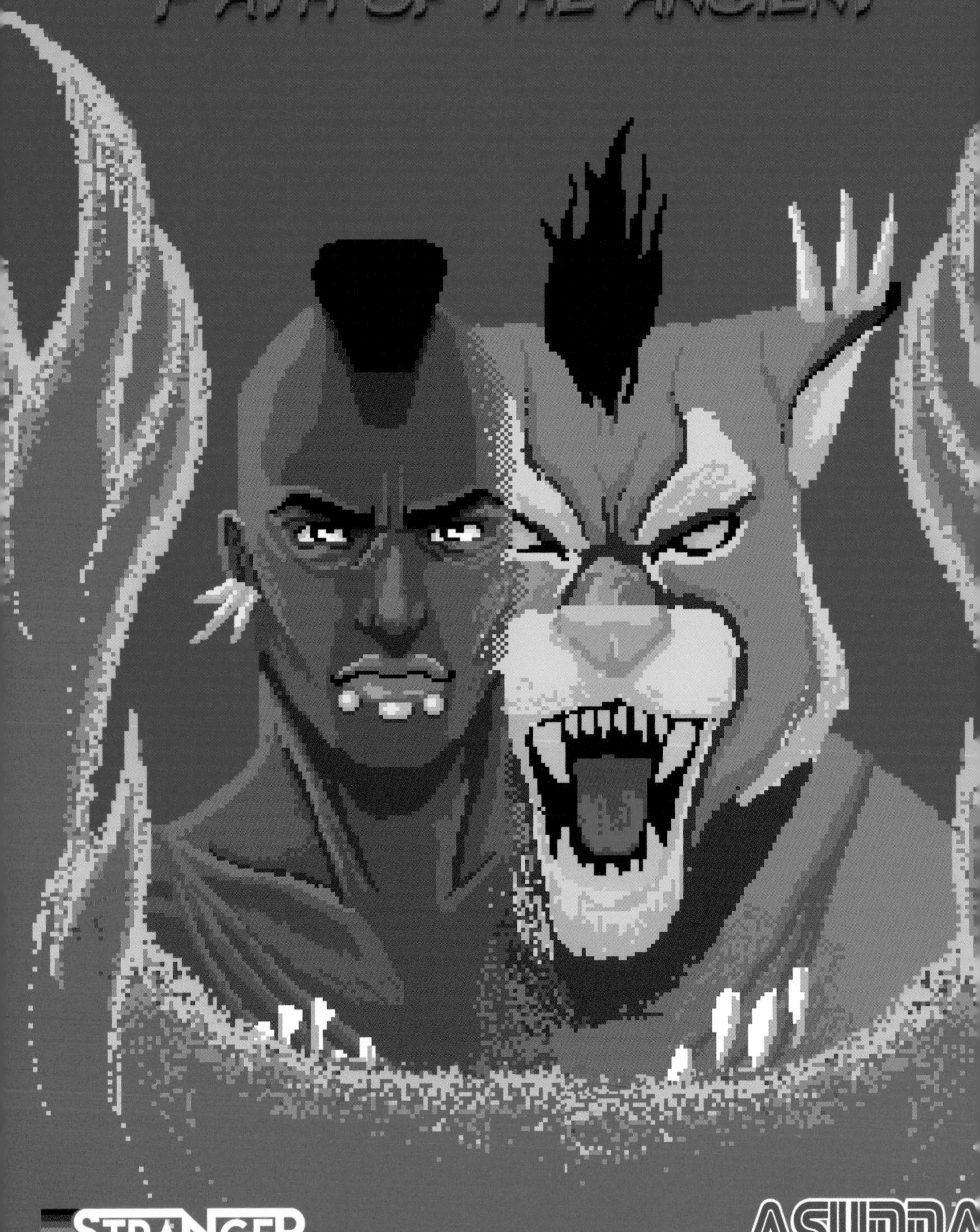

STRANGER

ASUNDA

Terrance Bouldin-Johnson

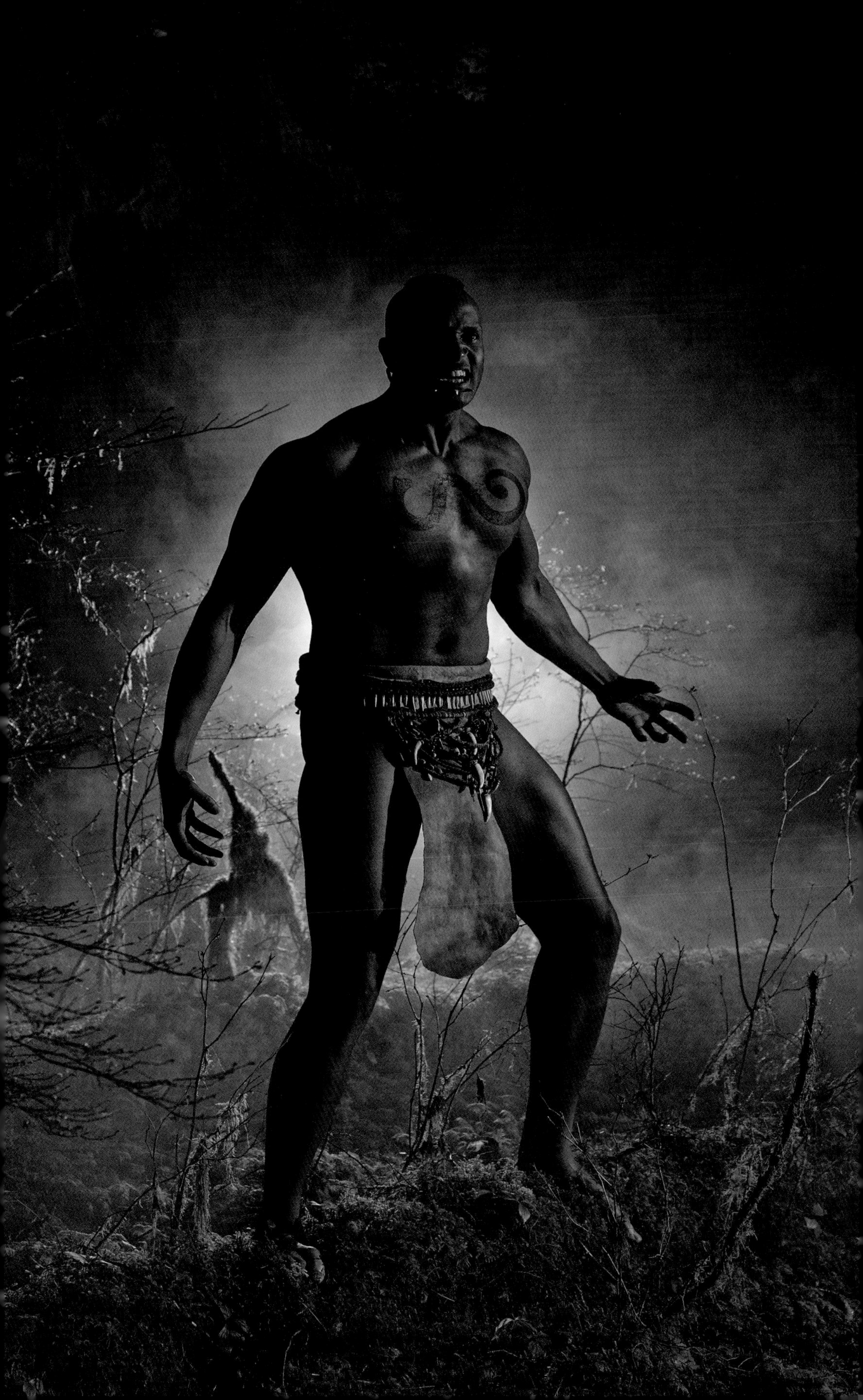

James T. Webster

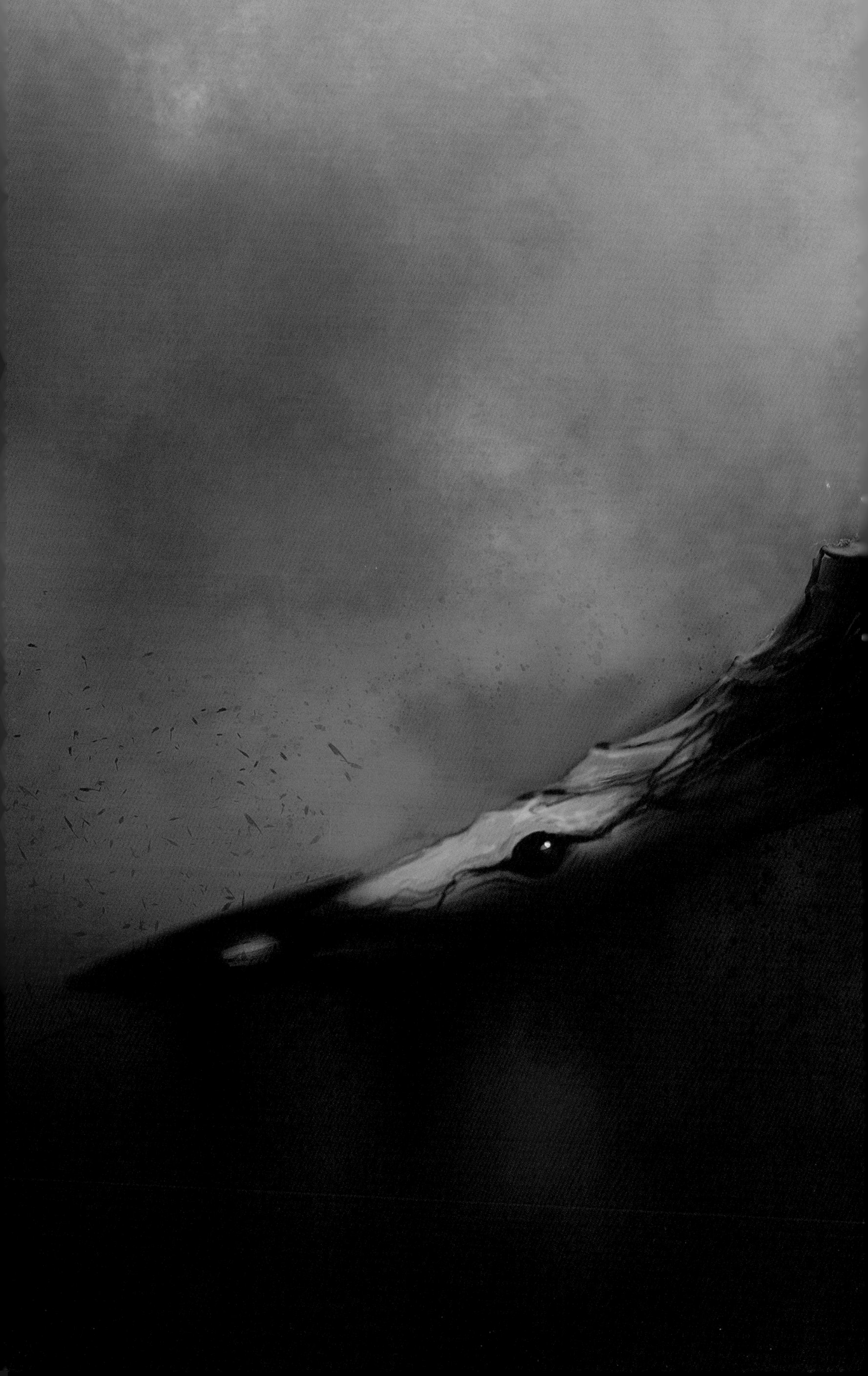

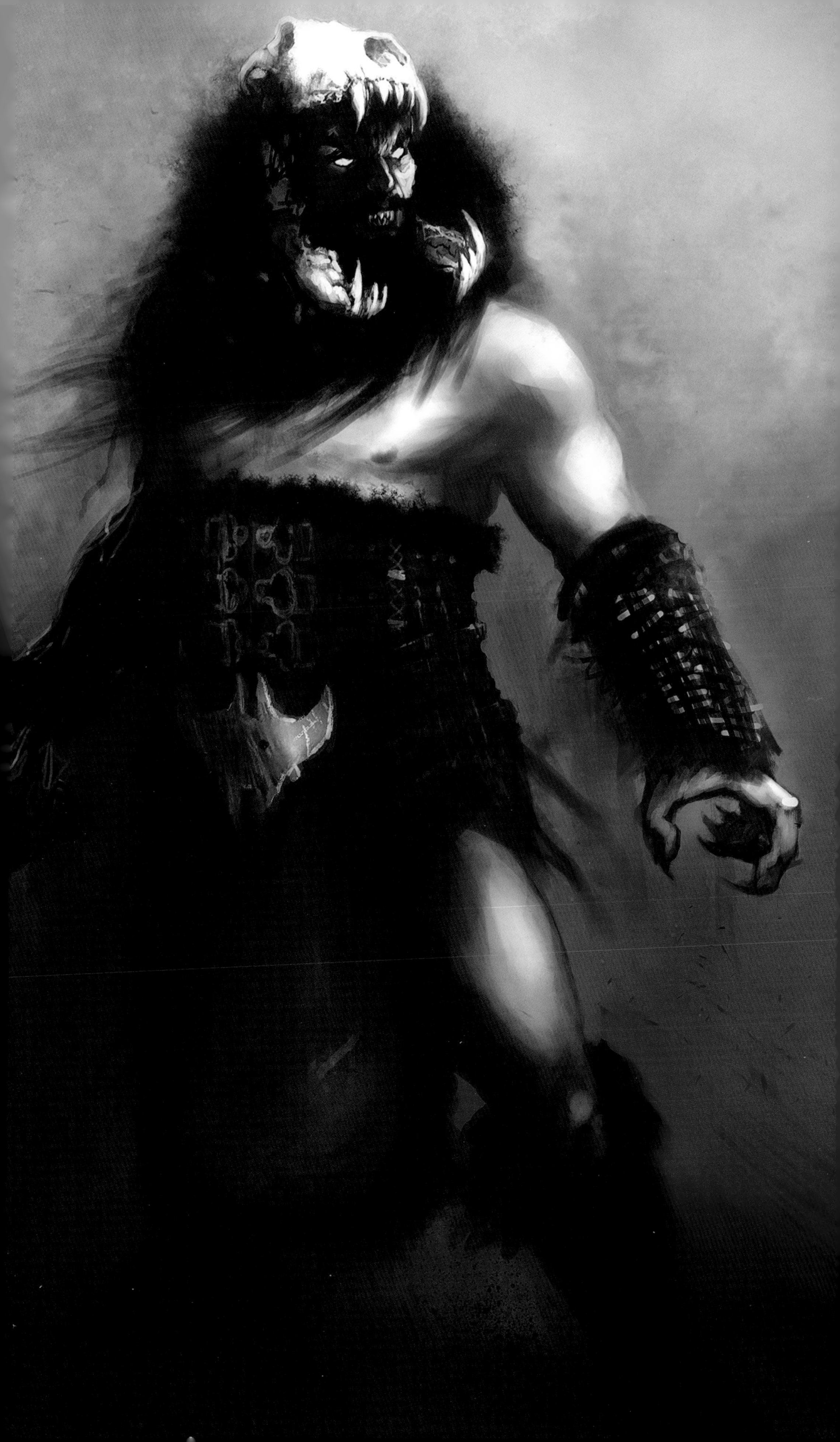

THE PATH OF THE ANCIENT HAS JUST BEGUN...